HE THAT BE

He That Believeth

Establishing the Truth
of Eternal Security

Paul McCauley

JOHN RITCHIE LTD
CHRISTIAN PUBLICATIONS

40 Beansburn, Kilmarnock, Scotland

ISBN-13: 978 1 910513 31 6

Copyright © 2016 by John Ritchie Ltd.
40 Beansburn, Kilmarnock, Scotland

www.ritchiechristianmedia.co.uk

Typeset by John Ritchie Ltd., Kilmarnock
Printed by Bell & Bain Ltd., Glasgow

Contents

Foreword

In extensive areas of Eastern Europe and the African continent, there are professing believers who have never heartily espoused the doctrine of the Eternal Security of the Believer in Christ. In the Western World, the large part of evangelicalism that is dominated by Arminian theology also rejects the concept that once a person has genuinely repented and believed on the Lord Jesus, they cannot be "unsaved" again, they can never be lost.

Paul McCauley addresses the issue head on, but in a very balanced way. He is at pains to show that not all who have *professed* to be saved can regard themselves as secure, for he demonstrates from Scripture that it is possible for people to claim to have been converted, but there has been no subsequent evidence of "fruit" for God. The alleged "conversion" has been a mere emotional response to defective gospel preaching and later there has been a drift into spiritual disinterest. It is not that they have been saved and then lost again, but the plain fact is that they were never saved in the first instance. On the positive side, he lines up arguments from the Word of God to demonstrate that genuine repentance and faith place people in an unassailable position of security from the judgment of God.

Paul is in a position to understand what people in general are thinking about these issues because of his own experience. He is at the sharp end of evangelical activity, not only conversing with those who attend his outreach meetings, but also encountering individuals at their own homes. He is alert to trends in the religious world, and from his knowledge of current thinking he has set out to put in place reasons for rejecting what is generally called "the fall-away doctrine", the idea that a genuinely saved person could thereafter be lost. It is done with the conviction that the doctrine is not just some minor doctrinal aberration, but rather a fundamental error, because among other things, it impinges on the efficacy of the work of the Lord Jesus at the cross.

Paul's arguments are laid out in a scholarly way. As he states, he does not rely on appeals to what may be regarded as "proof texts", but rather, much space is devoted to the context of these statements. For example, the reader will find that the arguments of certain parts of the Epistle to the Romans or the Epistle to the Hebrews are followed through meticulously. Following these lines of reasoning leads to the conclusion that the true believer can never perish. The same contextual approach is adopted towards Bible passages that may appear to support the "fall away" theory. Context is the keynote.

The volume will appeal to the thoughtful reader. Much research has been done as writers ancient and modern have been consulted and quoted appropriately. It is hoped that the perusal of the book will help the reader to form his own convictions about the sufficiency of the activity of The Triune God in not only providing salvation, but the assurance of that salvation, and the confidence that it can never be lost.

Jack Hay
June 2015

Introduction

It's a most unpleasant way to live; insecure and uncertain, with the dark cloud of dread hovering over you, threatening that something you love could be lost, or someone you love could leave.

We all recognise how important security is: we have National Security, Online Security, Social Security, Security Guards, Security Alarms, Security Lights, Security Cameras, Security Services, Security Forces, Security Fences, Security Doors, etc. etc. And yet, have people ever felt less secure and more threatened?

Many a person has gone into work content and happy that he had job security only to have his employer tell him there is no longer a position for him in the company. Heartbreaking stories can be told of how a husband or wife has gone home to a spouse to whom vows were made and with whom life was to be shared and dreams were to be fulfilled, only to hear that spouse say that the relationship is over. Many can tell of people who made investments in ventures that were a sure thing, and deposited savings in banks without a worry, but the investments have been squandered and the deposits gone. We can read about people who built on an inadequate foundation and their houses have subsided, the very ground beneath their feet literally going out from under them, and the structure of their home falling in round them.

Positions, relationships, deposits, foundations; lost, severed, gone, destroyed. It makes a mockery of the phrases we use to express the thought of security: 'A job for life', 'Till death do us part', 'It's in the bank', 'Safe as houses'.

It's not only the case that people have lost things they thought they would never lose, but also people fear the loss of things they now have. Insecurity is the thief of joy, the murderer of peace, and the destroyer of hope. If you are not sure of your job security, if you don't have faith in your spouse's fidelity, if you don't have confidence in the bank, if you don't feel safe in your own home, then you can't actually enjoy what you have.

What about the matter of our salvation? As a believer in the Lord Jesus you have a position. The Bible states it as being 'in Christ'. Can you ever be dismissed from it? Will you ever be told there's no room for you anymore? Upon repenting you entered into a relationship; you are a child of God and part of the Church, Christ's Bride. Is there any possibility of that bond being broken and the relationship ending? When you trusted Christ you made a deposit; you committed the matter of your soul's salvation to the Lord. Can that which you have committed to Christ ever be lost? You have built upon a foundation. Can that foundation ever be shaken, destroyed or undermined? Do you need to live in fear of losing what you have? I believe the Bible's answer is clear to all these questions, it is a conclusive *No!* We can live in the calm certainty and joyful confidence of eternal security.

That is not to say there are no difficulties. There is absolutely no doubt that there have been great men of God who have believed that salvation can be lost, and there are Scriptures (and stories) that certainly appear to lend support to that view. However, the issue cannot be settled by pointing to great and godly men, by placing our finger on proof-texts or passing on our experiences. We must go back to the Bible and go forth from the Bible. While we must admit that there are some Scriptures that can be read more than one way, nevertheless, when we look at the Scriptures closely, contextually, and consistently[1] we will be led in one direction and will draw one conclusion, that the Bible teaches eternal security.

It is my prayer that this book will help Christians to emerge from the darkness of doubt and the fetters of fear into the freedom and joy of their security in Christ, and that as a result they will love

---

[1] By looking at the text closely I mean seeing exactly what the writer said; by looking at it contextually I mean seeing it in the context of the particular book, taking note of the genre and style, and seeing how it contributes to the theme of the book; by looking at it consistently I mean ensuring that we don't come to a conclusion that jars with other passages of Scripture. The Word of God speaks with one harmonious voice and has one united message.

Him more fervently and live for Him more faithfully until that promised day when God will perfect His work in us and all the justified will be finally glorified.[2]

---

[2] Phil.1:6; Rom. 8:30.

Watching your Language

In examining this issue of whether a Christian can lose his salvation our terminology can be a big help or hindrance.

Some people speak about the *perseverance of the saints,* and others use the slogan *once saved, always saved.* Although there is no error expressed by the terms themselves, there are certain erroneous connotations that might have attached themselves to the terms that we must try to prise off.

Perseverance of the saints

This phrase is intended to communicate the fact that all those who are regenerate will persevere in faith, and that their lives will, to one degree or another, show that they are regenerate. This is, as we will seek to show, exactly what the Bible teaches, so what is the problem? Well, the problem is that the phrase (inadvertently and unintentionally) seems to put the emphasis on the *saint persevering* rather than on the *Saviour preserving*. It focuses on the believer and his need to keep on going, and thus he does not have the complete assurance that he is truly saved. Although the believer would say that it is the Lord who keeps him going, and it is the Lord's faithfulness that holds him, it can in practical terms lead to him having the attitude 'I have to keep going, and I have to hold on or else I'm not saved', and so, although he says his salvation depends on the Lord, he acts and feels as if his salvation depends on him. He knows if he is saved he will persevere, but he can't be sure he will persevere so it would be presumptuous of him to say he is sure he's saved. R. T. Kendall summarises the problem:

> If that is what the Bible teaches [that the true
> believer will persevere in godliness to the end],
> then faith gives very little purpose or comfort

whatever. I would simply be back to the original view of my own background and assume that, though I am saved by trusting Jesus' death on the cross, I will have no assurance that I am saved unless I am also in a state of godly living at every moment.[3]

Many believers from the Reformed tradition will object that they do have peace about their standing before God, and assurance of their salvation, and that's fine; I'm not disputing that at all, but many, too many, will testify that perseverance of the saints means one cannot say he is saved. Their focus is in the wrong place and on the wrong person.

I am not so enthusiastic about the...expression, "The perseverance of the saints." I believe in it, I believe that all saints, all really belonging to God, will persevere to the end, for the Book tells me, "He that shall endure unto the end, the same shall be saved" Matt.24:13, and if a man starts out and makes a profession but gives it all up, he will never be saved, because he was never born again to begin with, he was never truly changed by grace divine. On the other hand, the reason he endures to the end is not because of any particular perseverance of his own. What I believe in, and what the Word of God clearly teaches, is the perseverance of the Holy Spirit. When He begins a work, He never gives up until it is completed. That is our confidence.[4]

Once saved always saved

Again, there is nothing wrong with what these words state, but there is something wrong with what this phrase communicates. It is a popular slogan in evangelical circles where repentance is neglected and easy-believism is promoted. It seems to have come into vogue around the time of big gospel "revivals", around the

---

[3] R. T. Kendall, *Once Saved, Always Saved*, CrossBooks, 2013, Kindle location 212.
[4] H. A. Ironside, *The Eternal Security of the Believer*, p.12 http://www.wholesomewords.org/etexts/ironside/eternal.pdf.

same time that lifelong "backsliders" began to appear more and more. People "make a decision for Christ" and they are told that they are saved, and their lives subsequently yield no fruit for God, they show no evidence of a changed attitude or a new life, but they are comforted by the thought *once saved, always saved!* They tell themselves and others *I'm a backslider*, even though there was hardly any forward motion from which they could slide back. Salvation is viewed as a momentary transaction rather than a momentous transformation, merely the act of a moment rather than the fact of a lifetime. We will try to show in this book that once a person is saved he is always saved, but once a person is saved there will be evidence of it in the life. I think it is important to underscore, highlight, emphasise and circle this point; this book is not intended to give a slice of solace or a crumb of comfort to the person who has made a profession of faith in Christ, but gives no evidence of being born again; if this is you, if you have no love for the Lord Jesus, if you have no appetite for God's Word, if you have no interest in getting to know Christ more, if you have no real capacity for true prayer and spiritual worship, if you have no love for holiness, if you don't feel comfortable amongst the Lord's people, then, rather than read this book, read instead the Lord's words in Matt.7:13-27 and have a good, honest look and a real, hard think about where you really stand before God.

> When we speak of the eternal security of the believer, what do we mean? We mean that once a poor sinner has been regenerated by the Word and the Spirit of God, once he has received a new life and a new nature, has been made partaker of the divine nature; once he has been justified from every charge before the throne of God, it is absolutely impossible that that man should ever again be a lost soul. Having said that, let me say what we do not mean when we speak of the eternal security of the believer. We do not mean that it necessarily follows that if one professes to be saved, if he comes out to the front in a meeting, shakes the preacher's hand, and says he accepts the Lord Jesus Christ as his Saviour,

that that person is eternally safe. It does not mean that if one joins a church or makes a profession of faith, is baptised, becomes a communicant, takes an interest in Christian work, that that person is forever secure. It does not mean that because one manifests certain gifts and exercises these gifts in Christian testimony, that that person is necessarily eternally secure.[5]

So without being petty about it, I'm not comfortable using either of these phrases. I think they both turn our eyes in the wrong direction. *The perseverance of the saints* puts the focus on us; *once saved, always saved* puts the focus on a past experience. *Eternal security* puts our focus on a living, powerful Saviour and that's where it should be. *The perseverance of the saints* may lead us to think that *we* have to produce fruit in order to say we're saved; *once saved, always saved* may lead us to think there need not be any fruit in order for us to say we're saved; in the doctrine of *eternal security* we will see there will be fruit, and it will be produced *in* us not *by* us. *The perseverance of the saints* minimises the truth that the believer still has the old, sinful nature which is always capable of manifesting itself; *once saved, always saved* minimises the truth that the believer has a new nature which will inevitably manifest itself. The doctrine of *eternal security* affirms the truth that the believer has two natures, and seeing this truth will be a means of assuring those who need not be doubting, while at the same time awakening those who should be doubting.[6]

---

[5] Ibid. pp.6,7.
[6] See Appendix 2: *Does the believer have two natures?*

The Case for Eternal Security

> "Salvation!" "Saved!" O blessed, peace-inspiring words to him who knows the reality of them! What do they mean? Do they leave still the doubt that, after all, by that from which we are saved we may still be overtaken, overcome, and perish? Then, for pity's sake, and in the interests of truth itself, let us not use the words; let us not inspire a hope which may be so mistaken![7]

We have mentioned how many people, in the everyday things of life, live in the grip of fear and the gloom of worry and doubt. Why is this? Well, if we are thinking in terms of personal relationships it is because they are not assured of the love of the person they have trusted. "Is he really committed to me?" "Will she leave me when she finds out what I'm really like?" If we are thinking in terms of personal safety it is because they are not assured of the power of the person or thing they have trusted. "Can the Government really save us from these terrorists?" "Will this alarm scare off any intruders, etc.?" I think all would agree that if you had a relationship with one whose very nature was love then you would not need to doubt that person's commitment, and I think you would likewise agree that if you were trusting one who was all-powerful you would be left with no reason to fear for your personal safety.

For these reasons I suggest our investigation into the case for eternal security has to begin with the God we have trusted. This is the one of whom it is said, "God is love" (1 Jn.4:8, 16), and the one who is described as "the Almighty" (e.g. Rev.1:8).

---

[7] F. W. Grant, *Christian Holiness*, http://www.stempublishing.com/authors/FW_Grant/FWG_Christian_Holiness5.html.

One of the great truths of the Bible is that God is a Trinity. There is only one true God, but there are three distinct Persons who share that Being. As we turn our attention to God we will take time to focus on each of these three divine Persons and see how secure the believer really is.

God the Father guarantees our Eternal Security

'Tis God that justifies!
Who shall recall His pardon or His grace,
Or who the broken chain of guilt replace?
'Tis God that justifies!

(Horatius Bonar)

As we travel down the path of investigating how God the Father guarantees our eternal security we come to a junction, one road is signed *The purpose of God* and the other *The power of God*.[8] Whatever route we take we will arrive at the same destination and come to the same conclusion, so we will take a walk down both of them in turn.

The Purpose of God

Romans 8:28-30

The course of history is not merely a series of random events meaning nothing and heading nowhere. The hand of divine providence is on the helm of human history and He is steering all things toward His intended destination. The Bible speaks of God's purpose in relation to nations, kingdoms, governments and rulers, but also in relation to individuals, and that is what I want us to consider now. Rom.8:28-30 is a passage that presents God's purpose for His people.

> And we know that all things work together for
> good to them that love God, to them who are

---

[8] As I was writing this and turning to different writers for help I noticed that Charles C. Ryrie took a similar approach when dealing with the subject of eternal security in his useful book, *Basic Theology*, Moody Press.

> the called according to His purpose. For whom
> He did foreknow, He also did predestinate to be
> conformed to the image of His Son, that He might
> be the firstborn among many brethren. Moreover
> whom He did predestinate, them he also called:
> and whom He called, them He also justified: and
> whom He justified, them He also glorified.

Now this is a good place for us to start because this is a passage which sets out to give assurance to believers. We are not drawing strained lessons from obscure passages, we are not making descriptive passages prescriptive, we are not taking a narrative that relates events under one dispensation and trying to derive doctrine from it and apply it to us. What Paul writes in this passage applies directly to us, and what he is saying is that every single soul who is justified will be glorified,[9] indeed, as far as God is concerned, the believer already is glorified, it is as good as done because it is a matter of divine purpose.[10]

So we have to look at what Paul teaches in this epistle about the *meaning* of justification and the *means* of justification.

Justification means to be declared righteous. We need to understand that it does not mean to be made righteous. This is evident from the fact that Paul actually speaks about God being justified:

> What advantage then hath the Jew? or what
> profit is there of circumcision? Much every way:
> chiefly, because that to them were committed the
> oracles of God. For what if some did not believe?
> shall their unbelief make the faith of God without
> effect? God forbid: yea, let God be true, but every
> man a liar; as it is written, "That Thou mightest be
> justified in Thy sayings, and mightest overcome
> when Thou art judged." (Rom.3:1-4)

Paul is anticipating and answering objections to the truths he has

---

[9] Paul's chain of divine purpose goes back before justification, but I am focusing solely on the last two links because no matter what view a true Christian takes of the first three he will agree on how someone is justified, and that is all that is required to prove eternal security.
[10] See Rom. 4:17.

presented thus far in the epistle and he responds to some who may be questioning God's faithfulness. Paul emphatically rejects any suggestion that God could ever fail in regard to His promises. He says that if it were the case that every man contradicted what God said then we must reckon God to be true and every man a liar. It is at this point he quotes from Psalm 51 and says that God is to be justified in His sayings. Clearly Paul is not saying God is unrighteous and needs to be made righteous. Rather he is saying that God is righteous and needs to be declared righteous.[11]

So when a man is justified before God he is declared by God to be righteous, God's justice has no claim against him and can pronounce no condemnation upon him; that's the meaning of justification, but let us look now at the means of it.

In the early chapters of Romans Paul is presenting the universal guilt and condemnation of mankind before a righteous God. This is a section that spans 1:18-3:20, and it is vital that we see everything within that section as part of Paul's argument that the whole world is guilty before God, because it is in that section we read the following words:

> For not the hearers of the law are just before God,
> but the doers of the law shall be justified. (2:13)

Paul is not here teaching the *way* of justification, he is teaching the *need* of justification. He is saying that if someone were to continually and completely keep the law then he would be declared righteous by God. However, as Paul goes on to show, no one has met the standard and kept the law, and the section is concluded in this way:

> Now we know that what things soever the law
> saith, it saith to them who are under the law: that
> every mouth may be stopped, and all the world
> may become guilty before God.

---

[11] In Deut.25:1 God's command to the judges is to justify the righteous and condemn the wicked, thus showing that justification is a declaration of righteousness; the law has nothing against this person. Furthermore, if justification meant to make someone righteous then it would be a very strange thing that God would find it abominable for men to justify the wicked (Prov.17:15), surely God would be delighted for the wicked to be made righteous. For more information the reader can go to Additional Note D: Justification, in Leon Morris's commentary, *The Epistle to the Romans*, PNTC, Apollos, 1988.

> Therefore by the deeds of the law there shall no
> flesh be justified in His sight: for by the law is the
> knowledge of sin. (3:19,20)

So there is no one who can stand before God and be accepted by
Him on the basis of the life they have lived and the law they have
kept. God's law condemns every man and closes every mouth; we
are guilty, without exception and without excuse, and (if God had
not intervened) without escape.[12]

This introduces us to one of the most glorious sections in God's
Word:

> But now the righteousness of God without the
> law is manifested, being witnessed by the law
> and the prophets; even the righteousness of God
> which is by faith of Jesus Christ unto all and upon
> all them that believe: for there is no difference: for
> all have sinned, and come short of the glory of
> God; being justified freely by His grace through
> the redemption that is in Christ Jesus: whom God
> hath set forth to be a propitiation through faith
> in His blood, to declare His righteousness for
> the remission of sins that are past, through the
> forbearance of God; to declare, I say, at this time
> His righteousness: that He might be just, and the
> justifier of him which believeth in Jesus.
> Where is boasting then? It is excluded. By what
> law? of works? Nay: but by the law of faith.
> Therefore we conclude that a man is justified by
> faith without the deeds of the law. Is He the God
> of the Jews only? is He not also of the Gentiles?
> Yes, of the Gentiles also: seeing it is one God,
> which shall justify the circumcision by faith, and
> uncircumcision through faith. Do we then make

---

[12] I had a letter from an atheist some time ago which included a list of supposed Bible contradictions.
On his list was 2:13 along with 3:20. He thought this was a clincher: in one chapter Paul says we
are justified by law-keeping, and in the next chapter he says we aren't! Of course it would have
been helpful if my correspondent had read what came between 2:13 and 3:20! In one chapter he
says we would be justified by law-keeping if we'd kept it; in the next chapter he says we won't be
justified by law-keeping because we haven't kept it. (None of his other "contradictions" were any
harder to deal with.)

> void the law through faith? God forbid: yea, we
> establish the law. (3:21-31)

There we stood, our past exposed, our heads bowed, our mouths shut, our future bleak, guilty before God, with nothing to say in our defence and no ability to pay for our deliverance; it's a hopeless scene.

I'm sure Paul dictated the words of verse 21 to Tertius with a stamp of the foot and a smile on his face, *"But now..."* Into such a scene shines the light of God's glorious gospel telling the guilty that there is a way they can be brought into a right standing before God, because there is a righteousness from God, a righteousness that God has provided apart from the principle of law,[13] and it is received by faith in Jesus Christ.[14]

Now let us linger here a while and see what is said about God justifying the guilty:

> Being justified freely by His grace through the
> redemption that is in Christ Jesus... (v.24)

Paul says we are justified *freely*. That word *freely* is used by Paul when he speaks of how he didn't eat anyone's bread *for nought* (2 Thess.3:8). He didn't take anyone's bread without working for it, earning it or buying it. Elsewhere the word is translated *without a cause* (Jn.15:25). Thus we can see that the word can have the idea of without cause or it can mean without cost. Which of those two meanings is in Rom.3:24? Well, both actually. Paul is saying that justification is *without cause in us* and it is *without cost to us*. But look at the rest of the verse: although justification is without cause in us, there is a cause: "being justified freely *by His grace*..." The cause of our justification is the grace of God, His free, unmerited favour. Picture the courtroom scene again: you stand before the righteous Judge, the charges have been read out, the evidence has been presented, the witnesses have testified, the verdict has been

---

[13] Please let all take note: the righteousness God has provided is not only apart from the deeds of the law (v.28), but it is apart from law altogether. This proves conclusively that the believer does not have the righteousness of Christ imputed to him. We do not stand before God on the basis of Christ's perfect law-keeping. That would be a "law righteousness", and it denies the teaching that God has brought an end to Adamic manhood, and we have our standing in a risen Christ.

[14] Righteousness without law was always available in Old Testament times, as Paul says here and shows in Romans 4 with Abraham and David, but now man's probation is over and this righteousness is manifested.

given, and the sentence is about to be handed down. The Judge asks you if you have anything to say in your defence, any reason why He should let you go free. Imagine yourself stammering about trying your best, not being as bad as others, going to church, being sorry, etc. and the Judge showing you that none of those things excuses your sins or pays for your crimes. When every excuse has been exhausted, you confess that you cannot give one reason why the Judge should let you go free. It is *then* the Judge says, "I'm prepared to let you go free anyway." Why? *Because it is by grace*; this is the cause of our justification. The cause is not in us, it is in Him.

Look again at the verse; although justification is without cost to us, there is a cost: "being justified freely by His grace *through the redemption that is in Christ Jesus*". Thayer and Vine both define that word *redemption* as a releasing effected by payment of a ransom. So although justification is freely bestowed, it was not free to bestow. The righteous Judge could not just let the guilty go free, the penalty had to be paid, and so Christ Jesus stepped in and by His sacrifice at Calvary He paid the infinite price and put God in the position of being "just and the justifier of the one who has faith in Jesus" (Rom.3:26, NKJV). The believer thus walks free from the courtroom in the knowledge the penalty has been paid. This is something that is brought up again in 5:9:

> Much more then, being now justified by His blood, we shall be saved from wrath through Him.

When Paul says in 3:24 that Christ paid the price it is not that Christ sacrificed something, but rather He sacrificed Himself, He held nothing back. Nothing less than the self-giving of the Son of God could pay the penalty our sins deserved and God's justice demanded, and we can thank God that nothing more than the self-giving of the Son of God was needed to pay that price.

There was a story in the press that caused a bit of a stir.[15] It involved a Judge actually paying the fine of the guilty criminal. There were several good reasons why people had cause to be

[15] http://www.telegraph.co.uk/news/uknews/law-and-order/9837688/Judge-branded-insensitivefor - paying-thiefs-1-penalty.html

upset. Firstly, people thought the fine was too small and it was all a bit of a farce. Secondly, the criminal, although not rolling in wealth, could have paid the fine himself. Thirdly, the offended parties were not consulted to see if they were satisfied with the arrangement. Fourthly, the criminal may not have been the least bit repentant and could have left the court laughing over the whole thing. Thankfully, every one of these problems is addressed by the gospel of God. The penalty sinners have to pay is no trifling token gesture: they are deserving of nothing less than the wrath of a sin-hating God, and this is a penalty they can never pay, no matter how many ages roll their course; they will never be able to satisfy divine justice. The Judge is able to pay the penalty, and He also has the moral right to do so because He is also the offended party. Every sin we commit is an offence to God, and as the one who has been robbed, so to speak, He can, if He chooses, pay the penalty His law demands. And the guilty will not go free unless and until they are truly repentant. So the justifiable objections to the Judge's action are overruled in God's courtroom. He has acted in perfect justice, rich grace and divine wisdom.

Paul goes on to say about the Lord in 4:25:

> [He] was delivered for our offences, and was raised again for our justification.

What does it mean that He was raised for our justification? The point is this, the grace of God and the work of Christ go beyond merely the pardoning of a criminal. It is not just the case that our penalty is paid and we are looked upon as those whose sentence has been served. No, by means of the death of Christ the guilty sinner is actually removed altogether from before God's face, and we have a standing of righteousness in the risen Christ.

But I haven't really got to the intended destination yet. By now you may have forgotten where we started and where I intended to take you. Let me just remind you. We noticed in Rom.8:30 that all whom God justifies are, in divine purpose, already glorified. Therefore, if we can get amongst the company of the justified we can be completely assured of our future and final glorification; that's why we looked back into Romans to see what Paul means when he talks about being justified, and how it actually happens.

We have seen we are justified by God's grace, that's *why* we're justified; we are justified in virtue of Christ's blood, that's *how* we're justified; we are justified in union with the risen Christ, that's *where* we're justified. But what we need to focus our attention on now is *when* we're justified. Over and over again in Romans Paul will tell us, justification is by faith, and so takes place the moment we believe.[16] But what does that mean? The word "faith" has been so misused and distorted in our day that we have to sweep away some wrong notions before we get a proper understanding.

Facts about faith
It has been common for atheists (and sadly, some professing Christians) to define faith in a way that the Bible doesn't recognise or endorse. Faith, according to many, stands in contrast to reason. For example, Friedrich Nietzsche defined faith in this way: "the will to avoid knowing what is true"[17] and says that faith "as an imperative vetoes science".[18] A typically moderate and thoughtful quote from Richard Dawkins is apt here, "Faith is the great cop-out, the great excuse to evade the need to think and evaluate evidence. Faith is belief in spite of, even perhaps because of, the lack of evidence."[19] Christopher Hitchens, in an equally fair-minded way said "Faith is the surrender of the mind; it's the surrender of reason, it's the surrender of the only thing that makes us different from other mammals."[20] Penn Jillette weighs in with this, "Religion is faith. Faith is belief without evidence. Belief without evidence cannot be shared. Faith is a feeling."[21]

I don't want to get off our track here, but let's just see these quotes for what they are. They are either misunderstandings born of ignorance or misrepresentations spawned by malice, but by no stretch of the imagination can they be thought to be accurate representations of what the Bible means when it speaks about

---

[16] 1:16, 17; 3:21-31; the whole of chapter 4; 5:1.
[17] Friedrich Nietzsche, *The Antichrist*.
[18] Ibid. It is strange and striking then that modern science sprang from the Christian worldview in which believers expected to see law and order in nature based on the immutable character of God. As we see Nietzsche fly in the face of the facts, it leads us to think perhaps he was exercising his own definition of faith.
[19] A lecture by Richard Dawkins extracted from *The Nullifidian* (Dec. '94).
[20] http://en.wikiquote.org/wiki/Christopher_Hitchens
[21] http://www.nytimes.com/roomfordebate/2013/01/22/is-atheism-a-religion/atheism-should-end-religion-not-replace-it

faith.[22] All of the people quoted above are divorcing faith in a "religious" context from faith in an everyday context, and this should not be done. The writers of Scripture did not speak about faith because it was a foreign concept shrouded in mystery. They used it because it was a term everyone understood and a faculty everyone used. But the new atheists prefer to view "religious" faith as shutting one's eyes to the evidence, closing one's ears to the facts, turning the other way and taking a mad run and jump. However, in their everyday lives they see faith simply as an act or attitude of trust in someone or something. This is precisely what the Bible is calling us to when it calls us to have faith; it is an appeal for us to place our trust in the Lord, and the Bible gives us many reasons and much evidence to allow us to do that sensibly. Atheists are keen to give the impression that as facts increase faith decreases, but when you reflect on the nature of faith in your own everyday life you discover that this is entirely false. Do you have faith in your spouse? Hopefully your immediate response is "Yes, absolutely." Is that because you don't know much about your spouse? Of course not! Your faith isn't based on what you *don't* know; it's based on what you *do* know. You have a vast wealth of evidence and experience to show that your spouse is trustworthy and that your faith is factually based and wisely placed. The same is true in the medical sphere. If you were in need of life-saving surgery you would want to find out something about the surgeon. It is manifestly obvious that if you didn't know much about him your faith would be very small, not big. The more you hear about him, his expertise, his experience, etc. the more you would have faith in him. Faith increases with evidence and reason, it does not decrease. At the beginning of Paul's letter to the Romans he gives us facts upon which we can confidently stand. For example:

> Paul, a servant of Jesus Christ, called to be an
> apostle, separated unto the gospel of God, (which

---

[22] "So let's set the record straight. Faith is not the opposite of reason. The opposite of faith is unbelief. And reason is not the opposite of faith. The opposite of reason is irrationality. Do some Christians have irrational faith? Sure. Do some skeptics have unreasonable unbelief? You bet. It works both ways." Greg Koukl in *Is God Just a Human Invention? And Seventeen Other Questions Raised by the New Atheists* by Sean McDowell & Jonathan Morrow, Kregel, 2010, p.30.

He had promised afore by His prophets in the
Holy Scriptures,) concerning His Son Jesus Christ
our Lord, which was made of the seed of David
according to the flesh; and declared to be the
Son of God with power, according to the spirit
of holiness, by the resurrection from the dead: by
whom we have received grace and apostleship,
for obedience to the faith among all nations,
for His name: among whom are ye also the
called of Jesus Christ: to all that be in Rome,
beloved of God, called to be saints: Grace to
you and peace from God our Father, and the
Lord Jesus Christ.

First, I thank my God through Jesus Christ for
you all, that your faith is spoken of throughout
the whole world. (Rom.1:1-8)

This is not an apologetics book, but what material there would
be for one in these eight verses. I only mention them and pass
on. He speaks about the gospel of God which was promised
before by the prophets in the Holy Scriptures; the prophecies
of the Old Testament stand as irrefutable evidence of the
existence of God and the inspiration of Scripture. Consider just
three of the many prophetic passages in the Old Testament:
Psalm 22 prophesied *how* Christ would die (hundreds of years
before crucifixion was ever devised); Dan.9:24-27 prophesied
when He would die, counting it out to the very year, and telling
us it would be before the destruction of the temple and the
city of Jerusalem; Isaiah 53 prophesied *why* He would die,
as a sacrifice for our sins. These are things that none of these
writers would have naturally known or could have luckily
guessed. How are these prophecies to be explained? The
only explanation that makes sense is the one the Bible itself
gives:

[For] prophecy never came by the will of man,
but holy men of God spoke as they were moved
by the Holy Spirit. (2 Pet.1:21, NKJV)

He also makes reference to the Lord being declared the Son of God by the resurrection.[23] The truth of the resurrection of Christ is the corner stone of Christianity. Paul elsewhere says, "if Christ be not raised, your faith is vain; ye are yet in your sins."[24] Many people have sought to disprove this fact and have ended up resting on it rather than wrestling against it. The evidence for the resurrection stands without a scratch after all the venomous but vacuous attacks of unbelievers throughout the centuries. There simply is no naturalistic theory that can account for the historical facts. The case stands undented, allowing the Christian to stand undaunted: the Lord is risen indeed (Lk. 24:34)!

Again, Paul makes reference to the testimony of the believers in Rome. He says their faith is spoken of throughout the known world. A remarkable transformation had occurred that left people shocked. What was it that made such a powerful, positive, permanent change in the lives of these Romans? It was nothing other than the gospel of God. Millions since have been able to testify to the life-changing, soul-saving power of the risen Christ. This shows us that the reality of the claims of the gospel cannot only be examined evidentially, but can be experienced personally. The gospel doesn't merely promise forgiveness for the past and heaven in the future, it promises new life in the present, so that we can know it is true.

Further down the chapter Paul speaks about the evidence of creation pointing to the Creator.

> For the invisible things of Him from the creation of the world are clearly seen, being understood by the things that are made, even His eternal power and Godhead; so that they are without excuse: because that, when they knew God, they glorified Him not as God, neither were thankful; but became vain in their imaginations,

---

[23] Some see this as a reference to those whom the Lord raised from the dead, however, there are many reasons to see this as a reference to His own resurrection as the firstfruit of the harvest to come, see Acts 26:23. However, we can go along with William Kelly, who, having spoken of Christ's own resurrection and those whom He raised and will raise, said, "Thus in every way resurrection marks Him out as Son of God in power..." (*Notes on the Epistle to the Romans*, Bible Truth Publishers, 1978, p.4.)

[24] 1 Cor.15:17. Let the New Atheists read 1 Corinthians 15 and try to say faith is belief without evidence and evades the need to think! Paul's point is that Christianity is founded on historical fact, not floating on esoteric fancy. He is saying if it is not true then it is useless.

> and their foolish heart was darkened. Professing
> themselves to be wise, they became fools, and
> changed the glory of the uncorruptible God into
> an image made like to corruptible man, and to
> birds, and fourfooted beasts, and creeping things.
> (1:20-23)

Paul is saying that in the blaze of God's glorious creation people are without excuse for their unbelief and idolatry. It is still true today; in fact it is increasingly true. As technology advances, telescopes can see further and microscopes can peer closer than people in past generations ever would have dreamed possible, and their discoveries only uncover more of God's majestic handiwork. The origin of the universe out of nothing, the fine-tuning of the universe for life, the information in the DNA, the complexity of the cell, and so much more, declare the greatness and glory of God.

He speaks at the end of chapter 1 and in chapter 2 about the subject of morality.

> Who knowing the judgment of God, that they
> which commit such things are worthy of death,
> not only do the same, but have pleasure in them
> that do them. (1:32)

> For when the Gentiles, which have not the law, do
> by nature the things contained in the law, these,
> having not the law, are a law unto themselves:
> which shew the work of the law written in their
> hearts, their conscience also bearing witness, and
> their thoughts the mean while accusing or else
> excusing one another... (2:14,15)

The reality of the existence of right and wrong, good and evil, needs explanation. This realm of objective morality is another proof of God. We all recognise there are some things that are really evil, and that evil is a departure from the way things *ought* to be, but if we are just collections of chemicals banging around which arose with no purpose, then there is no way things *ought* to be, there's just the way things *are*. Furthermore, if there is no soul distinct from the body, no mind distinct from the brain, and we are 100% material beings, then we are not acting freely, we are reacting deterministically; we are merely doing what molecules do under these conditions. If atheism is true then there is no evil and there is no responsibility, and no one believes that is true. The existence of evil in the world tells us there is a righteous God whose law has been broken.

So there are five evidences of God found right at the start of Paul's letter to the Romans, fulfilled prophecy, the resurrection, personal experience, creation and conscience: historical proofs, scientific proofs, existential proofs. Therefore we can safely conclude that, in the Biblical context, faith is not belief *without evidence*, it is *trust*, and in the reckoning of the Biblical writers it is trust because of facts, reason and evidence, not in spite of them. Paul was not a man who engaged in or encouraged blind faith.

We have to be clear on this too, while faith is not *anti*-intellectual, it is not *only* intellectual; it is an act of the will as well as an acceptance in the mind. At the beginning and end of the epistle to the Romans Paul speaks about "the obedience of faith" (1:6; 16:26), showing us that the faith that saves is a faith that submits to the Lord. This is made clear in chapter 10 of the epistle.

> Brethren, my heart's desire and prayer to God for Israel is, that they might be saved. For I bear them record that they have a zeal of God, but not according to knowledge. For they being ignorant of God's righteousness, and going about to establish their own righteousness, have not submitted themselves to the righteousness of God. For Christ is the end of the law for righteousness to every one that believeth. For Moses describeth the righteousness which is of the law, That the man which doeth those things shall live by them. But the righteousness which is of faith speaketh on this wise, Say not in thine heart, Who shall ascend into heaven? (that is, to bring Christ down from above:) or, Who shall descend into the deep? (that is, to bring up Christ again from the dead.) But what saith it? The word is nigh thee, even in

> thy mouth, and in thy heart: that is, the word of
> faith, which we preach; that if thou shalt confess
> with thy mouth the Lord Jesus, and shalt believe
> in thine heart that God hath raised Him from the
> dead, thou shalt be saved. For with the heart man
> believeth to righteousness; and with the mouth
> confession is made to salvation. (10:1-10)

Notice how Paul says the Jews (generally) have not submitted themselves to the righteousness of God, that is, there has not been a bowing of the will in acknowledgement of their own guilt and helplessness, and a dependence on Christ for salvation. Later down that passage he says that salvation comes through confessing Jesus as Lord and believing in one's heart that God raised Him from the dead. To confess Jesus as Lord is to recognise who He is, the one who came down from heaven (according to verse 6), and bow to Him as such. To believe in the heart that God raised Him from the dead is to rest on the fact that the work is done, nothing needs to be added (see verse 7).[25] The last verse of the chapter shows us the contrast:

> But to Israel He saith, All day long I have stretched
> forth My hands to a disobedient and gainsaying
> people. (10:21)

Rather than believing, Israel is marked by unbelief,[26] and rather than confessing (literally *speaking the same word*) they are gainsaying (literally *speaking against*).[27]

So faith is not mere intellectual assent or the belief of historical facts. Many people are confused on this point. They have heard preachers say "Just believe that He died for you", and they say to themselves, "I do believe He died for me, but I'm not saved."[28] This then leads them to think they haven't got the right kind of faith or the right amount of faith, and they start trying to *really* believe it. The problem is they have been given wrong information. The

---

[25] Rom.10:9 is Paul's own experience of salvation. On the Damascus Road we see him confessing Jesus as Lord Acts 9:5,6, believing then and there that God had raised Him from the dead.
[26] "Disobedient" really is "unbelieving".
[27] See 6:17; 10:16 for other instances of saving faith being linked with the idea of obedience.
[28] A more tragic outcome is that they say "I do believe He died for me so I am saved" when they aren't at all.

Bible nowhere says that merely (or *really*) believing He died for you brings salvation. Charles Haddon Spurgeon said, "Saving faith is an immediate relation to Christ, accepting, receiving, resting upon Him alone, for justification, sanctification, and eternal life by virtue of God's grace."

When Paul teaches that justification comes to the sinner by faith he contrasts faith with something so that we can better understand what faith means. He says justification is by faith, *apart from the deeds of the law* (3:28), *to him who does not work* (4:5), *without works* (4:6). Faith stands in contrast to works. We exercise faith when we place our trust in someone or something. It is depending upon another to do for us what we cannot do for ourselves. You have faith in the pilot when you step aboard the plane; you have faith in the surgeon when you commit your case to him and allow him to operate on you; and you have faith in Christ when you depend on Him to save your soul and forgive your sins.[29] This leaves us with nothing of ourselves to boast of or glory in. See how Paul emphasises this point:

> Where is boasting then? It is excluded. By what law? of works? Nay: but by the law of faith. Therefore we conclude that a man is justified by faith without the deeds of the law. (3:27,28)

> What shall we say then that Abraham our father, as pertaining to the flesh, hath found? For if Abraham were justified by works, he hath whereof to glory; but not before God. For what saith the scripture? Abraham believed God, and it was counted unto him for righteousness.
> Now to him that worketh is the reward not reckoned of grace, but of debt. But to him that worketh not, but believeth on Him that justifieth the ungodly, his faith is counted for righteousness. Even as David also describeth the blessedness of the man, unto whom God imputeth righteousness without works, Saying, Blessed are they whose

---

[29] Paul has said twice in the preceding context that Jesus Christ is the object of faith (verses 22 and 26).

> iniquities are forgiven, and whose sins are
> covered. Blessed is the man to whom the Lord
> will not impute sin. (4:1-8)

Paul argues that faith means boasting is excluded; if you trust another then you get no credit if the thing you trust him to do gets done; you didn't accomplish it. If there was some work that we had to do, or standard of goodness to which we had to attain, then we would be able to take some credit and do some boasting. But faith eliminates all that. Does a beggar puff out his chest with pride when he receives a gift? Well, faith is the empty hand of the bankrupt sinner that receives God's gift.

> If we must keep ourselves saved in order to not be lost, the simple conclusion is that we have something to boast about concerning the quality of our performance in comparison to those who have never kept themselves saved. Salvation is ultimately dependent upon us for, in the end, even God cannot save us unless we allow it. But in effect, isn't this a form of earning our salvation by our own righteousness? And isn't such a teaching thoroughly rejected in Scripture? Granted, most Christians who believe that salvation can be lost do not think in these precise terms, but if they are trusting in their own performance to keep themselves saved, isn't this the only logical conclusion?[30]

In chapter 4 Paul enlarges on this by taking the two greatest figures in Israel's history, Abraham and David,[31] and showing how they both confirm the truth he has just been teaching: God justifies on the principle of faith.[32] The example of Abraham proves it is not by our working, he had been given a promise about having descendants as numerous as the stars. At this stage in life neither

---

[30] John Weldon, John Ankerberg, *Knowing the Truth about Eternal Security*, ATRI Publishing, loc. 108.
[31] Matthew wrote primarily for a Jewish audience, and when he commences his presentation of the Messiah he calls Him "the Son of David, the Son of Abraham" Matt. 1:1. With Abraham, justification by faith is the emphasis; with David, justification by grace is the emphasis.
[32] This chapter shows the truth of what Paul has said in 3:21, this righteousness which is apart from the law is witnessed by the law and the prophets. The experience of Abraham is recorded in the law section, and the experience of David would fall under the heading of the prophets.

he nor his wife had the ability to produce a child, it was going to require a miracle, and Abraham simply believed God; he trusted God to do what he and Sarah could not do.

It is at this point Paul brings in this wonderful illustration about works and wages. If you are contracted to do 40 hours work each week for your employer, every hour you work you are putting your employer more and more into your debt; he owes you. At the end of the week or the month he gives you your wages. This is not an act of grace on his part, he is just paying his debt; you have earned that money. However, if you were sick and could not work, and that same man came along with the wages and gave them to you, that is not debt, that is grace; you didn't earn that money, you couldn't earn that money, yet it is given to you anyway. That's the way justification works. There is no way anyone of the guilty members of this rebel race can stand before a holy God and say "I have earned your acceptance. I deserve your blessing." All we have earned is His wrath (2:5,6). All we deserve is to be cut off and cast away from Him forever (6:23). But even though we cannot earn His acceptance or deserve His blessing He offers it anyway. I heard a great illustration of this by the late J Boyd Nicholson. His grandfather lived in a coal mining community in Scotland back in the days when there was no sick-pay. Things were tough and the limited resources of large families were stretched. If someone in the locality was sick and unable to go to work Boyd's grandfather would go into the mine and do the work, he would then go to the sick man and give him the wages. Likely there would have been some men who would have been too proud to take such charity, but if those who were prepared to humble themselves and take something they couldn't earn, they would benefit from his work. So it is with the gospel. There are multiplied millions who are too proud to accept what God says about them and accept that they are charity cases. God is a God who justifies the one who does not work for it but simply trusts, and unless and until someone is prepared to accept his helplessness and receive justification as a gift he will never benefit from the offer. Paul says that the people God justifies are ungodly people.[33] This is perhaps what brings him to speak about David.

If the example of Abraham proves justification is not by our works, the example of David proves it is not by our worthiness. The incident with Bathsheba, and all that followed it, makes for very sad reading,[34] but nevertheless Psalm 32 is a song David wrote following his repentance, and we find such a man rejoicing in justification. We learn then in the case of Abraham that we are not justified on the basis of how hard we try, and we learn from David that we are not justified on the basis of how good we are. No, the answer to our guilt is not trying harder or doing better. The answer to our guilt is the grace of God and the blood of Christ, and we need to trust in the greatness of God's grace and depend on the value of Christ's blood for our acceptance with God. The fact that justification is by faith leads to wonderful assurance, as Paul details in chapter 5.

> Therefore, having been justified by faith, we have peace with God through our Lord Jesus Christ through whom also we have access by faith into this grace in which we stand, and rejoice in hope of the glory of God. (5:1,2, NKJV)

This is Paul commencing his conclusion to all that has gone before. He has shown that we can't be justified by law because the law condemns us. But the grace of God and the blood of Christ have intervened, and by trusting in Christ our record of guilt is cleared and we are declared righteous before God. I want to underscore the point that Paul does say that justification happens at a point in time, not over a period of time. It is God declaring us righteous, not making us righteous. Twice over in Romans 5 (verses 1 and 9) Paul says that we have been (aorist tense) justified. True, in 3:24 and 4:5 he does speak about it in the present tense, and the Roman

---

[33] Note the two-fold description: "him that worketh not" and "the ungodly"; our helplessness and our hostility are emphasised. These are descriptions Paul uses again in 5:6, "For when we were yet without strength Christ died for the ungodly." We find this two-fold description again in 8:7,8: Paul speaks there about our enmity against God and our inability to please Him, but in place of helplessness the Spirit of God gives life and in place of enmity He brings peace. Thus the Triune God meets our need as helpless, hostile sinners: in chapter 4 it is what God does, in chapter 5 it is what Christ does, in chapter 8 it is what the Spirit does.

[34] 2 Samuel 11 & 12.

Catholic Church bases its doctrine about justification as a process on this point, but in neither of these references is Paul citing a specific case of justification but rather he is stating how people are justified in 3:24 and about God as the God who justifies in 4:5. It would make no sense to say "having been justified by His grace" when he is not speaking about a specific instance of justification, and it would likewise give the wrong sense to speak of God as the God who justified the ungodly. But when Paul is dealing with real instances of justification, as he is in 5:1,9 ("we" occurs in both verses), he is crystal clear, it is done, we have been justified. So, according to 5:1,2, the person who has put his faith in Christ has been justified (an act in the past, at the moment faith was placed in Christ), he stands in grace (a reality in the present), and he rejoices in hope of the glory of God (a prospect for the future).

This is one of the many unique things about the message of the gospel, salvation is by faith. In all the religions of the world salvation is something you must attain by your own efforts, and for that reason no religion offers what the gospel offers, the present certainty of acceptance with God. If our standing before God was based on our performance then we could never have peace, but if I have abandoned all hope of meriting God's favour, recognising my guilt and helplessness, and have put my trust in Christ to make me right with God, then why would I ever doubt? If you trusted me to do something for you, you would be well within your rational rights to doubt and fear. You could justly wonder if I was really up to the task, but if you trust the Son of God then what sensible reason is there for worry? As one has said, "The truth of eternal security is inherent in the nature of salvation itself."[35]

Too easy?
Many people, when faced with the truth of justification by faith respond by saying it's too easy. The reality is it's anything but easy. It's the simplest thing in the world, but it certainly isn't easy to admit that I am a hell-deserving sinner. It isn't easy to accept there is nothing I can do to merit or contribute to my salvation. It isn't easy to take my hands off the matter and trust Christ to do it all. Our pride recoils and resists, desperately wanting some of the

---

[35] Lewis Sperry Chafer, *Systematic Theology*, Kregel, vol.3, p.272.

credit. The gospel does not massage our ego or cater to our pride. Justification by faith is a humbling thing, but then we have a lot to be humble about!

Another common reaction to the presentation of justification by faith is to say that it allows us then to live whatever way we like. I will not take time right now to actually answer that objection, (we will come to that later),[36] but I do just want to point out that I am always very pleased when someone responds in that way, it shows me that I have been presenting the Biblical gospel. After Paul had set out God's way of justifying sinners he anticipates an objection in 6:1:

> What shall we say then? Shall we continue in sin,
> that grace may abound?

Paul's presentation of the gospel should therefore invite this question, and if it doesn't then you haven't got the right gospel.

Martyn Lloyd-Jones said it well:

> There is no better test as to whether a man is really preaching the New Testament gospel of salvation than this, that some people might misunderstand it and misinterpret it to mean that it really amounts to this, that because you are saved by grace alone it does not matter at all what you do; you can go on sinning as much as you like because it will redound all the more to the glory of grace. That is a very good test of gospel preaching. If my preaching and presentation of the gospel of salvation does not expose it to that misunderstanding, then it is not the gospel. Let me show you what I mean.
>
> If a man preaches justification by works, no one would ever raise this question. If a man's preaching is, 'If you want to be Christians, and if you want to go to heaven, you must stop

---

[36] See the section *Getting away with murder?* Suffice it to say right now that the reason Paul gives for why we don't continue in sin is not because we would lose our salvation but because we have been set free from the power of sin in our lives.

committing sins, you must take up good works, and if you do so regularly and constantly, and do not fail to keep on at it, you will make yourselves Christians, you will reconcile yourselves to God, and you will go to heaven'. Obviously a man who preaches in that strain would never be liable to this misunderstanding. Nobody would say to such a man, 'Shall we continue in sin, that grace may abound?', because the man's whole emphasis is just this, that if you go on sinning you are certain to be damned, and only if you stop sinning can you save yourselves. So that misunderstanding could never arise....

...Nobody has ever brought this charge against the Church of Rome, but it was brought frequently against Martin Luther; indeed that was precisely what the Church of Rome said about the preaching of Martin Luther. They said, 'This man who was a priest has changed the doctrine in order to justify his own marriage and his own lust', and so on. 'This man', they said, 'is an antinomian; and that is heresy.' That is the very charge they brought against him. It was also brought against George Whitefield two hundred years ago. It is the charge that formal dead Christianity – if there is such a thing – has always brought against this startling, staggering message, that God 'justifies the ungodly'....

That is my comment; and it is a very important comment for preachers. I would say to all preachers: If your preaching of salvation has not been misunderstood in that way, then you had better examine your sermons again, and you had better make sure that you really are preaching the salvation that is offered in the New Testament to the ungodly, to the sinner, to those who are dead in trespasses and sins, to those who are enemies of God. There is this kind of dangerous element about the true presentation of the doctrine of salvation.[37]

Some call this gospel the gospel of cheap grace. It's not at all, it's free grace. And the reason it is free is because it is the most costly thing in the universe, so costly we could never pay for it. Only the sacrificial, substitutionary death of Christ could pay the price. The only people who will come into the good of God's grace are those who are prepared to accept that they can do nothing to earn it, but Christ has done everything to provide it, and it is received as a free gift or it is not received at all. It is an insult to God to offer Him payment for that which cost Him His Son; that cheapens it.

> The great Protestant reformer Martin Luther was correct when he wrote that in the end there are only two religions in the world: the religion of grace and the religion of works. In essence, all non-Christian religions in the world, large and small, are religions of works. Only biblical Christianity teaches that salvation is a free gift resulting solely from God's grace. This makes Christianity unlike any other religion that has ever existed, past or present...this is also one of the great proofs that the Bible alone is a divine revelation. Were it not, it would teach the same approach to salvation found in every other religion devised by human beings or inspired by demonic spirits.[38]

That then is the answer to Job's question, "How should a man be just with God?" It is through faith. That's what brings us into this wonderful blessing of justification.

But what about James?
In a last ditch effort to evade the plain teaching of Romans on justification by faith, many will cite James and his teaching about justification by works. Now we have to point out a problem with this procedure that is very common with cultists and others who deny justification by faith: we have made our case thus far on the

[37] Martyn Lloyd-Jones, *Romans: The New Man, An Exposition of Chapter 6*, cited in *The Grace Awakening*, Charles R. Swindoll, W Publishing Group, pp.33,34.
[38] Weldon, Ankerberg, *Knowing the Truth about Eternal Security*, loc 56.

fact that Paul says those who are justified are (as good as) glorified, and then we noticed that people are, according to Paul, justified by faith apart from works. If someone jumps to another part of the Bible and shows that another author speaks about justification being by works then we have to conclude one of two things, either there is a contradiction in the Bible or justification is being used in a different sense, but in no way does it follow that Paul didn't mean what he said. We have walked carefully through the argument of the epistle to the Romans and have observed the plain teaching of Paul that our works do not come into the matter of being made right with God. When those opposed to that teaching go to James they are not showing you that your understanding of Romans is incorrect, they have to deal with Paul's words and show how he isn't actually teaching what he appears to teach over and over again. Honesty and consistency demand that they deal with the texts from Romans, and that is something they are utterly unable to do. Knowing then that the Bible does not contradict itself, we can safely conclude that James is speaking about justification in a different sense to Paul.

So what did James mean when he spoke of justification by works? Let's look at the text:

> What doth it profit, my brethren, though a man say he hath faith, and have not works? can faith save him? If a brother or sister be naked, and destitute of daily food, and one of you say unto them, Depart in peace, be ye warmed and filled; notwithstanding ye give them not those things which are needful to the body; what doth it profit? Even so faith, if it hath not works, is dead, being alone.
>
> Yea, a man may say, Thou hast faith, and I have works: shew me thy faith without thy works, and I will shew thee my faith by my works.
>
> Thou believest that there is one God; thou doest well: the devils also believe, and tremble. But wilt thou know, O vain man, that faith without works is dead?

> Was not Abraham our father justified by works, when he had offered Isaac his son upon the altar? Seest thou how faith wrought with his works, and by works was faith made perfect? And the scripture was fulfilled which saith, Abraham believed God, and it was imputed unto him for righteousness: and he was called the Friend of God. Ye see then how that by works a man is justified, and not by faith only.
>
> Likewise also was not Rahab the harlot justified by works, when she had received the messengers, and had sent them out another way?
>
> For as the body without the spirit is dead, so faith without works is dead also. (Jms.2:14-26)

Look at how James commences this section, "though a man *say* he hath faith, and have not works" (emphasis added). James is clearly calling into question whether the man has faith at all. His spiritual antennae are up and twitching nervously, he detects a fake in our midst. Here is a man who says he has faith and there is nothing in his life that backs that up, there is nothing in the man's behaviour that would tie up with his professed belief. James then injects a shot of sarcasm and spoons a dose of scepticism into his words and says in effect, *OK, you say you have faith, let's call it that, can that kind of faith save?* Unfortunately the KJV misses this vital point by leaving out the definite article, and having James merely say "can faith save him?" If that were the question then the answer would be a resounding yes! Indeed, twice over the Lord Jesus said, "Thy faith hath saved thee" (Lk. 7:50; 8:48).

The definite article is there in the original text and is reflected by most translations, for example:

> What doth it profit, my brethren, if a man say he hath faith, but have not works? can that faith save him? (ASV, RV)

> What good is it, my brothers and sisters, if someone claims to have faith but does not have works? Can this kind of faith save him? (NET)

James is referring to that which the man claims to have, and he is saying, *If you call that faith then I want you to know, that kind of faith cannot save you.* In reality, people will live out and act on their core beliefs. You can tell what someone believes by watching how they live, seeing what is most important to them, what drives them, etc. James is saying here that if a man does not live in accord with his professed faith then that is just an empty faith. Where saving faith is exercised it will be manifest in works because salvation brings new life. This is something Paul readily affirms and confirms:

> For by grace are ye saved through faith; and that not of yourselves: it is the gift of God: not of works, lest any man should boast.
> For we are his workmanship, created in Christ Jesus unto good works, which God hath before ordained that we should walk in them. (Eph.2:8-10)

So if there is not fruit in the life or evidence in the walk of the professing believer, it shows that the faith is empty and insincere, just the same way it is empty and insincere to say to someone in need "be ye warmed and filled" and you do nothing about it; you are showing that the words which have come from your lips haven't actually come from your heart. So if someone professes to be a believer but his life is no different then it shows that his profession has not come from his heart.

James goes on to give further proof that saving faith is not a mere intellectual faith:

> You believe that there is one God. You do well. Even the demons believe – and tremble! (v.19, NKJV)

The demons are theologically orthodox! There is belief, but there is not actual trust. He then issues the challenge again, if your "faith" isn't manifesting itself in your life then it is not saving faith. It's at this point he introduces the two very interesting examples of Abraham and Rahab.

The striking point about Abraham and Rahab is this: the works by which James says they were justified were not works that we would consider good! James isn't saying that Abraham and Rahab were justified by giving to charity, helping their neighbours and living upright lives. Abraham was about to offer up his son, Rahab betrayed her own nation! How did these actions justify them? Quite simply because there is absolutely no way Abraham and Rahab would have done what they did if they did not trust God. The fact that they carried out these actions was the proof of their faith in the promise and power of God. Would Abraham ever have raised the knife to kill his beloved son if he did not trust God? Of course not! Would Rahab ever have betrayed her nation if she was not sure that Yahweh was going to give the Israelites the land? Not a chance! These actions declared these people to be true believers, thus they were justified (or vindicated) by their works.[39] James says that Abraham's sacrifice of Isaac fulfilled the Scripture, "Abraham believed God, and it was imputed unto him for righteousness." But of course that faith was exercised and that imputation made many years before (Gen.15:6), but we see that it was a true faith by what he did on Mount Moriah. So, far from this passage teaching that we are justified by how much we do or how hard we try or how good we are, it is teaching the very opposite; your life should show your faith is in the Lord alone. How would such faith be manifested? Imagine someone who is brought up in a system in which he is taught that a certain ritual or ceremony needs to be carried out every week to ensure his salvation. That person then hears the gospel and makes a profession of faith in Christ. What happens next? If the professor continues to carry out the ritual week by week it shows he has not really put his faith in Christ to save him, but if he abandons the system and never observes the ceremony it is showing that he has real faith. He never would have dared give up that religion if he did not have genuine faith in the Saviour, thus his work showed his faith, he is justified by works.

To conclude then, notice the difference: Paul in the epistle to the Romans is speaking in a legal sense; we are in the courtroom before the Judge, but James is not speaking about justification in

---

[39] D. Edmond Hiebert points out that in this context the word translated *justified* means *vindicated*: "But the point of James's argument here clearly does not imply a forensic declaration of justification; rather, he is pointing to the divine vindication of the righteous nature of his character manifested by the deeds flowing from his faith." *James*, Moody Press, 1992, p.171.

that forensic sense, he is speaking about justification in a practical sense. Remember that the word *justification* means a declaration that the person is righteous. Paul is saying that legally that declaration takes place the moment faith is exercised in the person of Christ and the provision He made, but James is saying that practically you are declared righteous when that faith manifests itself.

The final link in the chain
We have spent quite a bit of time setting out how a sinner is justified because Paul's teaching is crystal clear, if you're justified then you're glorified, it's a *fait accompli*.

> *He glorified us.* This is the clincher in the five-linked chain of argument! The Holy Spirit daringly puts the verb in the past tense – He glorified us – even though our present infirmities remind us all too vividly that we have not yet reached the glorified state. The point is that if a person has been justified, his glorification is as certain as if it had already taken place.[40]

> 'Glorified' is a marvellous past tense. It reminds us that in this passage we are placed, as it were, upon the mountain of the throne of God; our finite thought is allowed to speak for once (however little it understands it) the language of eternity, to utter the facts as the Eternal sees them. To God, the pilgrim is already in heaven; the bondservant is already at the end of his day's work receiving his Master's 'Well done, good and faithful'. He to whom time is not as it is to us thus sees his purposes complete, always and forever. We see through His sight, in hearing His word about it. So for us, in wonderful paradox, our glorification is presented, as truly as our call, in terms of accomplished fact.[41]

So the all important issue is to make sure you are justified. Paul

---

[40] William MacDonald, *Once in Christ, in Christ Forever*, Gospel Folio Press, 1997, p.24.
[41] H. C. G. Moule, *Romans*, Marshall Pickering, 1992, p.162.

reaches this point and we can see him shaking his head in wonder as he says, "What shall we then say to these things?" Looking at the glorious scope of divine purpose Paul is almost lost for words. He says "If God be for us, who can be against us?" If this is the plan of God for His people then who could ever stop it?

The argument of Paul is so watertight and the purpose of God so certain that we could really finish the book here, but we'll not, there's still much more to be said.

Ephesians 1:1-14

Let's briefly stop here without delving into all the details. It will be enough for our purpose to lift a few key points.

> Paul, an apostle of Jesus Christ by the will of God, to the saints which are at Ephesus, and to the faithful in Christ Jesus: grace be to you, and peace, from God our Father, and from the Lord Jesus Christ.
> Blessed be the God and Father of our Lord Jesus Christ, who hath blessed us with all spiritual blessings in heavenly places in Christ: according as He hath chosen us in Him before the foundation of the world, that we should be holy and without blame before Him in love: having predestinated us unto the adoption of children by Jesus Christ to Himself, according to the good pleasure of His will, to the praise of the glory of His grace, wherein He hath made us accepted in the beloved.
> In whom we have redemption through His blood, the forgiveness of sins, according to the riches of His grace; wherein He hath abounded toward us in all wisdom and prudence; having made known unto us the mystery of His will, according to His good pleasure which He hath purposed in Himself: that in the dispensation of the fulness of times He might gather together in one all things in Christ, both which are in heaven, and which are on earth; even in Him: in whom also we have

> obtained an inheritance, being predestinated according to the purpose of Him who worketh all things after the counsel of His own will: that we should be to the praise of His glory, who first trusted in Christ.
>
> In whom ye also trusted, after that ye heard the word of truth, the gospel of your salvation: in whom also after that ye believed, ye were sealed with that Holy Spirit of promise, which is the earnest of our inheritance until the redemption of the purchased possession, unto the praise of His glory.

Paul ascribes praise to the Triune God for our salvation, and, in regard to God the Father, Paul takes our minds back before creation, and tells us about election and predestination. He tells us that God chose us in Christ before the foundation of the world that we should be holy and without blame before Him in love, and He has predestined us to sonship through Jesus Christ to Himself. In short then, it is God's purpose to have *saints before Him* and the Father's purpose to have *sons toward Him*. This is God graciously and gloriously undoing all the effects of the fall. When Adam and Eve sinned they experienced two things they had never known before, shame and fear, and rather than walk with God they fled from His presence and hid. But God was not defeated nor was He taken by surprise, for before the foundation of the world He had determined there would be saints before Him without shame and sons toward Him without fear, and this then is the position and prospect of every Christian, because every Christian is in the enjoyment of sainthood and in the place of sonship.[42]

Further down the passage he tells us that we have obtained an inheritance in Christ, having been predestined according to the purpose of Him who works all things after the counsel of His will. It is clear that when the Bible speaks in this context about God's purpose it is not talking about a mere desire. God desires many things that don't take place,[43] but when Paul speaks of God's

---

[42] Even the carnal Corinthian believers were saints (1 Cor. 1:2), and we are all the sons of God by faith in Christ Jesus (Gal.3:26).

[43] e.g. 1 Thess.4:3; 5:18; 1 Tim.2:4.

purpose he is talking about the very reason God brought creation into existence. God is working all things after the counsel of His will in order to fulfil His purpose. It would be nothing less than a failure on God's part then if a single soul whom He had chosen and predestined were ever to be lost. Whatever difficulties may surround the glorious truth of election, everyone should be able to see that it is a guarantee of our eternal security. Let me give Fred Saunders the last word on Ephesians 1:

> What would it take to lose your salvation?
> Sometimes I think the fact that we can pose that question in such a short sentence, with so few words, is part of the problem of talking about the question well. The brevity of the formulation ("Lose your salvation? Yes or no.") lends itself to taking the question less seriously than it deserves. The five syllables of "lose your salvation" don't have enough gravity or complexity to prepare our minds for what the Bible teaches.
> A mental discipline I've imposed on my own thinking, and which I sometimes inflict on students, is to replace the phrase "lose your salvation" with the thought project, "run Ephesians 1 backwards." Instead of asking, "can you lose your salvation," ask, "if Ephesians 1 is true of you, how could it reverse its momentum and come untrue of you?"
> By Ephesians 1, I mean specifically the one long Greek sentence that is verses 3-14, which explores the "complete spiritual blessing" with which God has blessed us in Christ. As far as I can tell, for it to run in reverse would require something like this:
> The guarantee on our inheritance has been voided and its possession will now be forfeited; God has removed His seal, the Holy Spirit, from us. We no longer believe the word of truth, so it is no longer the gospel of our salvation. We have been un-predestined, have lost the inheritance, and

are back outside of Christ. The mystery of God's will for the summing up of all things in Christ in the fullness of time has gone opaque and become irrelevant. An unlavishing of grace has taken place. We do not have redemption through the blood of God's beloved Son, so our trespasses are not forgiven. We are unadopted, have stepped out of our predestination to that goal, so we will never stand holy and blameless before God in love. We have been unchosen from before the foundation of the world. No longer being in Christ, we are no longer recipients of every spiritual blessing in Him. And perhaps God's glorious grace, and His wisdom in salvation, will still be praised, but not by looking at us. Avert your eyes.

This is the mental vision in the back of my mind when I discuss the topic of losing salvation. It transmits some sense of the scope and complexity involved, and rules out in advance a number of facile blunders.[44]

Before we conclude this section on the purpose of God I want briefly to stop in John's Gospel to show that what Paul teaches about God's purpose guaranteeing our salvation confirms ministry the Lord Jesus had already given, which we'll look at now.

John 6:35-40

The purpose of God was supreme in the life of the Lord Jesus, and it is this that guarantees that we can never be lost.

And Jesus said unto them, I am the bread of life: he that cometh to Me shall never hunger; and he that believeth on Me shall never thirst.

But I said unto you, That ye also have seen Me, and believe not. All that the Father giveth Me shall come to Me; and him that cometh to Me I will in no wise cast out. For I came down from heaven, not to do Mine own will, but the will of Him that sent Me. And this is the Father's will

[44] http://www.patheos.com/blogs/scriptorium/2013/06/eno-snaisehpe-ephesians-one-backwards/

which hath sent Me, that of all which He hath
given Me I should lose nothing, but should raise
it up again at the last day. And this is the will of
Him that sent Me, that every one which seeth the
Son, and believeth on Him, may have everlasting
life: and I will raise him up at the last day.

The Lord had been preaching in the synagogue in Capernaum.
The response was less than enthusiastic. As you read the
discourse you discover that the people were more than happy
to have a miracle-working King, but they were turned off by the
idea of Him being the Saviour from heaven who would give His
life for their salvation. But despite the lack of response the Lord
knew that God's purpose would be fulfilled and all was not in
vain. Although most in His audience would not believe, the Lord
declared that all that the Father gave Him would come to Him,
and that anyone who came to Him would never be cast out. This
tells us something then about what it means to come to Christ.
It is to come to Him as He is in reality, as He has been revealed
in the Word. Many people have made a move toward a Jesus
they can have as an example, a Jesus who can help them through
their difficulties, or a Jesus who gives great guidance for living a
fulfilled life, but when it comes to the Jesus of Scripture, the Son
of God who calls on us to repent and bow to Him as Lord, the one
who speaks about our defilement and condemnation, the one who
presents Himself as the only Saviour and His sacrifice as the only
means of salvation, many of those people would run a mile. The
one who thus comes to Christ on His terms is the one who can
claim the comfort of these words, "him that cometh to Me I will in
no wise cast out."

This lovely text is not just telling us that the Lord will never turn
anyone away who comes to Him, gloriously true though that is,
but rather it is telling us that, having taken a sinner in, under no
circumstances will the Lord ever subsequently cast him out. He takes
sinners in and never casts them out, they are His forever. In fact, the
Lord emphasises the point by the use of a "strong double negation",[45]
giving the expression this force, "I will never, never cast out."

----

[45] *Robertson's Word Pictures*, e-Sword.

The strong negative "in no wise" suggests that, so far from casting out a believer, the Lord will embrace and protect him; it conveys something more than the promise to receive, it carries with it the assurance of eternal security, and intimates the delight of the Lord in this grace toward what is given Him by the Father.[46]

The last clause "I will in no wise cast out" assures the eternal preservation of everyone that truly cometh to Christ. These words of the Saviour do not signify (as generally supposed) that He promises to *reject none* who really come to Him, *though that is true*; but they declare that under no imaginable circumstances will He ever expel one that *has* come. Peter came to Him and was saved. Later, he *denied* his Master with an oath. But did Christ "cast him out"? Nay, verily. And can we find a more extreme case? If Peter *was not* "cast out," *no* Christian ever was, or will be. Praise the Lord![47]

No limit is set to the duration of this promise. It does not merely say, "I will not cast out a sinner at his first coming," but, "I will in no wise cast out." The original reads, "I will not, not cast out," or "I will never, never cast out." The text means that Christ will not at first reject a believer; and that as He will not do it at first, so He will not to the last.[48]

While we rejoice in the fact that Christ is devoted to His people, the force of this passage is not that it is His devotion to us that ensures we are never cast out, but rather it is His devotion to His Father. He says He came down from heaven to do His Father's will, and the Father's will is that none given to the Son / believing

[46] W. E. Vine, *John: His Record of Christ*, *The Collected Writings of W. E. Vine*, Thomas Nelson Publishers, vol.1, p.253.
[47] A. W. Pink, *Exposition of the Gospel of John*, Zondervan Publishing House, pp.330, 331, emphasis his.
[48] C. H. Spurgeon, *Morning and Evening: Daily Readings*, Evening, 30th July.

on the Son should be lost.[49] The Lord's commitment to His Father is unqualified, and for that reason we ought to have no fear, it's not just the case that we will not be cast out, but we cannot be cast out; a believer losing his salvation would rend the Godhead asunder. The chain that links us to salvation is as strong and secure as the relationship of God the Father with His beloved and eternal Son. We really are as safe as that.

I heard about a woman and her son who went to a gospel meeting and heard a message on John 6:37. Both the mother and son came to Christ that night and were rejoicing in salvation. About a week later the boy came home from school and found his mother sitting at the table looking very troubled and upset. When he asked her what was wrong she told him she didn't know if she was still saved. The boy went over to the table, lifted the Bible and turned to John 6. He ran his eye down the passage until he got to verse 37, then he looked up and said, "Mum, it's still here!" That's one of the great things about the God we have, His purpose is eternal and His promise never changes. When the emotions go on a roller coaster ride we can still point to His Word and say "It's still here." When the dark clouds of sorrow gather, it's still there. When the storm of suffering breaks, it's still there. When the world seems to be falling apart around you, God's Word is still there. And when we come to the threshold of eternity, pushing against the very door of death, we can rest secure knowing "it's still here." Someone has said that the believer has a firmer foundation for his faith than he does for his feet. How true that is. The Saviour said, "Heaven and earth shall pass away, but My words shall not pass away" (Matt 24:35).

It is great to know that our security rests on divine purpose. It is possible for us to have plans that look good on paper and seem good in theory but then as time goes on we realise there were factors we hadn't considered, issues we didn't know about, and problems we never anticipated, and the plan had to be scrapped. Many of us look back to purposes we had in our childhood, things we wanted to do and be, and now such ambitions would be the furthest things from our minds, we have changed with the passing

---

[49] Just as v.37 presents the divine side then the human side, v.39 is the divine side and v.40 the human side.

years. It is also the case that many plans remain unfulfilled, not because they are bad ideas or we no longer want to implement them, but because we just can't; there are obstacles we are not able to overcome and so we have to admit defeat. Our ignorance, our changeable natures and our weaknesses all combine to make our purposes very shaky. How we should rejoice that with God there is none of that uncertainty. The God we trust is omniscient. Every detail about the past, present and future is fully known by Him, so there will never be any unforeseen events.

> Remember the former things of old: for I am God, and there is none else; I am God, and there is none like Me, declaring the end from the beginning, and from ancient times the things that are not yet done, saying, My counsel shall stand, and I will do all My pleasure… (Isa.46:9,10)

Not only can nothing ever surprise an omniscient God, but nothing can ever change an immutable God. God will never change His mind regarding His purpose. He is the great I AM.

> For I am the LORD, I change not... (Mal.3:6)

> Every good gift and every perfect gift is from above, and cometh down from the Father of lights, with whom is no variableness, neither shadow of turning. (Jms.1:17)

We know God's purpose will never change because He is omniscient, because He is immutable, and also because He is omnipotent. Here is a God who cannot be knocked off course by any foe.

> For I know that the LORD is great, and that our Lord is above all gods. Whatsoever the LORD pleased, that did He in heaven, and in earth, in the seas, and all deep places. (Ps.135:5,6)

This attribute of His omnipotence will be considered in more detail in our next section, but we can pause here in reverent worship before our great God and rest absolutely secure in the knowledge that "The counsel of the Lord standeth forever, the thoughts of

His heart to all generations" (Ps.33:11). His purpose is to glorify all who have been justified, to share His inheritance with every son, to keep all who have come, and His purpose will be fulfilled; it cannot fail.

The Power of God

When we speak about someone having power we usually mean one of two things. We can either be talking about the strength of the person (like a power-lifter), or we can be talking about the authority of the person (e.g. the Prime Minister is a very powerful man). When it comes to the subject of our eternal security both these ideas are relevant.

The strength of God
Peter was writing to strangers who had been scattered abroad. They likely felt that there wasn't too much that was stable and secure in their lives. Peter's first epistle was written with the intention of establishing, strengthening and settling them (1 Pet.5:10). He does this right from the commencement by telling them how secure they really are. Though their circumstances seemed very shaky Peter tells them they are being kept by omnipotence:

> Blessed be the God and Father of our Lord Jesus Christ, which according to His abundant mercy hath begotten us again to a lively hope by the resurrection of Jesus Christ from the dead, to an inheritance incorruptible, and undefiled, and that fadeth not away, reserved in heaven for you, who are kept by the power of God through faith unto salvation ready to be revealed in the last time. (1 Pet.1:3-5)

The assurance for these believers was that there was an inheritance that was kept for them; it was reserved in heaven for them. But more, they were kept for it, and the power that kept them was nothing less than the power of God Himself. The word Peter uses, here translated kept, is the word Paul uses in 2 Cor.11:32, translated *garrison*.

> In Damascus the governor under Aretas the king
> kept the city of the Damascenes with a garrison,
> desirous to apprehend me:

The governor deployed the king's military might to ensure that Paul would be kept in Damascus and would not escape. However, Paul was too wily and managed to escape his hands. But the Christian is garrisoned by the power of God, and there is therefore no possibility of escape from the inside.[50] Neither is there any possibility of invasion from the outside. We can find examples in Scripture of garrisons being broken through,[51] but none can break through this garrison. The believer is therefore as secure as an all-powerful God can make him.

The Lord Jesus makes a similar point to this in Jn.10:27-30:

> My sheep hear My voice, and I know them, and
> they follow Me: and I give unto them eternal life;
> and they shall never perish, neither shall any
> man pluck them out of My hand.
> My Father, which gave them Me, is greater than
> all; and no man is able to pluck them out of My
> Father's hand.
> I and My Father are one.

In this chapter in which the Lord presents Himself as the Good Shepherd we see how much He loves His sheep. He gives His life for them (v.11), but He also gives His life to them (v.28). It is worth taking our time and examining what the Lord says carefully.

"My sheep hear My voice" – Please don't take the Lord's words here in the sense so many understand them today as they "learn to hear from God". Trying to hear God's voice and decipher His "leading" is not a Scriptural motif for Christian living. The Lord was simply saying that His sheep respond to His voice, they heed His call. The previous verse makes that clear, "But ye believe not, because ye are not of My sheep, as I said unto you." What this tells us is that someone who claims to be a Christian, but consistently

---

[50] The fact that we are kept by the power of God *through faith* unto salvation does not introduce any thought of insecurity into the doctrine. When we come to look at the section on the unfinished work of Christ we will see how Peter would know better than anyone that the faith that links the believer with the Lord can never be broken.
[51] e.g. 2 Sam.23:13-17

has no regard for what the Bible teaches, does not actually belong to Christ at all.

"and I know them" – This is a statement not of the extent of knowledge the Lord had, but of the personal relationship He has with His own. Again, if the Lord is a stranger to you, if you have not come to know Him personally, the doctrine of eternal security has no comfort for you.

"and they follow Me" – This is not an imperative but an indicative, that is, it is not setting out eternal life as being conditional upon us following Him, it is saying that those who have eternal life are those who follow. The verse shows that eternal life actually affects the life; it puts people on a different path going a different direction. Those who have eternal life show it. If someone says he is saved yet the course of his life has never altered and he has no desire to be close to the Shepherd, I wouldn't like to be in his shoes.

"and I give unto them eternal life" – "Not, 'I will give,' as if the bestowment of life was a promise conditional upon following Him. That interpretation has been put forward by some, but it is contradictory to 5:24, where the Lord declared that eternal life was imparted upon hearing His word and believing. The present tense indicates the possession of life already enjoyed."[52]

The Lord says eternal life is something *He* gives.[53] That means it is not dispensed through any third party, but comes directly from the Lord. It is not administered through any ordinance. If someone is going to have eternal life he needs to come directly to Christ for it.

Notice too, it's something He *gives*. It is not a prize to be won, an item to be bought or a reward to be earned. It is a free gift to be received by those who deserve the very opposite. As Paul says in Rom.6:23:

> For the wages of sin is death; but the gift of God is
> eternal life through Jesus Christ our Lord.

He goes on to say in Rom.11:29 that "the gifts and calling of God

---

[52] Vine, *John: His Record of Christ*, p.277.
[53] The pronoun "I" in the sentence is emphatic.

are without repentance." This means that once God gives a free gift it is never recalled.

So what then does He give? He gives eternal life. This is a big point we need to get. John's Gospel is full of teaching about eternal life, and it is taught again and again that eternal life is not merely a future prospect, but for the person who believes in Christ it is a present reality. It is something *living*, after all, it's called eternal *life*. This is one of the many unique things about the Christian gospel, and it is also one of the many reasons why we can be sure Christianity is true and that we are saved, it offers new life *now*. God is not just saying if you trust Christ to save you then you'll be in heaven when you die. That would leave some people still in a state of anxiety: *Is the whole thing true? Have I interpreted it right? Have I really trusted?* etc. but God gives eternal life as a present possession so that we can know for sure that this is real. It is a life from God, indeed it is the very life of God, and it is communicated to us in the new birth. In this passage, as well as Jn.3:16, it is set in contrast to perishing. When we get a grasp of what it means to perish it will help us understand by contrast what it means to have eternal life.

To perish has the idea of being marred, spoiled, ruined or lost. When that is applied to us it has a present and eternal aspect to it. Without Christ we are perishing now,[54] and without Christ we will ultimately and eternally perish.[55] In the present we are not fit for God's purpose, we can't live for Him, know Him, enjoy Him, or please Him, we are ruined. And then eternally we are not fit for His presence, we can't live with Him, we are lost to Him forever. So sin spoils us for God and separates us from God. Eternal life is the perfect answer to this. It's a life that enables us to live for God now and entitles us to live with God forever.

A man I worked with asked me on one occasion if it would be possible for him to be saved and still go on living the same kind of life he's living now. I told him it would be more than he would be able to do to be saved and keep living the same life. Eternal life is something *living*.

---

[54] e.g. 1 Cor.1:18
[55] e.g. Rom.2:12

But eternal life is also something *lasting;* after all, it's called *eternal* life. For that reason it can never be lost.

"and they shall never perish" – This is His guarantee to all who have eternal life. The word *never* is another example of that double negative we noticed in Jn.6:37, we shall never, **never** perish, is the force of it. "Never say never" is good advice for us. Many a time we say "Never" only to have to eat our words and retrace our steps later. But when God says "never" you can rest your soul and stake your eternity on it.

"neither shall any man pluck them out of My hand" – You may well think that all that has gone before is adequate to assure us, but the Lord isn't finished. He speaks about His sheep being held by His powerful hand. So although practically we are following Him, positionally we are held by Him, and it is His hold on us that makes us secure, not our hold on Him. Earlier in the chapter the Lord Jesus told us about the danger of thieves and robbers who are seeking to get the sheep (vv.1,8). Thieves use stealth to get what they want, robbers use strength to get what they want. Thieves operate on the ignorance of their victims;[56] robbers operate on the weakness of their victims.[57] Isn't it great to know that the one who keeps and cares for us is the omniscient Shepherd who can never be outsmarted by any thief, and He is the omnipotent Shepherd who can never be overpowered by any robber?

Some have countered this clause by saying that it only says no other person can take us out of His hand, it doesn't say we can't take ourselves out. Harry Ironside brings a bit of clear thinking and common sense to bear on such a notion:

> Some may say, "Well, I know a devil cannot pluck me out, no angel would want to, and man could not, but I might pluck myself out." Then you would perish, would you not? And He says, "They shall never perish," before He tells you,

---

[56] See Matt.24:43: "But know this, that if the goodman of the house had known in what watch the thief would come, he would have watched, and would not have suffered his house to be broken up."

[57] See Lk.10:30: "A certain man was going down from Jerusalem to Jericho; and he fell among robbers, which both stripped him and beat him, and departed, leaving him half dead" (RV).

"Neither shall any pluck them out of My hand."[58]

Have you got a sense of that security yet? You have eternal life, you will never, never perish, you are in Christ's hand and no one can pluck you out, but there is more.

"My Father, which gave them Me, is greater than all; and no man is able to pluck them out of My Father's hand. I and My Father are one" – Not only is there a double negation in regard to perishing, but there is a double security in regard to salvation; the Lord does not want any of His people to be in any doubt about their safety. The teaching is as clear as could be: if someone has eternal life then there's not the slightest possibility of them losing it or Christ losing them.

> Nothing can be more touching, nothing more precious or wonderful! The grace is infinite, the love knows no bounds, and the power by which all is secured is the almighty power of the Eternal God.[59]

The idea of the Lord as the Shepherd is a prominent one in the Bible and is full of assurance in regard to our subject. Think of the lovely story the Lord told in Lk.15:3-7:

> And He spake this parable unto them, saying, What man of you, having an hundred sheep, if he lose one of them, doth not leave the ninety and nine in the wilderness, and go after that which is lost, until he find it? And when he hath found it, he layeth it on his shoulders, rejoicing. And when he cometh home, he calleth together his friends and neighbours, saying unto them, Rejoice with me; for I have found my sheep which was lost.
> I say unto you, that likewise joy shall be in heaven over one sinner that repenteth, more than over ninety and nine just persons, which need no repentance.

---

[58] Ironside, *The Eternal Security of the Believer*, p.25.
[59] J. N. Darby (the authorship isn't certain), *The Fold and the Flock, Present Testimony* 8 (1856), http://www.stempublishing.com/authors/darby/Magazines/JND_possibles.html.

The point I want us to see from this story is that the security of the sheep depended entirely on the shepherd. When the shepherd found the sheep he didn't send it home, nor did he lead it home, but he carried it the whole way home. He picked it up and never set it down until he was across the threshold of his door.

> As sheep, our security is the responsibility of our Shepherd (1 Pet.2:25). Of each saved sheep it is written, "When He hath found it, He layeth it on His shoulders, rejoicing" (Lk.15:5). The struggles of the sheep would not be to keep on, but to get off. We are not saved by our "holding on", for sheep have no hands to hold on by. Now all the Lord's sheep are borne along on the shoulders of the rejoicing Shepherd, and thus all are equally saved. The Shepherd will take care that not one shall slip off His shoulders. When danger is past, the journey ended, and home reached (v.6), the Shepherd's note of joy is this: "I have found My sheep which was lost." Thus the eternal safety of every sheep is the blessed Lord's own personal responsibility and care.[60]

The point is clear, when it comes to the matter of our salvation He is carrying us. He lifted us at the moment of salvation and He will never let us go or let us down for one single step or one single second of life's pathway. He will set us down safe in heaven's glory. Think about that sheep for a moment, is there any way it could have been lost again once the shepherd found it? Well, if the shepherd wasn't strong enough to carry it. Is there any possibility of one who has rested on Christ for salvation ever being lost? It seems that could only happen if the Lord was not strong enough to completely save us. Is that something we ought to worry about? Of course not! We are trusting in one of whom it is said, "He is able to save to the uttermost..." (Heb.7:25, RV).

A similar truth is presented in Philippians 1:

---

[60] Walter Scott, *Eternal Security, Holding on or eternally held?* http://www.stempublishing.com/authors/Walter_Scott/WS_Eternal_Security.html.

> I thank my God upon every remembrance of you,
> always in every prayer of mine for you all making
> request with joy, for your fellowship in the gospel
> from the first day until now; being confident of
> this very thing, that He which hath begun a good
> work in you will perform it until the day of Jesus
> Christ... (vv.3-6)

Paul is thanking God for the work that the Philippian believers were engaged in on behalf of the gospel. They had been marked by consistency, "from the first day until now" their fellowship had been expressed and enjoyed. This led Paul to think of something even greater, a work that God was doing in them that not only had continued up to that present moment, but would continue until, and be completed at, the day of Jesus Christ.[61]

> No other agent is at work but He alone, and what
> He does covers the beginning, the continuation
> and the completion of Christian experience.[62]

God had commenced His saving work in the lives of these Philippians, and He would see it through to the end. Any sheep lifted by the Lord is taken all the way home.

Let's bring this section to a close with a lesson from a parable the Lord told, recorded in Lk.11:21, 22:

> When a strong man armed keepeth his palace,
> his goods are in peace: but when a stronger than
> he shall come upon him, and overcome him,
> he taketh from him all his armour wherein he
> trusted, and divideth his spoils.

Here is a strong man keeping his palace safe and his goods secure. The goods are under threat only if a stronger man comes along. When the Lord came to earth there were many who were the spoil of Satan, under his authority and in his dark domain. We are glad for the one who is stronger than the strong man and was able to overcome him and take his goods. We are now in the keeping

---

[61] The day of Jesus Christ (or the day of Christ) is a reference to a period of time in heaven that commences with the rapture of the Church.
[62] Alec Motyer, *The Message of Philippians*, The Bible Speaks Today series, IVP, Second edition, 1997, p.43.

power of God. The question then is this, is there anyone stronger than Him? Is there anyone who can overcome God and take His property? To ask the question is to answer it, of course there isn't. That means therefore "his goods are in peace". There is no need for us to worry, the strength of God guarantees our eternal security.

The authority of God
You could imagine someone having great strength but nevertheless being outranked and overruled by someone of superior authority, but we don't need to have any worries in that regard. The almighty God in whom we trust is the Sovereign of the universe, the King of the ages, the Judge of all the earth. He doesn't answer to anyone, He is inferior to none. This means then that His authority is unchallenged and unchallengeable. There is no one who can reverse a decision that He has made or revoke a decree He has issued.

This is the basis of our assurance according to Paul's words in Rom.8:33:

> Who shall lay any thing to the charge of God's
> elect? It is God that justifieth.

Paul had a well-trained, finely-tuned legal mind, and, as we see in the book of Acts, he was well used to being in courtroom dramas. In the first eight chapters of his letter to the Romans he presents two court cases. We have already spent a good deal of time looking at the first one: we were the accused and the verdict was not in our favour. However, as we saw, because of the blood of Christ, God *could* provide justification, and, because of His grace, He *would* provide it. Now in this section we are brought back into the courtroom to show that every claim against us has been met, every objection answered and we are free. The challenge is issued, "Who shall lay anything to the charge of God's elect?" And we imagine some satanic accuser rising up to present a list of sins. You gasp in horror, blush with shame and tremble with fear as you realise these sins are your sins. You wait for the Judge to change His verdict in light of this new evidence, but then you breathe a sigh of relief as you realise the Judge is God; this evidence is not new evidence, God is not shocked or surprised, He knew it all along, so nothing can ever make Him change His mind. Our justification is irreversible because it is *God* that justifies!

> It is God that justifieth His own elect; can wicked
> men or lost spirits or Satan himself call again to
> account those whose case has been favourably
> decided in the highest place of judicature? Even
> to speak against God's people impeaches the
> Judge and is in contempt of court – heaven's
> court. His decision of justification in favour of
> him who believes is final and irreversible.[63]

Today, as I write this, I have been looking at a story in the news
in which a woman in another country who had previously been
acquitted of a crime could possibly be retried following an appeal.
Can you imagine how uneasy you would feel? You have been set
free but you have to live with the fear that at any moment you
could be called back into court again. We can offer a prayer of
thanks to God that we do not have to live with such uncertainty.

> To attempt to bring any charges against those
> whom God has justified is to question the
> judgment of the Supreme Judge of the universe.
> In the purpose of God and through the death
> of His Son, the grounds of justification have
> been perfectly laid. No charges therefore can be
> entertained against any who are in Christ. Paul's
> words remind us of what Balaam was made to
> say concerning Israel long ago. 'How shall I curse
> whom God has not cursed?' (Num. 23:8)[64]

There can never be any appeal. There is no higher court, there
is no greater authority. The Supreme Judge of the highest court
has spoken and His verdict is final, the case is closed and we
are free.

Summing up
In this chapter we have been looking at how God the Father
guarantees our eternal security. We have seen that God has a
purpose that cannot be challenged and will not be changed. His

---

[63] James M. Stifler, *The Epistle to the Romans*, Fleming H. Revell Company, 1897, p.158.
[64] James B. Currie, *Paul's Epistle to the Romans*, John Ritchie Ltd, 2001, p.152.

purpose is that everyone who has been saved will be ultimately and eternally glorified.

We then considered the subject of the power of God and saw that, whether we think of power in terms of His might or His authority, the result is the same; our eternal security is unassailable.

How firm a foundation, ye saints of the Lord,
Is laid for your faith in His excellent Word!
What more can He say than to you He hath said,
To you, who for refuge to Jesus have fled?

"Fear not, I am with thee, O be not dismayed,
For I am thy God, I will still give thee aid;
I'll strengthen thee, help thee, and cause thee to stand,
Upheld by My righteous, omnipotent hand.

"When through fiery trials thy pathway shall lie,
My grace, all sufficient shall be thy supply;
The flame shall not hurt thee, I only design
Thy dross to consume, and thy gold to refine.

"The soul that on Jesus hath leaned for repose,
I will not, I will not desert to his foes;
That soul, though all hell should endeavour to shake,
I'll never, no never, no never forsake!"

(Richard Keen)

The Son of God guarantees
our Eternal Security

What from Christ the soul can sever,
Bound by everlasting bands?
Once in Him, in Him forever,
Thus th' eternal covenant stands.
None shall pluck thee, none shall pluck thee
From the Strength of Israel's hands.

(John Kent)

The Triune God is a God of perfect consistency and harmony. We are not surprised then that as we look at truths connected to the Son and the Holy Spirit we arrive at the same conclusion as we have already reached in connection with God the Father. The Son of God Himself said that it was impossible that He could act independently of His Father,[65] so if the Father ensures our eternal security then we can have no doubt, the Son does as well.

The way we will approach this chapter is going to be similar to our approach to the last one. We have two paths that both lead us to the same place. These paths are the finished work of Christ and the unfinished work of Christ.

The Finished Work of Christ
The cross stands at the centre of the Christian gospel. While many religions want to get Jesus on their side to support their cause, it is the wise teacher, the great prophet, the inspiring example, the fearless leader that they want, not the substitutionary sin-bearer.[66] Give them Christ on the mountain delivering His sermons, give

---

[65] Jn.5:19
[66] e.g. He is merely a prophet according to Islam, a manifestation of God according to the Baha'i faith, the bringer of knowledge according to Gnosticism, an enlightened man according to Buddhism.

them Christ in the towns healing the sick, give them Christ in the synagogue challenging the authorities, give them Christ in the villages abiding with the poor, give them Christ in the Judgment Hall exemplifying non-violence; they will take all of that, but give them Christ on the cross suffering under the judgment of God, satisfying the justice of God, and they turn away in disgust. But this is where the gospel shines the spotlight and fixes our focus:

> For the preaching of the cross is to them that perish foolishness; but unto us which are saved it is the power of God. (1 Cor.1:18)

> And I, brethren, when I came to you, came not with excellency of speech or of wisdom, declaring unto you the testimony of God. For I determined not to know any thing among you, save Jesus Christ, and Him crucified. (1 Cor.2:2)

> Moreover, brethren, I declare unto you the gospel which I preached unto you, which also ye have received, and wherein ye stand; by which also ye are saved, if ye keep in memory what I preached unto you, unless ye have believed in vain. For I delivered unto you first of all that which I also received, how that Christ died for our sins according to the scriptures; and that He was buried, and that He rose again the third day according to the scriptures... (1 Cor.15:1-4)

> O foolish Galatians, who hath bewitched you, that ye should not obey the truth, before whose eyes Jesus Christ hath been evidently set forth, crucified among you? (Gal.3:1)

> But God forbid that I should glory, save in the cross of our Lord Jesus Christ, by whom the world is crucified unto me, and I unto the world. (Gal.6:14)

So what is it about the cross that is so important? What's so good about Good Friday? The answer of course is that the Lord Jesus was there to pay sin's penalty so that the guilty could go free. Sin could not be overlooked or ignored, it had to be dealt with for two reasons; firstly, because God is holy, and secondly, because God is righteous. God's holiness demands that sin be banished from Him; God's righteousness demands that sin be punished by Him. The Lord went to the cross to answer fully to the demands of a holy and righteous God against sin. These are the themes of the two great prophetic portraits of the cross of Christ: Psalm 22 and Isaiah 53. In Psalm 22 we find the Lord Jesus answering to the demands of God's holiness as He is forsaken by God:

> My God, My God, why hast Thou forsaken Me? why art Thou so far from helping Me, and from the words of My roaring? O My God, I cry in the daytime, but Thou hearest not; and in the night season, and am not silent. But Thou art holy, O Thou that inhabitest the praises of Israel. (Ps.22:1-3)

In Isaiah 53 we see the Lord Jesus answering to the demands of God's righteousness as He endures the punishment our sins deserve:

> Surely He hath borne our griefs, and carried our sorrows: yet we did esteem Him stricken, smitten of God, and afflicted. But He was wounded for our transgressions, He was bruised for our iniquities: the chastisement of our peace was upon Him; and with His stripes we are healed. All we like sheep have gone astray; we have turned every one to his own way; and the LORD hath laid on Him the iniquity of us all.
>
> ...
>
> Yet it pleased the LORD to bruise Him; He hath put Him to grief: when Thou shalt make His soul an offering for sin, He shall see His seed, He shall prolong His days, and the pleasure of the LORD shall prosper in His hand. He shall see of the travail of His soul, and shall be satisfied: by His knowledge shall My righteous Servant justify many; for He shall bear their iniquities. Therefore will I divide Him a portion with the great, and

> He shall divide the spoil with the strong; because
> He hath poured out His soul unto death: and He
> was numbered with the transgressors; and He
> bare the sin of many, and made intercession for
> the transgressors. (Isa.53:4-6, 10-12)

Had the Lord Jesus Christ not gone to the cross to experience
the banishment and endure the punishment sin deserved then
none could be saved. His sacrifice was absolutely necessary, but
the relevant question for our subject is this, was it absolutely
sufficient?

> The question resolves itself to one issue: did Christ
> do enough on the cross to make it possible for God
> righteously to *keep* one saved, as well as righteously
> to save at all? Since this question strikes at the
> very heart of the revelation regarding the cross, its
> importance cannot be overestimated.[67]

Romans 8:34

We are returning to the majestic environment of Romans 8. Paul
has told us about God's purpose to glorify all who have been
justified. We have stood as the satanic antagonist has pointed
his accusing finger in our direction and told God that we aren't
righteous. That objection has been overruled because God has
justified us. He has declared us righteous and His decision is final;
no charge can ever be laid against us. But look now, the accusing
finger now moves from us to God and our opponent's complaint is
now that God isn't righteous. Imagine his challenge to the Judge:
"These people You have justified are actually guilty. This is not
a righteous verdict." He might even have the temerity to quote
God's own Word back to Him, "Does not Your very own Scripture
say that he that justifies the wicked and he that condemns the
righteous are an abomination to the Lord, and yet this is the very
thing You are doing?"[68]

What is the answer? Is God fudging on justice? Is God

---

[67] Lewis Sperry Chafer, *Salvation*, Moody, 1917, Kindle edition, loc. 1098.
[68] Prov.17:15. In Rom.4:5 He is explicitly said to justify the ungodly, and in Rom.8:3 He is said to condemn the righteous. The glorious truth of the gospel is that God has done this righteously.

compromising with sin? Not at all!

> Who is he that condemneth? It is Christ that died,
> yea rather, that is risen again, who is even at the
> right hand of God, who also maketh intercession
> for us. (Rom.8:34)

If someone were to demand our condemnation the answer is, "It is *Christ* that died".

> It is Christ, superior to all finite beings, who
> died. The death of such as He is the undisputable
> answer to the condemning power of every sin;
> and He is risen. Oh blessed Presence! Oh eternal
> safety! No condemnation can ever pass His nail-
> scarred body. What priceless consolation to the
> imperfect and sin-conscious saint![69]

Yes, I have broken God's law, but it is Christ that died. Yes, I am hell-deserving, but it is Christ that died. God is not overlooking my sin or lowering His standard. There is one who has stepped forward to meet the claims of God against me. All that my guilt deserved and God's justice demanded was fully met in the death of God's Son. Think again of the language of Isa.53:5,6:

> But He was wounded for our transgressions, He
> was bruised for our iniquities: the chastisement
> of our peace was upon Him; and with His stripes
> we are healed.
> All we like sheep have gone astray; we have
> turned every one to his own way; and the LORD
> hath laid on Him the iniquity of us all.

Ours were the transgressions, His was the wounding. Ours were the iniquities, His was the bruising. All that should have been mine became His, and faith reckons it to be enough and rests on it, saying, *with His stripes I am healed.*

This is the glorious truth of substitution. A substitute does not merely act in the interests of another but actually in his place. If someone is your substitute then whatever it is that substitute is

---

[69] Chafer, *Salvation*, loc. 1490.

doing for you, you don't do it, he does it instead, e.g. consider the substitute on a football team, as he sits on the bench he is nobody's substitute in reality, but when he comes on the field he is only actually the substitute of the person who goes off. The point Paul is making in Rom.8:34 is that the Lord Jesus Christ is our Substitute and thus we can never experience the condemnation for our sins; He took it instead. Now it is important to recognise this doesn't entail the error of a limited atonement, for the Lord Jesus gave Himself a substitutionary ransom on behalf of all, 1 Tim.2:6. The self-giving of the Person of Christ, of necessity, is a sacrifice of infinite worth, and makes possible the freedom of all sinners, and any will go free if they claim Him as their Substitute and rest on the value of His sacrifice.[70] This is precisely what F. W. Grant had in mind when he said:

> What then is meant by substitution? It is one taking the place of others, so that they for whom He stands shall be delivered from all that in which He stands for them. The cross is thus the complete taking of death and judgment for those whom there He represents, so that for them salvation is absolutely insured...A substitution in death and judgment can mean nothing less than the necessary salvation of those for whom it is made...Christ is not a substitute for the world, for substitution implies the actual bearing and bearing away of the sins of those who are represented in the Substitute, and the sins of the world are not so borne away. He is the Substitute of His people, but a people not numerically limited to just so many, but embracing all who respond to the invitations of His grace, though it were indeed the world for multitude...Propitiation is, then, by substitution, and only so; yet the substitution itself is not for a fixed number before-determined, but for a people to whom men can be freely invited to

---

[70] It is not just the case that there is enough in the sacrifice of Christ for all that believe. There is enough in it for all that don't believe, but they don't come into the good of it unless and until they believe.

join themselves, because of the infinite value of
the work accomplished, and of the infinite grace
which that work expresses.[71]

F. B. Hole gave a helpful illustration:

> Years ago a popular accident insurance scheme
> was much advertised in the daily press as offering
> benefits for practically nothing. All you had to
> do was to give a definite order for the paper in
> question to a newsagent, and then register as
> having done so. "A registered reader is an insured
> reader," is what one of the papers said.
>
> "How very simple!" you might have exclaimed,
> "have I nothing to do beyond that?" Nothing!
> But you must not overlook the fact that the
> newspaper proprietors had a very big thing to
> do before the offer was made. The thousands of
> little registration transactions cost but the stamp
> that posts them to the office, but behind these
> lies the great transaction when the newspaper
> proprietors drew the big cheque running into
> many thousands of pounds in favour of the
> insurance company that undertook the liability.
>
> Now that big premium payment, in view of
> which the offer went freely forth to all buyers of
> the paper, is not a bad illustration of propitiation.
> The offer of God's forgiveness goes forth on the
> ground of Christ's propitiatory sacrifice, and its
> scope and bearing is nothing less than all men.
>
> When the premium was paid, no questions, as
> to any particular individuals benefiting under
> the scheme, were raised. The point was that the
> insurance company was so satisfied that it was
> able to issue the offer upon a sound basis.
>
> The act of registering under the scheme was on
> the other hand, purely individual. After all, only

---

the registered reader was the insured reader, and therefore only the one who had registered had the right to speak of the premium paid by the proprietors as a substitute for the premium they otherwise must have paid, had they as individuals approached the insurance company to insure against similar risks. The registration very well illustrates what takes place when a sinner turns to God in repentance and faith. He registers, so to speak, under God's great salvation scheme. Such an one alone can rightly speak of Christ as being a Substitute for himself, and bearing his sins in His own body on the tree.[72]

So the Substitute is available for and offered to all without exception, and, the moment I put my faith in Christ, God reckons what Christ did to be in my place, and the condemnation that hung over my head is removed, Christ bore it instead. Consequently, when Satan accuses, when memory condemns or when conscience convicts, I can say with relief and joy, *"It is Christ that died"*.

In Old Testament Israel if a man came to the altar to offer a sacrifice for his sin, the priest didn't examine the man to see if the man was good enough, the priest examined the sacrifice to see if the sacrifice was good enough. If the sacrifice was good enough the man went free.[73] The question then is this, is the sacrifice you are depending on good enough? Many people are depending on the sacrifice of their time, effort, energy, money, and 101 other things. I met a woman who told me she had spent a couple of weeks on a retreat eating nothing but dry toast and drinking nothing but black tea. When I asked her why, she said she wanted to make some sacrifices to atone for her sins. Sin is far more costly than that. God looks at all the sacrifices we make and says they are not good enough. You may be satisfied that they are good enough, but it is God who needs to be satisfied, and nothing we offer can ever satisfy God's righteous demands against our sin.

What sacrifice am I depending on? It is the sacrifice of the Lord

---

[72] F. B. Hole, *Propitiation and Substitution*, available at http://www.stempublishing.com.
[73] I read that illustration years ago in a UCB daily devotional.

Jesus offered at Calvary. For those who are depending on the value of that sacrifice the question has to be asked, is the sacrifice good enough? Paul answers that emphatically, "It is Christ Jesus that died, yea rather, that was raised from the dead..." I have quoted the verse here from the Revised Version because it captures the original more accurately than the AV at this point. It is not just that the Lord is risen, but that He was raised by the God who judged Him for our sins. Had the Lord Jesus not fully atoned for sin He would still be in the grave, but the fact that God raised Him from the dead is God's stamp of approval on His work, His sign of acceptance of His sacrifice and the signal of His agreement to the Lord's word "Finished".

> If my acceptance depended on my growth in grace I could never have settled peace. It would be egotism of the worst kind to consider myself so holy that I could be satisfactory to God on the ground of my personal experience. But when I see that "He hath made us accepted in the Beloved", every doubt is banished. My soul is at peace. I have quietness and assurance forever. I know now that only
>
> > *That which can shake the cross,*
> > *Can shake the peace it gave;*
> > *Which tells me Christ has never died,*
> > *Nor ever left the grave.*[74]

This is the same truth Paul is presenting in Rom.10:9.

> That if thou shalt confess with thy mouth the Lord Jesus, and shalt believe in thine heart that God hath raised Him from the dead, thou shalt be saved.

As we have shown before,[75] Paul's point in speaking about God raising the Lord Jesus from the dead is to show that God is satisfied with the sacrifice He offered, so death could not hold Him, the glory of the Father demanded His resurrection.

---

[74] H. A. Ironside, *Full Assurance*, Moody Publishers, Kindle edition loc 244-250.
[75] See section on *The Purpose of God*.

> Christ's bodily resurrection is the divine token that all has been dealt with to God's satisfaction. Jesus bore our sins on the cross. He made Himself responsible for them. He died to put them away forever. But God raised Him from the dead, thereby attesting His good pleasure in the work of His Son. Now the blessed Lord sits exalted at the right hand of the Majesty in the heavens. He could not be there if our sins were still upon Him. The fact that He is there proves that they are completely put away. God is satisfied![76]

As Charles Swindoll put it, "First, those most unqualified to condemn you, will ... Second, the One most qualified to condemn you, won't."[77] Remember the incident with the woman caught in adultery?

> Jesus went unto the mount of Olives. And early in the morning He came again into the temple, and all the people came unto Him; and He sat down, and taught them. And the scribes and Pharisees brought unto Him a woman taken in adultery; and when they had set her in the midst, they say unto Him, Master, this woman was taken in adultery, in the very act. Now Moses in the law commanded us, that such should be stoned: but what sayest Thou? This they said, tempting Him, that they might have to accuse Him. But Jesus stooped down, and with His finger wrote on the ground, as though He heard them not. So when they continued asking Him, He lifted up Himself, and said unto them, He that is without sin among you, let him first cast a stone at her. And again He stooped down, and wrote on the ground. And they which heard it, being convicted by their own conscience, went out one by one, beginning at the eldest, even unto the last: and Jesus was left alone, and the woman standing in the midst.

[76] Ironside, *Full Assurance*, loc 224-228.
[77] Charles R. Swindoll, *The Owner's Manual for Christians*, Thomas Nelson, 2009, p.185.

> When Jesus had lifted up Himself, and saw
> none but the woman, He said unto her, Woman,
> where are those thine accusers? hath no man
> condemned thee? She said, No man, Lord. And
> Jesus said unto her, Neither do I condemn thee:
> go, and sin no more. (Jn.8:1-11)[78]

This account is so touching and instructive. They drag this woman before the Lord and think they have got Him inescapably pierced on the horns of a dilemma. What should be done with this woman? *Moses in the law commanded her to be stoned, but what do **You** say?*[79] If He says she should be stoned then He will be in trouble with the Romans for the Jews didn't have the authority to put anyone to death while under Roman jurisdiction, and also He would alienate the many *publicans and sinners* who had come to Him in their guilt. On the other hand, if He says she shouldn't be stoned then He is setting Himself against Moses and the divinely-given law. He seemingly takes no notice and begins writing with His finger on the ground. They start badgering Him like little children, then He rises and issues the famous challenge, "He that is without sin among you, let him first cast a stone at her." He then stoops and writes again. What is it He is writing? When we watch this interplay and the actions of the Lord our minds surely are supposed to go racing off to Mount Sinai where, on two occasions, the law was written with the finger of God.[80] By His action in this scenario the Lord was indicating that He was the one who gave the law to Moses. It was also a challenge to these men; the Lord was saying in effect, *You want to uphold the law? Well, if you measure up to its demands then you can execute its judgments.* None of them of course could stand up to the challenge. The same law that condemned that women condemned them too and they could not endure the conviction, so they all left. The Lord then tells the woman that He didn't condemn her, and He sent her out to live a new life of holiness. The Lord wasn't setting aside the law, but the condemnation the law pronounced upon her was

---

[78] I'm well aware of the doubt over this passage based on its omission from the most ancient manuscripts, however, the internal evidence and marks of inspiration persuade me of its authenticity. See note on the passage here - http://www.livingwater.org/about-the-logos-21-translation.html.
[79] The 2nd person singular pronoun in the text is emphatic.
[80] Ex.31:8; Deut.10:1-5

a condemnation He Himself would bear on the cross, allowing the repentant to go free. Thus the gospel upholds the demand of the broken law and sees it fulfilled in the work of Christ. In Romans 3 Paul has pronounced the universal guilt of mankind and presented the answer in the atoning blood of Christ. Having shown that justification is by faith in Christ, he says:

> Do we then make void the law through faith?
> God forbid: yea, we establish the law. (Rom.3:31)

The law demands the penalty for sin be paid, the Lord Jesus paid it in full on the cross, evidenced by the resurrection from the dead. This is why that woman in John 8 could go free, and it's why we can too, for the Lord said in that very same chapter, "If the Son therefore shall make you free, ye shall be free indeed" (v.36).

Our Lord is now on the other side of judgment, and those who are linked with Him by faith are seen as being on the other side of judgment too, never to come into condemnation. John takes up this theme in his first epistle: let's look at what he has to say.

1 John 4:17

> Herein is love made perfect with us, that we may
> have boldness in the day of judgment; because as
> He is, even so are we in this world. (1 Jn.4:17, RV)

In this section John is dealing with the great subject of the love of God. He speaks about how the love of God has been expressed in the past (vv.9,10), how it is experienced in the present (vv.11-16), and then the expectation it gives us for the future (vv.17-19). John is telling us in verse 17 that God's love reaches its goal with us when we have boldness in the light of that future day of judgment. God wants us to live without dread: "no one can rest while in terror of eternal damnation."[81] Imagine how hurt you would be if your spouse or child lived in constant fear of your rejection; she obviously is not secure in your love. If that kind of questioning of our love causes hurt to us, think how much more hurtful it is to God; His love could not be demonstrated in any greater way. Think of what He has given to us:

---

[81] Chafer, *Salvation*, loc. 1098-1107.

> In this was manifested the love of God toward us,
> because that God sent His only begotten Son into
> the world, that we might live through Him. (v.9)

He has given the very thing we needed: life! This is evidence of love; we were undeserving, indeed, hell-deserving, and God has brought us into His family by giving His Son, and His Son has given His life to us. But there's more, John tells us not only of what God gave to us but what He gave for us:

> Herein is love, not that we loved God, but that He
> loved us, and sent His Son to be the propitiation
> for our sins. (v.10)

The Son has not only given His life to us, but in order for that to happen He had to give His life for us. God was prepared to pay the ultimate price to make us His own; He sent His Son to bear His wrath at Calvary. Love is seen in what it is prepared to give and what it is prepared to take. In the sacrifice of God's Son on the cross we see that there was nothing more that could be given; the Lord Jesus gave Himself and held nothing back. We also see there was nothing more that could be taken; He took the sin of the world and all the judgment for it. This is love that can never be changed or challenged. Thus as we look back to the past we should rest secure.

But John tells us that this love which has been expressed in the past can be experienced in the present. John is exhorting us to exhibit that self-sacrificial Calvary-love to others. If we are going to do that then we need to know that the story of the cross is true. John shows us how we know it is.

> Beloved, if God so loved us, we ought also to love
> one another. No man hath seen God at any time.
> If we love one another, God dwelleth in us, and
> His love is perfected in us. Hereby know we that
> we dwell in Him, and He in us, because He hath
> given us of His Spirit. And we have seen and
> do testify that the Father sent the Son to be the
> Saviour of the world. Whosoever shall confess
> that Jesus is the Son of God, God dwelleth in him,

> and he in God. And we have known and believed
> the love that God hath to us. God is love; and he
> that dwelleth in love dwelleth in God, and God
> in him. (vv.11-16)

How do we know the reality of God's love? Because of an internal witness and an external witness. The internal witness is the Holy Spirit of God. Upon believing the gospel God gives us His Spirit who brings us into the enjoyment of God's love and gives us the capacity to express it.[82] The Holy Spirit makes an undeniable change in the life of the believer, thus giving the assurance that this is real.

The external witness to the love of God is the testimony of the apostles. John says, "We have seen and do testify..." The testimony of the apostles is a rock solid guarantee of the truthfulness of the message. These men couldn't have been mistaken about what they witnessed and they wouldn't have been lying about it, and so the only conclusion that can be reached is that their message about the love of God is really true.

This brings us to verse 17. Assured of such love we need not fear judgment, because God's love has provided the very thing that we need: a sacrifice. And so the reason the believer can look ahead with boldness is because "as [Christ] is, even so are we in this world." The Lord Jesus has passed through judgment and is far beyond its reach, never to enter into it again, and we are positionally "as He is", just as secure as the risen Christ. When we see the Lord worrying about future judgment then, and only then, does the Christian need to worry about it.

So His sacrificial death was not only essential, it was enough, and the resurrection proves that. Therefore the believer can never be condemned because Christ has paid for all his sins. The thought that calms my fears as a Christian is the very same thought that caused my fears before my conversion, i.e. God is righteous. Before I was saved this thought gave me no comfort, there is a righteous God who demands payment for my sin, but now that I am saved the righteousness of God is the source of my comfort; He cannot punish me because the Lord Jesus took the punishment instead.

---

[82] See also Rom.5:5.

It seems to be one of the very principles of our enlightened nature to believe that God is just; we feel that it must be so, and this gives us our terror at first; but is it not marvellous that this very same belief that God is just becomes afterwards the pillar of our confidence and peace! If God be just, I, a sinner, alone and without a substitute, must be punished; but Jesus stands in my stead and is punished for me; and now, if God be just, I, a sinner, standing in Christ, can never be punished.[83]

In bringing Israel into direct fellowship with Himself, God shewed, by putting the blood on their doorposts (Ex.12), that when He executed judgment on Egypt He secured deliverance from it to His people. And just so in God's dealings with us; the judgment that has passed on Christ because of sin is the security of the church (of every believer) against judgment. When the soul apprehends the Lord Jesus as the one offering for sin, it has confidence in God; and that on the very ground of His knowing thoroughly our sinfulness. It is impossible that God should pass over the blood of the Lord Jesus, and impute to sinners those sins which He has washed away. He cannot impute sin to a believer without condemning the value of His blood-shedding, and virtually denying the efficacy of it. And if that be true when He judges men by and by, it must be true now. Faith knows that death is God's own sentence against sin, and that it has been executed on Christ in the sinner's stead. Faith "sets to its seal that God is true," and receives His thoughts who has said about the blood-shedding of Jesus, "When I see the blood, I will pass over."[84]

---

[83] Spurgeon, *Morning and Evening*, Morning reading, 25th September. Sadly he espoused limited atonement, seeing substitution as something historic and fixed at the cross, rather than provisional and applied at conversion. This leads to an interesting question; if his view of substitution is true then how could one of the elect ever have been under the wrath of God?

[84] J. N. Darby, *Collected Writings*, vol.12 *Evangelic, Wilderness Grace*, http://www.stempublishing.com/authors/darby/EVANGEL/12028E.html.

The trembling sinner feareth
That God can ne'er forget;
But one full payment cleareth
His mem'ry of all debt;
When naught beside could free us,
Or set our souls at large,
Thy holy work, Lord Jesus,
Secured a full discharge.

No wrath God's heart retaineth
To us-ward who believe;
No dread in ours remaineth
As we His love receive;
Returning son He kisses
And with His robe invests;
His perfect love dismisses
All terror from our breasts.

(Mary Bowley Peters)

This is what gives the believer assurance when faced with his own failure and bombarded by satanic attacks: "It is Christ that died..." Satan is the accuser of the brethren,[85] and he is a master at it. He is a crack shot with his deadly darts of doubt and his fiery arrows of accusation, and sadly we have supplied him with plenty of ammunition. How do we overcome the accuser of the brethren? Do we try to show him what good Christians we are? Do we rehearse to him a past experience we've had? Those are very flimsy shields against his onslaught. Scripture tells us "And they overcame him by the blood of the Lamb..." (Rev.12:11). That is what will shut him up and drive him back, when we have as our only plea the blood of the Lamb, because "the blood of Jesus Christ, His Son, cleanseth us from all sin" (1 Jn.1:7).

Let's look at another passage on the same theme.

Hebrews 10:1-18

> For the law having a shadow of good things
> to come, and not the very image of the things,

---

[85] Rev. 12:10

can never with those sacrifices which they offered year by year continually make the comers thereunto perfect. For then would they not have ceased to be offered? because that the worshippers once purged should have had no more conscience of sins. But in those sacrifices there is a remembrance again made of sins every year. For it is not possible that the blood of bulls and of goats should take away sins.

Wherefore when He cometh into the world, He saith, Sacrifice and offering Thou wouldest not, but a body hast Thou prepared Me:

In burnt offerings and sacrifices for sin Thou hast had no pleasure.

Then said I, Lo, I come (in the volume of the book it is written of Me,) to do Thy will, O God.

Above when He said, Sacrifice and offering and burnt offerings and offering for sin Thou wouldest not, neither hadst pleasure therein; which are offered by the law; then said He, Lo, I come to do Thy will, O God. He taketh away the first, that He may establish the second.

By the which will we are sanctified through the offering of the body of Jesus Christ once for all.

And every priest standeth daily ministering and offering oftentimes the same sacrifices, which can never take away sins: but this man, after He had offered one sacrifice for sins for ever, sat down on the right hand of God; from henceforth expecting till His enemies be made His footstool.

For by one offering He hath perfected for ever them that are sanctified.

Whereof the Holy Ghost also is a witness to us: for after that He had said before,

This is the covenant that I will make with them after those days, saith the Lord, I will put My laws into their hearts, and in their minds will I write them;

> And their sins and iniquities will I remember no more.
>
> Now where remission of these is, there is no more offering for sin.

It is tempting to dive into these verses and soak our souls in the wonderful truths they present, but we must resist and merely dip in and have a paddle. The contrast is being presented between the animal sacrifices God had ordained and the ultimate sacrifice of His Son which those sacrifices foreshadowed. The animal sacrifices could never take away sins, and they were never intended to do so. The reason they were incapable of such a thing is at least fourfold. First, an animal could never be accepted in the place of a human. The only acceptable substitute for a human must be a human. Second, an animal could never volunteer to be the sacrifice, and as such could never be acceptable to God. The sacrifice must be voluntary. Third, animals are amoral creatures, and thus cannot take the place of a sinner. The sacrifice must be morally perfect. And fourth, the penalty for sin is infinite and thus no creature could ever pay that price. The sacrifice must be of infinite value, i.e. divine. All these necessary qualifications are fulfilled in one glorious Person, the Son of God. He says, "Lo, I come..." He is the uncreated Creator entering into His creation voluntarily, He takes a body, thus becoming truly human, and He expresses His devotion to the will of God, showing His moral perfection; so all four limitations of the animal sacrifices are overcome in the sacrifice of the Son of God. What then does this sacrifice accomplish for those who avail of it? Verse 10 tells us that "we are sanctified through the offering of the body of Jesus Christ once for all." The thought of being sanctified here is not to be looked at as practical sanctification but rather it is a positional term, that is, God has set us apart for Himself. It is saying that in accord with the will of God and through the sacrifice of Christ we have been made saints. In the letter to the Hebrews sanctification takes the prominent place that justification takes in Romans,[86] and this is not surprising. In Romans the emphasis is on our legal standing before a righteous God, but in Hebrews the emphasis is on our approach to a holy God.

---

[86] See for example Heb. 2:11; 3:1; 6:10; 9:13; 10:10, 14; 13:12, 24.

So He has sanctified us by the offering of His body, but we then move to verse 14 and discover that those who are being sanctified[87] are "perfected forever". To see what is involved in being perfected forever we will have to look at how the epistle uses the word *perfected* elsewhere.

> For the law made nothing perfect, but the bringing in of a better hope [did]; by the which we draw nigh unto God. (7:19)

> Which was a figure for the time then present, in which were offered both gifts and sacrifices, that could not make him that did the service perfect, as pertaining to the conscience... (9:9)

> For the law having a shadow of good things to come, and not the very image of the things, can never with those sacrifices which they offered year by year continually make the comers thereunto perfect. (10:1)

The meaning of these verses in their contexts is plain to grasp: the sacrifices of the old covenant could not bring about God's goal and desire for mankind, i.e. those sacrifices could never give a man peace in regard to sin. Sin was always being brought up for attention, or as 10:3 says, in the sacrificial ceremonies "there is a remembrance again made of sins every year." However, in identification with the sacrifice of the Saviour the believer is perfected forever, or, perfected permanently, perpetually, perfectly! That great once-for-all sacrifice has provided the perfect answer to the problem of sin, and therefore the beautiful words of v.17 belong to every Christian, "And their sins and iniquities will I remember no more."

Let's spend a bit of time looking at this assurance God gives here. He says He will not remember the believer's sins and iniquities. It hardly needs to be pointed out that God is not making a comment about His memory, He is not saying He will forget the believer's

---

[87] The present tense may indicate that what was positional in v.10 is worked out practically in the life. It in no way puts security in jeopardy because those who are being sanctified have been (and permanently are) perfected forever; that means the standing of perfection cannot be conditional upon the state of sanctification.

sins.[88] Some say, "No, God can't forget, but He can choose not to remember." That is little better and still no closer to the truth of the verse. As we have seen in v.3 the sacrifices were a remembrance of sins; it is a legal term saying that year by year sins were judicially remembered, that is, they were brought before God for attention.[89] Because of the limitation of the sacrificial system there was a remembrance every year. However, those who have availed of that perfect sacrifice are told that their sins will never be remembered; they will never be brought up before God as needing attention. They were remembered at the cross, and have been perfectly dealt with to the full satisfaction of God.

He says that He will remember their sins *no more*. The expression *no more* has this force behind it, *not at all hereafter*. This is telling us then that the believer's sins are *entirely* forgiven (*not at all*), and *eternally* forgiven (*hereafter*). Think of it, you are entirely forgiven. This is an unqualified statement, and nothing that follows can be allowed to blunt its force.[90] The sins of the believer, no matter their multitude or magnitude, whether before or after conversion, are dealt with entirely by the sacrifice of Christ. The glory of the gospel of the true and living God shines out all the more brightly and brilliantly when we set it against the background of man-made religion. Look at what the Koran teaches:

> Allah accepts only the repentance of those who do evil in ignorance and foolishness and repent soon afterwards; it is they to whom Allah will forgive...[91]

Aren't you glad that God is not like that? If He only forgave sins committed in ignorance then not one of us would be forgiven. We know there must be loads of sins we have committed in ignorance, but we are also aware that there have been more than just a few sins that were committed in downright deliberate defiance, yet the God of Scripture says that the value of the sacrifice of Christ is so great that not one of them will be remembered against the believer.

---

[88] We are afflicted with various annoying phrases in evangelism, one of which is "our sins are cast into the sea of God's forgetfulness". May that phrase sink into the depths of the sea of every Christian's forgetfulness, never to rise again.

[89] See too 1 Kgs.17:18 – to call sin to remembrance is to take action against it.

[90] We will deal with v. 29, see *Warning! The letter to the Hebrews*.

[91] Surah 4:17.

But our sins are not just entirely dealt with, but eternally dealt with. Many have had the experience of a fault from the dim and distant past being brought up by someone and thrown back in their face. We need not have any fear that God will do that, for our sins will be remembered not at all hereafter, and that includes whatever sins people think would cause a believer to lose his salvation. It is interesting to weigh up what that fatal sin would be. How many sins can the grace of God forgive or the blood of Christ cleanse before God says "That's it, I could cope with all those other sins, but that one is just too much!" This then is to introduce human merit into the plan of salvation, and to weave self-righteous threads into the garment of salvation that God has provided. God will not and cannot allow such a thing.

> For by grace are ye saved through faith; and that not of yourselves: it is the gift of God: not of works, lest any man should boast. (Eph.2:8, 9)

> Where is boasting then? It is excluded. By what law? of works? Nay: but by the law of faith. Therefore we conclude that a man is justified by faith without the deeds of the law. (Rom.3:27, 28)

> Are ye so foolish? having begun in the Spirit, are ye now made perfect by the flesh? (Gal.3:3)

Lewis Sperry Chafer puts it this way:

> It is easily concluded by some, and because to them it seems reasonable, that the divine Person cannot remain in a heart where there is sin. Such are soon driven either to judge themselves to be absolutely without sin, or else to be lost. They evidently do not realise the value of the cross as the divinely provided answer to every challenge of righteousness that may arise because of sin...[92]

Now imagine if getting salvation was by faith, but keeping it was by us meeting some standard of morality. If we managed to hold on and meet the standard then the fact is we would have something to boast about. We would be able to stand in heaven

---

[92] Chafer, *Salvation*, loc. 1421.

and say "I did it! I was good enough!" It doesn't remove the problem to say that God helped me to be good enough, because if you could have refused that help then the fact that you didn't gives you some credit. The Bible categorically asserts the impossibility of such a thing ever happening and the impertinence of anyone ever thinking it could. Paul tells us there is only one thing the Christian boasts about:

> But God forbid that I should glory, save in the
> cross of our Lord Jesus Christ... (Gal.6:14)

The Christian has no boast or plea other than the work of Christ at Calvary; salvation is not a joint effort. But that aside, how deceived a person must be to suppose his life could ever be good enough! Does anyone really think that God will look at the life of an individual and say "Yes, those few slips didn't matter, he wasn't so bad."? If salvation depends at all upon us then any sin is enough to disqualify us, but if it depends on the value of Christ's precious blood then no sin can disqualify us. This is a terribly important point that strikes at both the righteousness of God and the value of the sacrifice of Christ. If our performance is, even in part, a factor in our acceptance with God then our performance must be perfect, God can accept nothing less, but if we stand before God in virtue of the blood of Christ then what could ever stand against its cleansing power? We need to recognise that it comes down to this, either the blood of Christ overcomes our sins or our sins overcome the blood of Christ.

> To claim that a child of God is not safe because of
> the supposed unsaving power of sin is to put sin
> above the blood and to set at naught the eternal
> redemption that is in Christ Jesus.[93]

Also, if there is a sin that forfeits salvation then presumably all the sins of the once-saved person's life are put back onto his record, which means he was *not* perfected forever and his sins *are* remembered again, and that is a straight-forward denial of what this passage teaches. Let there be no doubt in the minds of any, this passage explicitly affirms eternal security.

---

[93] Ibid. loc. 1402-1411.

My numerous sins transferred to Him,
Shall nevermore be found,
Lost in His blood's atoning stream,
Where every crime is drowned.

The person who has abandoned all merit of his own and is resting on the finished work of Christ can therefore have full assurance that he will never be lost. But there is more.

The Unfinished Work of Christ

The Lord Jesus is engaged in ministry for His people now in heaven, and as we look at the offices He bears and the functions He fulfils, we will see that the Bible closes, locks and bolts the door against any idea that a Christian can ever lose his salvation, and it throws away the key.

Our Great High Priest

Once again I am taking you back to Romans 8 and into verse 34. We have already seen in this chapter a purpose that will never be revised; all of the justified will be glorified; we have listened to a verdict that can never be reversed; God has justified us and that is final. In verse 34 we have proven that in the death of Christ sin has been dealt with, and is an issue that will never be revisited; all our sins are atoned for forever. Now we will see that the Lord Jesus gives the Christian a standing that can never be revoked.

Let's have the verse before us again:

> Who is he that condemneth? It is Christ that died,
> yea rather, that is risen again, who is even at the
> right hand of God, who also maketh intercession
> for us.

Paul tells us that the Lord Jesus is at the right hand of God and He is there making intercession for us. We can't be certain what this intercession practically entails for the Lord Jesus, but it seems to be that the idea is that His very presence there is a continual act of intercession for all His people; He is there as our representative, and what that means then is that we are as safe and secure as Christ Himself is. Please let that sink into your mind and settle in your soul; we are as safe and secure as Christ Himself is. The

Lord is there *for us*[94] and while He is accepted before God, we are too, because as Paul puts it in Eph.1:6 we are "accepted in the Beloved". If God has something against me then it is Christ that bears it, so if I see the Lord at the right hand of God then I know that while He is there God has nothing against me. The implication of this is that the only way a saved soul could ever be lost is if the Lord Jesus Christ was lost. The only way one who has trusted the Saviour could perish is if the Saviour perished. Now if you agree with me that it is a blasphemous thing to suggest that the Lord Jesus could ever be lost then Rom.8:34 forces you to agree that it is blasphemous to suggest that one whom the Lord Jesus represents could ever be lost.

> *Now we see in Christ's acceptance,*
> *But the measure of our own;*
> *He who lay beneath our sentence*
> *Seated high upon the Throne.*

> *(G.W. Fraser)*

As Paul puts it in Rom.5:10:

> For if, when we were enemies, we were reconciled to God by the death of His Son, much more, being reconciled, we shall be saved by His life.

In the Lord's death He has removed the enmity between God and me. We are linked with one who has passed through death and lives forever, and our salvation is as secure as His life.

> As the first Adam transmitted what he was to those who were born after the flesh, so the last Adam transmits what He is to those who are born after the Spirit. The Christian's standing is in Christ, and there will be no fall in the last Adam. He is as secure as God can make him secure...[95]

---

[94] This is the fourth occurrence of the expression "for us" in Romans 8. In v.31 Paul issues that unanswerable challenge, "If God be *for us*, who can be against us?" – God for us. In v.32 He shows us that the Father is for us, "He that spared not His own Son, but delivered Him up *for us* all..." In v.34 the Son is for us, "...who maketh intercession *for us*." And in v.26 the Holy Spirit is for us, "... but the Spirit [Himself] maketh intercession *for us*..." The Father for us, the Son for us, the Spirit for us – no wonder Paul can truthfully and triumphantly say *"God...for us"*!
[95] Chafer, *Grace*, loc. 4758.

The epistle to the Hebrews makes a similar point in 7:25:

> Wherefore He is able also to save them to the uttermost that come unto God by Him, seeing He ever liveth to make intercession for them.

The Saviour we have trusted is one who saves to the uttermost, that is, He saves completely and continually, or as W. E. Vine says, the expression "combines the two ideas of time and degree".[96] This then guarantees an eternal and entire salvation; we are continually saved (i.e. He will never lose us) and we are completely saved (i.e. He will never lose any part of us. His saving work isn't a salvage job in which He recovers as much as He can from the wreckage of sin and the jaws of death. It is a full salvation in which the finished product will be untouched by any trace of sin). So this verse is teaching that every saved soul will be kept until he comes into the fulness of salvation,[97] there is no lack or let up in the Lord's saving ability. As we were thinking earlier on, when the sheep was being carried home by the shepherd, the sheep's security depended entirely on the shepherd. The sheep could only be lost if the shepherd got weak or died, but is such a thing possible with our Shepherd? Of course not! He is not weak, He is able; He will not die, He ever lives. Thus He saves to the uttermost the ones who approach God through Him; we are safe as long as He lives.

When we put Rom.8:34 and Heb.7:25 together we have the two references in the New Testament to the Lord interceding for His people. We recognise that this is a priestly function that directs our minds back to Israel's high priest. He bore the names of the tribes of Israel upon his garments and as he bore those names before God he was representing and interceding for them. Those names were on his breastplate, signifying the place of affection, and they were on his shoulders, signifying the place of strength.[98] Despite all the failures of Israel nationally, God never gave an instruction for any of those stones to be removed from the breastplate or the shoulders of the high priest's garments. In Rom.8:34 we see our names on His loving heart, for Paul goes on to say, "Who shall separate us from the love of Christ?" (v.35). In Heb.7:25 we see

---

[96] W. E. Vine, *Hebrews*, *The Collected Writings of W. E. Vine*, vol.3, p.284.
[97] That is, salvation from the very presence of sin as well as salvation from its penalty and power.
[98] See Exodus 28.

our names on his strong shoulders; He has power to save to the uttermost. And whatever failings and falls a child of God may have, God will never dislodge any name from the heart or shoulders of our Great High Priest. He lives forever to bring us safely home.

Another passage from Hebrews that expresses a similar thought is 9:24:

> For Christ is not entered into the holy places made with hands, which are the figures of the true; but into heaven itself, now to appear in the presence of God for us:

This confirms what we have already discovered, that the Lord Jesus has accepted all our liabilities and has undertaken to deal with them. If He is accepted then we are; if we are rejected then He is; He is in the presence of God *for us*. But rather than me repeating myself here and restating the teaching of the previous verses we have looked at, we'll hear from John Nelson Darby then David Gooding:

> He [Christ] is sitting, never having to get up again [to deal with sin], because the value of the sacrifice is uninterrupted in the presence of God, and the Holy Ghost comes out to show me the result of it. The person who had the sins must be shut out of heaven; then Christ is shut out, if they are not gone, for He took them.[99]

> He has entered heaven itself. And what He is now doing is appearing in the immediate presence of God 'for us' (9:24). Mark those two words 'for us'. It is not surprising that when the Lord Jesus ascended and entered into the presence of God, He was personally accepted for His own sake. But the point is that He did not enter merely for His own sake. He entered as our High Priest and representative; and He now appears in the presence of God for us, just as Israel's high

---

[99] J. N. Darby, *Notes on the Epistle to the Hebrews*, G. Morrish, p.96.

priest on the Day of Atonement appeared in the presence of God as the representative of the people who waited outside. In their case, if their representative high priest was accepted, it meant the people he represented were accepted. If he was rejected, they were rejected.

And so it is in our case too! If our representative has been accepted, so have we. The question I find myself asking is, 'Does God fully realise that as the Lord Jesus appears now in His presence, He appears not simply for His own sake, but as my personal representative?' The answer is, Yes, of course.

'But does God know all the sins I have done and will yet do?' The answer is, Yes, of course.

'Well, then – and here comes the crucial question – knowing the Lord Jesus has entered and is now appearing for me as the one who died for me at Calvary and now lives as my representative, has God accepted *Him*?' The answer once more is, Yes, of course. God has completely accepted Him, knowing Him to be representing me. Not once in all these 2,000 years has He ever been told that His sacrifice at Calvary is not enough to cover quite all the sins I shall yet do, and that He must leave heaven, come to earth again, and like Israel's high priest, supplement His original sacrifice with another. No, as my representative He sits at the very right hand of God, and not once in 2,000 years has He been asked to move back an inch. It means that all believers can know at this very moment that they are already accepted, and will ever remain so, at the highest level of God's heaven.[100]

Let's note as well, when Scripture says He *appears in the presence* of God for us, it is not simply saying He is there in the vicinity, but the

---

[100] D. W. Gooding, *An Unshakeable Kingdom*, IVP, 1989, pp.194,195 (now available at http://www.keybibleconcepts.org/).

word *appear* tells us He presents Himself, He is fully manifest,[101] and the expression *in the presence* means before the face of God.[102] The Lord Jesus, who died for our sins at Calvary, presents Himself to and is fully manifest before the face of an all-knowing, sin-hating God and there is no fear or dread on His part, neither then should there be any on ours.

> His work of sacrifice accomplished, He Himself carries in the token of it into heaven, the place henceforth of His priestly ministration. By Him we draw nigh to God: His acceptance, who is our representative there, the measure of our acceptance.[103]

> Think of that Man who walked this earth, who passed through all its trials, who magnified God in His daily life; He is now in the presence of God! He is not there for Himself, but appears in the presence of God for us! A Man before God, a Man as our representative, a Man who is God's delight, is the pledge that just so surely as He is there, so surely does God delight in every one of His redeemed people! If you want to know the measure of your acceptance before God think not of your poor, feeble, unworthy self, but look up yonder upon the throne and see One who has entered into heaven itself and appears in the presence of God for us. You remember in the fiftieth of Isaiah, the Lord asks, Who is it that will lay anything to His charge? God is near who justifies Him.[104] When you turn to the eighth of Romans, you find that identical language used of His people![105]

> He appears in the presence of God for us — how

---

[101] See, for example, Jamieson, Fausset and Brown commentary on Hebrews. Freely available on e-Sword.
[102] See RV or JND. Note Darby's footnote, "to the face of God", thus expressing and emphasising the thought of acceptance, approach and communion.
[103] F. W. Grant, *Atonement in Type, Prophecy, and Accomplishment*, loc. 584.
[104] Isa.50:8,9
[105] Rom.8:33,34

much that means! It means that the journey is already over, so far as our standing is concerned; that the whole question is eternally settled. Christ Himself would need to be dragged down from His place of glory before the acceptance of a believer in Him could be questioned. Doubts dishonour God's grace, and practically dethrone Christ! If we but realized it, to have a doubt of our perfect and eternal security is to have a doubt of Christ's place in the presence of God — He appears there for us.[106]

We'll look at one other passage from Hebrews before we look at another aspect of the Lord's unfinished work.

> For men verily swear by the greater: and an oath for confirmation is to them an end of all strife. Wherein God, willing more abundantly to shew unto the heirs of promise the immutability of His counsel, confirmed it by an oath: that by two immutable things, in which it was impossible for God to lie, we might have a strong consolation, who have fled for refuge to lay hold upon the hope set before us: which hope we have as an anchor of the soul, both sure and stedfast, and which entereth into that within the veil; whither the forerunner is for us entered, even Jesus, made an high priest for ever after the order of Melchisedec. (Heb.6:16-20)

What a passage of assurance. The Holy Spirit constructs an impenetrable fortress of protection for the Christian to rest and rejoice in here: "...willing *more abundantly* to show unto the heirs of *promise* the *immutability of His council, confirmed it by an oath*: that by *two immutable things*, in which it was *impossible for God to lie*, we might have *strong consolation*...an *anchor of the soul*, both *sure and stedfast*..." (emphasis added). I think you get the point here; our position of acceptance with God is not the least bit tenuous. Isn't it

---

[106] Samuel Ridout, *Hebrews Lectures,* available at http://www.stempublishing.com/authors/S_Ridout/SR_Hebrews09.html.

interesting that the two chapters in Hebrews to which people most frequently turn to try to prove a believer can lose his salvation (chapters 6 and 10) are the two chapters that most emphatically teach that we can't.

The Holy Spirit brings before us the counsel and character of God to give assurance, but the bit I want us to highlight here is that we are told that the Lord Jesus is our forerunner and has entered for us inside the veil. There is a mixing of metaphors here. We are to see ourselves on the stormy seas but our anchor is embedded in the Word of a God who cannot lie. That anchor is "within the veil", so we are also to see ourselves in the court of the tabernacle. So we have a hope that is within the veil, in the very presence of God, resting on the very promises of God, and the Lord Jesus has gone in, and He has gone in as our forerunner. This is something that was completely unknown in Judaism, a high priest going within the veil as a forerunner! But this is one of the things that make Jesus Christ a *Great* High Priest, His going in is the guarantee that others will follow.

So the Lord Jesus has entered within the veil as a forerunner for us, thus guaranteeing our safe arrival. "Christ Himself who is there and is the pledge of all that is coming, prevents us from making shipwreck."[107]

Our Advocate

John tells us about the Lord's unfinished work on our behalf in 1 Jn.2:1, 2:

> My little children, these things write I unto you, that ye sin not. And if any man sin, we have an advocate with the Father, Jesus Christ the righteous: and He is the propitiation for our sins: and not for ours only, but also for the sins of the whole world.

There are several views of what exactly the Lord's ministry as Advocate entails, but we don't need to come down on one of them here to prove our point. Whatever the ministry of the Advocate is,

---

[107] Vine, *Hebrews*, p.278.

it is not cancelled by our sin, in fact it is for us when we sin, and who the Lord Jesus is and what He has done ensures that no sin a believer commits will ever demand our condemnation, because He is the propitiation for our sins.

> "We have an Advocate with the Father, Jesus Christ the righteous." This never changes. The place which we have with God abides there, because Christ, the righteous One, is there. The perfectly accepted Person is in the presence of God, and God is honoured about the failure. "And He is the propitiation for our sins." So that the advocacy of Christ with the Father is founded upon this acceptance, first of His Person, and then of His work for us. We are accepted in the Beloved, and this never changes, because the righteous One always appears in the presence of God for us. And yet the Lord does not allow anything contrary to Himself. Sin is not passed over. "We have an Advocate." And yet if He is the Advocate for these persons who have failed, it is because He is the propitiation for their sins. There is perfect acceptance. Having met all requirements about sin on the cross, we are put in the presence of God in the acceptance of Christ Himself.[108]

Losing Faith?

But someone may still have a nagging concern despite all that has been said. One may say, That's all very well to say that the Lord guarantees the acceptance of His people, and He intercedes for His own, and He is in the presence of God for all Christians, but surely those ascriptions "His people, His own, Christians" etc. are all conditional upon us actually trusting Him, so what if we stop believing, what if we lose our faith? After all, the promises of salvation are not to whosoever *believed* but whosoever *believes*. That's a fair question, but before hitting it head on I want us to

---

[108] J. N. Darby, *Notes on the First Epistle of John*, available at http://www.stempublishing.com/ebooks/_catalog/79f2a652/79f2a652_books.html.

notice something: if the Lord intercedes for His own and one of them is lost then His intercession has failed. If the Lord appears in the presence of God for *us* and one of *us* is lost then the Lord's office as our representative forces Him out of the presence of God too. If God has said He will remember our sins no more, and then our sins are remembered against us then God's promise has been broken. If this doctrine that one can lose his salvation is true then it has massive ramifications that not only threaten us, but threaten the Godhead Itself.

Let me say as well, it is a great mercy that salvation is said to be for those who believe rather than for those that merely believed at a point in the past, for that would make for a very shaky ground of assurance, leading to endless backward glances and constant gnawing doubts, *Was that genuine faith? Was that real repentance? Was it true conviction or mere emotion?* And that then would lead to the scourge of people "getting saved again" when doubts come, because they are trying to go back in time and ascertain the reality of that moment of conversion, and since we can't perfectly relive the past, better just to "do it again" and make sure. But the Bible doesn't call on us to ask "Did we believe?" but "Do we believe?"

> Here's another way to think about it: if you are seated right now, there was a point in time in which you transferred the weight of your body from your legs to the chair. You may not even remember making that decision, but the fact you are seated now proves that you did. Salvation is the posture of repentance and faith toward the finished work of Christ in which you transfer the weight of your hopes of heaven off your own righteousness and onto the finished work of Jesus Christ. The way to know you made the decision is by the fact you are resting in Christ now. The apostle John almost always talks about "believing" in the present tense because it is something we do continually, not something we did once in the past (e.g., Jn.3:36; 9:36-38; 10:27,28; 1 Jn.5:13). The posture begins at a moment, but it

persists for a lifetime.[109]

So if I am a believer I am saved, but can a believer ever become an unbeliever? How do we deal with this issue?

I strongly suggest *not* dealing with it the way Charles Stanley does. He has written a book entitled *Eternal Security*,[110] which is helpful in some parts, but definitely not here. He says that while it is impossible for a Christian to ever lose his salvation, it is possible for a Christian to lose his faith. So according to Charles Stanley one who is saved can't be lost, but a believer can become an unbeliever.

He says that the use of the present tense does not necessarily mean that the action goes on continuously. He points to Jn.4:13 in support: "Whosoever drinketh of this water shall thirst again..." Obviously the Lord isn't saying that a person who continually drinks of the water from the well will thirst again, because if he were continually drinking from it he wouldn't thirst. Stanley says then it is unjustified to say that the present tense *believeth* indicates a continuous attitude of believing. There is a fair enough point being made here; you could make an offer and say, *Whoever comes and takes this can have it.* You don't mean someone has to keep on coming and taking, the present tense gives this idea, the person accepting. But this runs into a major barrier at Jn.1:12:

> But as many as received Him, to them He gave
> the right to become children of God, to those who
> believe in His name: (NKJV)

You will notice there are two descriptions of those who become the children of God, they are those who received Him (aorist tense) and those who believe in His name (present tense). This is not mere chance or an idle change. The God who inspires each tense as well as each word[111] has a purpose in this, and it is to show that receiving Christ is an act of a moment, but believing in His name is an attitude that continues permanently.

---

[109] J. D. Greear, *Stop Asking Jesus Into Your Heart: How to Know for Sure You Are Saved*, Kindle edition, p.43.
[110] Charles Stanley, *Eternal Security*, Thomas Nelson, 1990.
[111] e.g. Matt.22:31, 32 – "I am the God of Abraham..." not "I was".

Let's look a bit more at what Charles Stanley has to say on this issue.

> The Bible clearly teaches that God's love for His people is of such magnitude that even those who walk away from the faith have not the slightest chance of slipping from His hand.[112]

He goes on to say:

> To believe that a man or woman can lose his or her salvation is to believe that a human being can frustrate the eternal purpose of God...To hold a theology in which man can do something that throws him back into a state of spiritual deadness, thus denying God His predetermined purpose, is to embrace a system in which man is in the driver's seat and God is just a passenger.[113]

And then he gives this illustration:

> If I chose to have a tattoo put on my arm, that would involve a onetime act on my part. Yet the tattoo would remain with me indefinitely. I don't have to maintain an attitude of fondness for tattoos to ensure that the tattoo remains on my arm. In fact I may change my mind the minute I receive it. But that does not change the fact that I have a tattoo on my arm. My request for the tattoo and the tattoo itself are two entirely different things.[114]

I'll point something out in passing here about illustrations. Illustrations can be very helpful to *explain* your point of view, but illustrations can never *prove* your point of view. Stanley has given us a story about someone getting a tattoo and then immediately regretting it and being stuck with it for the rest of his life, but that's all that is, a story. He has to, but does not, prove that the story accurately illustrates the reality. You see the point is this, salvation

---

[112] Charles Stanley, *Eternal Security*, Kindle edition, loc. 938.
[113] Ibid. loc. 973.
[114] Ibid. loc. 1017.

is not like getting a tattoo, salvation is receiving a new life and entering into a real relationship with God, and the way one knows he has had the new birth is if he has the new life. Stanley says that he does not have a theology that teaches that man can do something to throw himself back into a state of spiritual deadness, but the fact is he does. To say a Christian can lose his faith, and become an atheist, Buddhist, Jehovah's Witness or Muslim, is to effectively and practically throw him into spiritual deadness, because there is no manifestation or evidence of divine life within. Life from God is not merely positional, legal or theoretical; it is powerful, living and practical. As William MacDonald said:

> The idea of a true believer ceasing to believe is purely hypothetical. The Bible knows nothing about it. It is unthinkable that one who is indwelt by Christ could or would drive Him out.[115]

John puts his apostolic authority against the notion that one can be a saved unbeliever:

> Who is the liar but the one who denies that Jesus is the Christ? This is the antichrist, the one who denies the Father and the Son. Whoever denies the Son does not have the Father; the one who confesses the Son has the Father also. (1 Jn.2:22,23, NASB)

> Whosoever transgresseth, and abideth not in the doctrine of Christ, hath not God. He that abideth in the doctrine of Christ, he hath both the Father and the Son. (2 Jn.9)

John is telling us here that holding erroneous doctrines about the Lord (e.g. denying that Jesus is the Christ, or denying that He is the Son) means that you do not have God, i.e. you are not saved. In John's writings, as we will see again later, one of the indispensable proofs of eternal life is that you believe the right things about the Lord Jesus. This is guaranteed by the Holy Spirit of God, because it is in the context of wrong doctrine about Christ that John tells the young children in the family of God (i.e. the new believers), "ye

---

[115] MacDonald, *Once in Christ, in Christ Forever*, p.194.

have an unction from the Holy One, and ye know all things" (1 John 2:20). He is saying that the Holy Spirit of God will alert them to errors regarding the person of Christ. This is something that is borne out in experience; a new believer may encounter a cultist and while they may not know *what* is wrong or *why* it's wrong, he will know *that* it's wrong; the Holy Spirit will not permit him to swallow it.

That is not to say that a Christian can't be stumbled, will never have doubts about his salvation, or may not question the existence of God. We are all prone to attacks from the enemy. Faith and doubt are not mutually exclusive, as a matter of fact, you can't have doubts unless there is faith but the Christian will maintain an attitude of trust. We all live out what we believe, and when I went through a period of doubts about what I believed I still lived as if it was true, that is, I still lived as if the Bible was the Word of God, because, although I had questions, they could not compel me to live as if there was no God. I was not prepared to step off that foundation of Christianity and say it's not true. And that is the vital point: a Christian can wonder, worry and waver, but he will not abandon the Christian worldview for any other.[116]

Consider what the Lord Himself said in another context:

> For there shall arise false Christs, and false prophets, and shall shew great signs and wonders; insomuch that, if it were possible, they shall deceive the very elect. (Matt.24:24)

Iniquity shall abound, deception will be widespread, but the Lord says that it will not be possible for the elect to be taken in by it. If that is true of future tribulation days, how much more true of this day in which the Holy Spirit of God permanently indwells all of God's people!

So that link of trust will never be broken because there is an indwelling Holy Spirit, but also because there is an interceding Great High Priest. Listen to what the Lord said in Lk.22:31,32:

> And the Lord said, Simon, Simon, behold, Satan

---

[116] I don't presume to venture into how genuine mental health issues touch on all this. All that I am saying presupposes that we are dealing with people of sound mind.

> hath desired to have you, that he may sift you as
> wheat: but I have prayed for thee, that thy faith
> fail not: and when thou art converted, strengthen
> thy brethren.

The Lord was warning Peter about a satanic attack that was looming, but this assurance was given, "I have prayed for thee, that thy faith fail not". The prayer was not that Peter would not fail, but that his faith would not fail, and that prayer was of course answered. Peter failed miserably, but he never stopped believing in who Jesus Christ was. This is a specific example of the intercessory ministry of Christ, He prays for the maintenance of the faith of all His own, so that that link of faith, which may seem so shaky and brittle, is actually as strong as the power of Christ can make it, and it will never be broken.

> ...the vital lifeline of their personal faith in the
> Saviour would be maintained by the intercessions
> of their King-Priest as in the case of Peter...[117]

Only if the Lord Jesus can have His prayers refused can a believer's faith fail, and we know the Lord Jesus can never have a prayer refused. Look at the reasons requests are refused and you will see that none of them can have any relevance to the prayers of our blessed Lord:

> If I regard iniquity in my heart, the Lord will not
> hear me... (Ps.66:18)

The idea in regarding iniquity is to see it with pleasure,[118] and so the thought in the verse is, "*If I had aimed at evil in my heart, the Lord would not hear.*"[119] Of course this could never be true of our Lord. He said, "the prince of this world cometh, and hath nothing in Me." God the Father Himself could look at the thoughts and motives of His Son and say, "in Thee I am well pleased." He never did or could look at sin with pleasure or aim at it in His heart. Sin is foreign and repulsive to His holy soul.

James gives us another couple of reasons why prayers are not

---

[117] D. W. Gooding, *According to Luke*, IVP, 1987, p.333 (now available at http://www.keybibleconcepts.org/).
[118] See Jamieson, Fausset and Brown commentary, e-Sword.
[119] See Keil & Delitzsch, *Commentary on the Old Testament*, Volume 5, Hendrickson Publishers, 2006, p.438.

answered, firstly, 1:5-8:

> If any of you lack wisdom, let him ask of God,
> that giveth to all men liberally, and upbraideth
> not; and it shall be given him. But let him ask in
> faith, nothing wavering. For he that wavereth is
> like a wave of the sea driven with the wind and
> tossed. For let not that man think that he shall
> receive any thing of the Lord. A double minded
> man is unstable in all his ways.

This passage is telling us that the man who is wavering in his
confidence in God cannot expect such an attitude to be honoured
or any request springing from that attitude to be granted.[120]
However, the Lord Jesus certainly could never be accused of
doubting the character of God. He knew God fully, and in His
pathway on earth He was the model of a life of faith, exemplifying
what it is to trust God completely.[121]

James has more to say on unanswered prayer:

> From whence come wars and fightings among
> you? Come they not hence, even of your lusts
> that war in your members? Ye lust, and have not:
> ye kill, and desire to have, and cannot obtain: ye
> fight and war, yet ye have not, because ye ask not.
> Ye ask, and receive not, because ye ask amiss, that
> ye may consume it upon your lusts. (Jms.4:1-3).

There were those James was addressing who were asking of God
in prayer but they weren't receiving what they asked because they
were asking with impure motives. Needless to say, the Lord Jesus
could never have a request refused on such a ground. He is the
epitome of self-sacrifice and the antithesis of self-centredness. He
always sought the glory of God and the good of others.

There is another condition given for prayer being answered; it is
found in 1 Jn.5:14,15:

---

[120] The man James has in mind perhaps isn't sure if he wants God's wisdom, he has his view on how
to deal with a problem and is fearful it is not God's way, so he doesn't ask in sincere faith. See Alec
Motyer, *The Message of James*, The Bible Speaks Today series, IVP.
[121] See Heb.12:1,2.

> And this is the confidence that we have in Him,
> that, if we ask any thing according to His will,
> He heareth us: and if we know that He hear us,
> whatsoever we ask, we know that we have the
> petitions that we desired of Him.

For prayer to be answered it has to be in accord with the will of
God, and there was no one so committed to the will of God as the
Lord Jesus Christ. It was His reason for coming into the world, it
was His motivation all through His life, and it was what took Him
on to the cross. The Lord Jesus certainly is not making requests for
us that are out of keeping with the will of God, and therefore what
He requests will without doubt be granted.[122]

> Since our Saviour always prays in perfect
> harmony with the will of the Father, we can be
> assured that keeping our salvation secure is the
> will of God.[123]

But are we not making an unjustified extrapolation of Lk.22:31,32
to take in all believers? After all, all those verses teach is that
Christ prayed that *Peter's* faith would not fail, why think He does
the same for all His people? The answer is found in John 17. In
this majestic passage we are allowed to hear the Son speak to His
Father about us.[124] He makes requests for all His people. Let's
have a look at some of them:

> While I was with them in the world, I kept them
> in Thy name: those that Thou gavest Me I have
> kept, and none of them is lost, but the son of
> perdition; that the scripture might be fulfilled.
> (v.12)

> I pray not that Thou shouldest take them out of

---

[122] The Lord's prayer in Gethsemane when He asked for the cup to be removed and the hour to pass from Him was qualified with "if it be possible…nevertheless, not My will, but Thine be done", and thus it is not an example of a request refused. No such qualifications are included in His intercessions for His people, He knows He is asking within the purpose of God.

[123] John MacArthur Jr, *Saved Without a Doubt: Being Sure of Your Salvation*, David C Cook, Third Edition, 2011, Kindle edition, p.24.

[124] The Lord prayed on two occasions on the night before His death, one in John 17 and the other in Gethsemane. The contrasts need to be noted. In Gethsemane He expresses His assumed dependence on the Father, but in John 17 He expresses His essential equality with the Father. In Gethsemane the language is, "Not My will…" but in John 17 His language is "I will" (v.24).

> the world, but that Thou shouldest keep them
> from the evil. (v.15)

When the Lord speaks here about *the evil*, the thought is the evil one.[125] He is praying that we would be kept from the dominion of the evil one, thus while Satan might desire to have us, He can't, because the Lord has not just prayed for Peter, He has prayed for all.[126]

> The only question each true believer nowadays needs to ask, therefore, is this: "Will the Father be less diligent, less effective in keeping me and preserving my faith, than the Lord Jesus was in keeping the faith of His eleven apostles?" The answer is self-evident: "Of course not!"
>
> ...
>
> So did our Lord's proud claim stand unbroken, and will stand firm for every true believer to the end of time: "Of all the Father has given Me, I have lost not one."[127]

He goes on to pray that all who believe "may be one" (v.21). Now this text has been a pretext for the ecumenical movement, but the point of course is that all true believers share an organic unity as members of one invisible and indivisible body. The Lord's request has been granted, it is not dependent on us. But the thing is this, if a believer lost his salvation then the Lord's prayer has been refused because it would mean that oneness has been divided.

In vv.22,23 He speaks about another oneness which has to do with manifestation in future glory.[128] His prayer is that all who believe will be one on that day, and this too ensures the security of everyone who has believed.

---

[125] Singular, masculine noun.
[126] It is true that at this stage He is still praying for the 11 disciples, but in v.20 He states that His prayer is not just for them but for all who will believe through their word, which comes down to us today. "He introduces those who should believe through their means into the enjoyment of their blessing." (JND, *Synopsis of the Books of the Bible*, vol.3, p.387).
[127] D.W. Gooding, *In the School of Christ*, Gospel Folio Press, 2001, pp.246,247 (now available at http://www.keybibleconcepts.org/).
[128] That this is referring to future manifestation is evident from the following: the mention of glory being given to us (see, for example, Col.3:4; 2 Thess. 1:10); being made perfect in one; the change from "that the world may believe", v.21 to "that the world may know" v.23.

Verse 24 is yet another glorious guarantee of our eternal security:

> Father, I will that they also, whom Thou hast given Me, be with Me where I am; that they may behold My glory, which Thou hast given Me: for Thou lovedst Me before the foundation of the world.

Listen to what the Lord is saying, every believer is a gift from the Father to the Son, and the Son is expressing His desire and asserting His divine right to have us with Him in His glory. He has made the request, and its fulfilment is as sure as the love of the Father for the Son.

> As Christ began to pray for His own while He was yet here in the world, so He has continued to pray for them, and will continue to pray for them, in heaven: "Seeing He ever liveth to make intercession for them" (Heb.7:25). Who can measure the security of the children of God when they are the objects of the ceaseless intercession of the Son of God, whose prayer can never be denied?[129]

Is there any room for doubt? He represents us before God; He has made specific requests to the Father for our security. Only if His person can be rejected and His prayers refused can one who has trusted Him ever be lost. That's good enough for me, I hope it's good enough for you too.

> *Before the throne of God above*
> *I have a strong, a perfect plea;*
> *A Great High Priest whose Name is Love*
> *Who ever lives and pleads for me.*
> *My name is graven on His hands,*
> *My name is written on His heart;*
> *I know that while in heaven He stands,*
> *No tongue can bid me thence depart.*

---

[129] Chafer, *Grace*, loc. 1235-1239.

When Satan tempts me to despair
And tells me of the guilt within,
Upward I look and see Him there
Who made an end to all my sin.
Because the sinless Saviour died,
My sinful soul is counted free,
For God the just is satisfied
To look on Him and pardon me.

Behold Him there the risen Lamb,
My perfect, spotless righteousness;
The great unchangeable I am,
The King of glory and of grace.
One with Himself I cannot die,
My soul is purchased by His blood;
My life is hid with Christ on high,
With Christ my Saviour and my God!

(Charatie de Cheney Lees Smith Bancroft)

The Holy Spirit guarantees our Eternal Security

The Comforter is come,
The earnest has been given;
He leads me onward to the home.
Reserved for me in heaven.
                    (Henry Bennett)

The Holy Spirit of God must be sorely grieved with so much of what is carried out in His name and purported to be done in His power. The Holy Spirit has neither part nor interest in making people blabber like babies, bark like dogs or behave like drunkards. However, the answer to charismatic insanity is not to ignore the ministry of the Holy Spirit, but to get a firm grasp on what His role is in the life of the believer. As we examine His ministry in our lives we discover that what He does has great relevance to this subject of eternal security. As with the Father and the Son, we will look at two truths that demolish any doubt and settle any questions about our security. These truths are *the seal of the Spirit* and *the earnest of the Spirit*.

The Seal of the Spirit

We have already had a dip into Ephesians 1 when we were considering the purpose of God, but we need to return to it for our present subject.

> In Him you also trusted, after you heard the word of truth, the gospel of your salvation; in whom also, having believed, you were sealed with the Holy Spirit of promise. (v.13, NKJV)[130]

---

[130] The KJV rendering "after that ye believed" gives the impression there is a period of time between faith and the reception of the Spirit, and that simply is not what the grammar of the verse means or what the Bible teaches. Paul says if anyone doesn't have the Spirit he is not saved (Rom.8:9).

In this section of assurance Paul tells them of something that happened to them at the moment of conversion. He says that upon believing they were sealed with the Holy Spirit of promise. This is a most important phrase that refutes a number of common errors. It shows, for example, that so much of charismatic teaching is erroneous; receiving the Holy Spirit is not an event for the believer to seek, Paul says it is at the moment of believing that we are sealed with the Spirit. Now Paul well knew all the events in the book of the Acts, and he is writing this letter under house arrest at the end of Acts, and what he is giving here is what is normative. We should not then be going to descriptive passages of unique events in the transitional period of Acts for our doctrine on the reception of the Spirit. Paul is giving teaching in Ephesians 1 regarding the order that pertains to all saints for the rest of this present age. Many of us have hunted the house looking for our wallet or keys only to discover them hiding in our pocket, likewise, many of the Lord's people earnestly seek the Spirit and they have had Him all along, but because they have been seeking Him they haven't been able to enjoy and use Him the way God intended.[131]

The phrase also contradicts the teaching that baptism or any other ordinance is required for salvation; we are sealed upon believing. You cannot be a believer without having the Spirit.[132]

But what we are interested in is seeing how it proves eternal security. We are *sealed* with the Holy Spirit. What are we to understand by this term *sealed*? A few illustrations from other parts of the Bible will help us in our appreciation.

A thing is sealed to provide a proof of purchase. In Jeremiah 32 the prophet was sitting in prison while the Babylonians were besieging the city. It was at this time the Lord gave him a most unexpected message. Jeremiah was told that his cousin Hanameel was going to come and see him and was going to offer to sell him a field in Anathoth. It seems Hanameel didn't think much of Jeremiah's intelligence that he would ask him to buy a field when Nebuchadnezzar and his army were ripping through the

---

[131] H.A. Ironside's *Holiness, The False and the True* is a really helpful and interesting treatment of these issues giving Ironside's own personal experience. It is available at http://www.wholesomewords.org/etexts/ironside/holiness.pdf.
[132] See Rom.8:9 – "Now if any man have not the Spirit of Christ, he is none of His."

land. However, the Lord had told Jeremiah that houses and fields and vineyards would yet again be bought in the land (v.15), so we read in vv.9,10:

> And I bought the field of Hanameel my uncle's son, that was in Anathoth, and weighed him the money, even seventeen shekels of silver. And I subscribed the evidence, and sealed it, and took witnesses, and weighed him the money in the balances.

So the seal is the proof of purchase. It is the means by which title deeds are kept safe. That field belonged to Jeremiah and the seal protected his purchase until he could actually take possession of it. So the Holy Spirit is given to every believer as a seal to protect what the Lord has purchased. There's an expression you'll be familiar with, *'easy come, easy go'*, and the point is that the degree to which you value something is dependent on what it cost you to get it. If something cost you little or nothing to acquire then you don't shed too many tears if you lose it, but how much did it cost the Lord to make us His? We weren't free and we weren't cheap. In Eph.1:7 we are told that we have redemption *through His blood*; He has paid an infinite price in order to make us His. Having paid such a price, He certainly does not want us to be lost. Therefore God places a seal upon us that can never be broken, the almighty Spirit of God. The Spirit protects what the Lord has purchased and marks us out as belonging to Him. Although we are redeemed now, the Bible teaches (and our own experience confirms) that redemption has not yet touched the body. We await the redemption of the body, and the Holy Spirit ensures our protection until that day. Paul writes in Eph.4:30:

> And grieve not the Holy Spirit of God, in whom
> ye were sealed unto the day of redemption. (ASV)

We were sealed with the Holy Spirit at the moment of believing, according to Eph.1:13, but He is the seal unto the day of redemption, until the day we enter into redemption in all its fulness. So from the moment of conversion until the glorious day when the Lord comes to take His people home we are sealed. This means there is not the slightest crack or smallest window of opportunity for the Lord's purchased possession to be lost. And please notice, in this very verse Paul speaks about the possibility of grieving the Holy Spirit of God, but the plain truth of the verse is this, even if we do grieve the Holy Spirit we are still sealed unto the day of redemption. Paul does not say, *"Grieve not the Holy Spirit or He will leave you."* He says, *"Do not grieve Him, because He will never leave you."*

> If salvation can be lost, then His sealing would not be until the day of redemption but only until the day of sinning, or apostasy, or disbelief.[133]

The motivation for holiness in the Old Testament seems to be that the Holy Spirit could leave you, so David prays in his psalm of repentance, "...take not Thy Holy Spirit from me" (Ps.51:11). But the motivation for holiness in the New Testament is that the Holy Spirit cannot be taken from you, that means then you had better behave yourself because He will not put up with sin without moving in discipline.

So we have been purchased, and the Holy Spirit is the proof that we belong to Christ, and that purchased possession can never be lost, He is the seal.

In Esther 8:8 we find another truth connected with the seal:

> Write ye also for the Jews, as it liketh you, in the king's name, and seal it with the king's ring: for the writing which is written in the king's name, and sealed with the king's ring, may no man reverse.

The seal of the king indicated that something was permanent. Once that seal was set on the writing, no one could reverse it. It's not difficult to see how this applies to us; God has done something to us and in us. We have been justified, we have been regenerated, we have been brought into His family, we are members of the church, Christ's body, we have been given an inheritance, etc. etc. and the Holy Spirit is the seal that says these things are permanent and stand forever. The King of the ages has sealed us, none can reverse it.

---

[133] Charles C. Ryrie, *Basic Theology*, pp.383, 384.

In Revelation 20 we find a seal used in another context:

> And I saw an angel come down from heaven, having the key of the bottomless pit and a great chain in his hand. And he laid hold on the dragon, that old serpent, which is the Devil, and Satan, and bound him a thousand years, and cast him into the bottomless pit, and shut him up, and set a seal upon him, that he should deceive the nations no more, till the thousand years should be fulfilled: and after that he must be loosed a little season. (Rev.20:1-3)

In this scene following the Lord's return to earth in judgment, Satan is cast into the abyss and a seal placed over him that he won't be able to get out. Now this mighty, malignant being can muster all his malicious fury and summon all his satanic strength but he will not be able to break that seal and emerge from that pit until God allows him. During that glorious Millennial reign no one needs to worry about the devil escaping, it can't happen. He won't be able to break God's seal then, and he isn't able to break God's seal now; we needn't worry.

One more example will suffice as an illustration:

> Now the next day, that followed the day of the preparation, the chief priests and Pharisees came together unto Pilate, saying, Sir, we remember that that deceiver said, while He was yet alive, After three days I will rise again. Command therefore that the sepulchre be made sure until the third day, lest His disciples come by night, and steal Him away, and say unto the people, He is risen from the dead: so the last error shall be worse than the first.
> Pilate said unto them, Ye have a watch: go your way, make it as sure as ye can.
> So they went, and made the sepulchre sure, sealing the stone, and setting a watch. (Matt.27:62-66)

The Lord had just died and been buried in Joseph's tomb. The

Jewish leadership had picked up on something the Lord's own disciples didn't seem to grasp, i.e. that the Lord said He would rise again. In light of this they wanted the tomb guarded and the stone sealed. Now the seal was the symbol of Roman authority, and breaking it would have been considered an act of treason, and thus a capital crime. The body was placed in the tomb, the stone rolled to the door, and the seal put on the stone. That seal was saying that all the imperial authority of Rome was invested in keeping that body in the tomb, and all the military might of Rome would descend upon the head of the one who violated it. Thus the seal signifies protection. However, there was one who did not care for Rome's authority or fear her power, this was the highest authority, the greatest power, God Himself. He raised His Son from the dead, and then sent an angel down to roll away the stone and show that Rome could not keep the body in the tomb; He is risen!

Here's the point, God has put a seal on us, and the seal is His own Holy Spirit. Is there any higher authority or greater power that could ever break that seal? Of course there isn't; what happened to Rome's seal will never happen to God's, and what that means then is that what is sealed is protected and can never be lost. Lewis Sperry Chafer certainly saw and felt the force of this truth:

> Nothing could be more final than this. The Spirit Himself is the seal. His blessed presence in every true child of God is the divine mark of ownership, purpose and destiny. The Spirit who was sent to abide in us will not withdraw. He may be grieved, or quenched (resisted), but He abides. This He does as the divine guarantee that there shall be no failure in any purpose of God and the sealed one will reach his eternal glory and the eternal blessedness of "the day of redemption."[134]

Let's just gather up the lessons from these illustrations: the seal is the proof of purchase, the evidence that we belong to God; the seal makes something permanent, irreversible and unchangeable; and the seal is a sign of authority intended to protect whatever it

---

[134] Chafer, *Salvation*, loc. 1421.

is placed upon. These are truths that are entailed in the thought of us being sealed with the Holy Spirit of promise, and it is God's intention that we relax our souls in the comfort and security these truths provide.

In 2 Corinthians 1 Paul refers to the Holy Spirit as the seal again:

> Now He which stablisheth us with you in Christ, and hath anointed us, is God; who hath also sealed us, and given the earnest of the Spirit in our hearts. (2 Cor.1:21, 22)

In this section Paul has been defending himself against charges of vacillation and duplicity. He refutes them by saying that he lived his life and conducted his service in the light of God's character, and therefore he sought to act accordingly.

> As God is faithful and true to His promises, therefore as His servant he had fully expected to fulfil what he had purposed.[135]

He is affirming the faithfulness of God and the dependability of His promises, and those who believe the gospel are given the Holy Spirit as the proof that those promises are to and for them.

Eph.1:13 shows us that only believers are sealed, (it is upon believing they were sealed), but in 2 Cor.1:22 we can conclude that all believers are sealed. Ryrie points this out:

> As with indwelling, sealing belongs to believers only and to all believers. In 2 Corinthians 1:22 Paul makes no exceptions in writing to a group in which exceptions could easily be justified.[136]

In Eph.1:13 the Spirit is called "the Holy Spirit of promise" which again is intended to convey to us that to have the Spirit is to be in receipt of the unchanging promises of God.

This thought of promise brings us on then to think about the earnest of the Spirit.

---

[135] J. M. Davies, *The Epistles to the Corinthians*, Gospel Literature Service, 1975, p.158.
[136] Ryrie, *Basic Theology*, p.414.

The Earnest of the Spirit

Ephesians gives us the ultimate rags to riches story. When we see what these Ephesians were "by nature" it is a shocking portrait:

> And you [hath He quickened], who were dead in trespasses and sins; wherein in time past ye walked according to the course of this world, according to the prince of the power of the air, the spirit that now worketh in the children of disobedience: among whom also we all had our conversation in times past in the lusts of our flesh, fulfilling the desires of the flesh and of the mind; and were by nature the children of wrath, even as others. (2:1-3)

These Ephesians were under the domination of sin, captive to and captivated by all things vile. Their whole personality was affected by sin: their minds were corrupt, their emotions (he speaks about their desires) were depraved, and their wills were rebellious (sons of disobedience). The three great enemies of God and godliness were having their way with them; they were dominated by the *flesh*, walking according to the course of this *world*, and obeying the orders of the *devil*. That is the unflattering, but brutally honest and completely accurate, portrait of the Ephesians (and us) *by nature*. But God intervenes in great love and rich mercy, and paints a new portrait of them *by grace*:

> But God, who is rich in mercy, for His great love wherewith He loved us, even when we were dead in sins, hath quickened us together with Christ, (by grace ye are saved;) and hath raised us up together, and made us sit together in heavenly

places in Christ Jesus: that in the ages to come
He might shew the exceeding riches of His grace
in his kindness toward us through Christ Jesus.
For by grace are ye saved through faith; and
that not of yourselves: it is the gift of God: not of
works, lest any man should boast. For we are His
workmanship, created in Christ Jesus unto good
works, which God hath before ordained that we
should walk in them. (2:4-10)

The grace of God intervenes and links them with the glorified
Christ. These very same people who had been sad examples of
the corruption of sin and the cruelty of Satan became instead the
exhibits of God's grace and power, and will be for all eternity.
Those who had been children (i.e. inheritors) of wrath have
been brought into a new family and have a new inheritance to
anticipate.

It was Paul's prayer in 1:15-23 that the Ephesians would enter into
the enjoyment of their riches in Christ:

Wherefore I also, after I heard of your faith in the
Lord Jesus, and love unto all the saints, cease not
to give thanks for you, making mention of you
in my prayers; that the God of our Lord Jesus
Christ, the Father of glory, may give unto you the
spirit of wisdom and revelation in the knowledge
of Him: the eyes of your understanding being
enlightened; that ye may know what is the hope
of His calling, and what the riches of the glory
of His inheritance in the saints, and what is the
exceeding greatness of His power to us-ward
who believe, according to the working of His
mighty power, which He wrought in Christ,
when He raised him from the dead, and set Him
at His own right hand in the heavenly places,
far above all principality, and power, and might,
and dominion, and every name that is named,
not only in this world, but also in that which is
to come: and hath put all things under His feet,

> and gave Him to be the head over all things to the
> church, which is His body, the fulness of Him that
> filleth all in all.

Paul prays that these saints would know three things: first, the hope of God's calling; second, the riches of the glory of His inheritance in the saints; and third, the exceeding greatness of His power toward us who believe. When we think of the hope of God's calling it directs us back to vv.4-6: what God is looking forward to is having saints before Him and sons toward Him, all in the enjoyment of His love. When we consider the riches of the glory of His inheritance we are directed back to vv.7-14; the word *inheritance* is mentioned twice over in those verses. Then when we look at the exceeding greatness of His power toward us who believe, it brings us on to 2:1-10. That power which raised and seated Christ has quickened, raised and seated us with Him.

But it is this thought of knowing the riches of the glory of His inheritance that we need to focus on. How can we be sure that this inheritance is really ours? The two references to inheritance in vv.7-14 let us know.

In v.11 Paul tells us we have this inheritance because we are in Christ, "In whom also we have obtained an inheritance..." Our standing in Christ guarantees this inheritance to us; this touches on what we covered in the previous chapter; us being linked with and accepted in Christ. But in v.14 the thought is that we have this inheritance because the Spirit is in us, He is *the earnest of our inheritance*.

What are we to understand by this word *earnest*? Vine defines it in this way, "originally, earnest-money deposited by the purchaser and forfeited if the purchase was not completed..."[137] Mounce has this to say, "Just as a down payment for a house today serves as a guarantee that the rest of the payment will come, so God sends His Holy Spirit into the hearts of believers as a deposit, guaranteeing that someday the full inheritance of salvation will be ours."[138] So

---

[137] W. E. Vine, *Expository Dictionary of New Testament Words*, Oliphants.
[138] William D. Mounce, *Mounce's Complete Expository Dictionary of Old and New Testament Words*, Zondervan.

an earnest is something that is given that guarantees more is to come.[139]

> ...and of this [inheritance] the Spirit of God is the pledge and earnest: an earnest, is what confirms an agreement, and assures the right to the thing agreed to, and is a part of it, and lesser than it, and is never returned; so the Spirit of God certifies the right to the heavenly inheritance, as well as gives a meetness for it; He is the firstfruits of eternal glory and happiness, and of the same kind with it; and as He is enjoyed in measure by the saints now, is lesser than the communion which they shall have with Him, and with the Father, and the Son, hereafter, for the best things are reserved till last; and being once given into the heart as an earnest, He always continues, He never removes more, or is ever taken away.[140]

Vine also points out that the word is used in modern Greek for an engagement ring, thus it is the token / pledge that the lady belongs to the one who gave her the ring and all he has belongs to her. That ring promises she will come into the possession and enjoyment of all that is his. An illustration of this can be found in Genesis 24. This is a great chapter in a great run of chapters that opens up to us a wonderful portrait of God's dealings with men. In chapter 22 we find Abraham's beloved son on the altar; in chapter 23 Sarah dies; chapter 24 Abraham sends his servant out to get a bride for his son, and escorting her home to be met by the son; chapter 25 Abraham marries another wife. It isn't difficult to see God's program pictured for us there: the sacrifice of His beloved Son, the setting aside of the nation of Israel; the Spirit sent forth to get a bride and bring her home, and we look forward to the Son coming out to meet us; God will then take up His dealings with the nation of Israel again. When the servant went in search

---

[139] Genesis 38 gives us an illustration, although I don't really want to go in to the details of this story. Judah's despicable treatment of his daughter-in-law, Tamar, led her to set a trap and play the harlot. When she asked him for payment he said he would send her a kid from his goats, but she wanted a pledge, that is, she wanted something she could have in the meantime that would be security for her, if he didn't fulfil his promise and send the kid she would keep the pledge.
[140] John Gill, *John Gill's Exposition of the Entire Bible*, Eph.1:14, e-Sword.

of a bride for Isaac he went out with treasures from home. He presented these treasures to Rebekah as a preview and promise of what was ahead.[141]

So when we believed the gospel the Holy Spirit was given as the pledge and guarantee that we would come into the enjoyment of the inheritance.

Paul uses the same language in 2 Corinthians 1 and again in chapter 5. We have already looked at the context of 2 Corinthians 1 in connection with the seal of the Spirit, but just to briefly recap and move on, Paul is defending himself regarding the alterations he made in his plans to come to them, and he assures them he had every intention of fulfilling his word when he gave it, but the reason he did not come was for their sake:

> It was that they would be spared the judgment that he, as an apostle, must have inflicted upon the unrepentant amongst them. His delay in coming to them allowed them time to turn from their evil ways and so be in such a state as to make the use of his rod unnecessary.
>
> ...
>
> It was no small mercy for the Corinthians that this imagined visit did not take place, and we are sure that when they read this part of this epistle, they were bowed in thanksgivings to God that He had given His servant grace and wisdom to stay away.[142]

Thus, Paul's coming would not have been for their good, but the Lord's coming will be for the good of all His people, and the Holy Spirit is the divine declaration that His plan will not be changed, the Lord will come to collect us; nothing can change that.

In chapter 5 Paul is talking about the glorious future every believer has, and how we don't get occupied with that which is merely temporal. He says the bodies we have are like tents: flimsy,

[141] Gen.24:53.
[142] A. McShane, *What the Bible Teaches*, vol. 4, *2 Corinthians*, John Ritchie Ltd, 1986, pp.262-263.

temporary, easily wrecked, but at the Lord's coming the believer will instead have a house, a body that is permanent, that will never know decay, experience disease or face death. In the meantime, we groan, quickened spirits in bodies of death, carrying the handicap of carnal flesh meaning we don't live as we should, impeded by the hindrance of mortal flesh meaning we can't live as we would. The desires our sinful flesh gives us and the demands our weak flesh makes upon us cause us to groan, longing for the day when we will be *clothed upon with our house which is from heaven* (v.2). The Spirit of God is the one who gives us such desires for the redemption of the body, and He is also the proof that it will take place. He has given us the foretaste and is the guarantee of the fullness.

But someone might say, "That's all well and good, but how do I know that I have the Holy Spirit? Is it through speaking in tongues or something like that?" No, it's not through speaking in tongues or *anything* like that. One does not require the Spirit of God to engage in what is known today as speaking in tongues:

> Today, ecstatic speech is found among Muslims, Eskimos, and Tibetan monks. A parapsychological laboratory at the University of Virginia Medical School reports incidents of tongues-speaking among those practising the occult.
> Those are only a few examples of the centuries-old tradition of glossolalia that continues today among pagans, heretics, and worshipers of the occult. The possibility of satanic influence is a serious issue, and one which charismatics ought not brush aside without sombre reflection.[143]

No, the presence of the Holy Spirit in a person's life is not manifested by something that can be generated by the flesh or inspired by the devil, it is manifested in a much deeper and far more miraculous way, by giving a person a real love for the Lord Jesus as He is revealed in Scripture, a delight in His Word, a desire for holiness, a capacity for worship, a new power in the life, and a kinship and true fellowship with other Christians. Those are

---

[143] John F. MacArthur Jr. *Charismatic Chaos*, Zondervan, 1992, p.292.

features that cannot abide in one who has never been born again.

I got a phone call one day from a lady who really wanted to be saved but she said she didn't think she would be able to live the Christian life. I informed her there was no way she could, no one could. It's like me saying I could never be a bird because I couldn't do the things birds do: I couldn't fly, build nests, eat worms, etc. But if I was born a bird then living a bird life would come naturally. So it is with Christianity, it's not that you have to live the Christian life, you have to take it, it's a gift.[144] When a person receives the Lord Jesus as Saviour he is born again, receives a new nature and discovers that things he previously found boring now captivate him, things he once hated now he loves, things he formerly thought he couldn't live without now no longer enslave him. This is the reality of the Holy Spirit of God in the life.

Another little example comes from an occasion when a colleague and I were asked to visit an elderly man who was having doubts about salvation. We went to see him and found him in a very distressed condition. After a while I asked him how long he had been in the fellowship of the assembly. He told me it was over 50 years. I asked him if, in all that time, he had ever enjoyed the breaking of bread meeting. He looked at me with surprise and told me he loved that meeting. I told him that it would be a very strange unbeliever who could sit for an hour in quiet contemplation of God's Son and love it. More than once we have had unbelievers come to the Lord's Supper to observe, and they haven't been able to stick it, they left before the meeting finished. When they've been asked for their opinion of the meeting the response has been, "That meeting was dead." The problem wasn't that the meeting was dead, the problem was that *they* were. They had no spiritual life to enable them to appreciate the remembrance of the Lord, and the meeting contained nothing that would appeal to the flesh or excite the emotions, it is a truly spiritual experience, and one would require the indwelling of the Spirit to enjoy it week by week.[145]

---

[144] e.g. Rom.6:23; Jn.10:10.

[145] It is so sad that many churches actually actively cater all meetings so that the unconverted can enjoy them. A meeting free from any soulish or fleshly adornments serves to expose those who are not truly born again and confirm those that are. Let us ensure we aren't propping up corpses by gearing meetings and messages toward making the lost comfortable in their sins.

At conversion the things of God come alive to us, or rather we come alive to them through the Spirit of God. He is the Person who leads us into the enjoyment of our heavenly, spiritual blessings and is the guarantee that we will come into the full enjoyment of them in the future. What we enjoy now is what we will be brought into in all its fulness by and by: "...a pledge may be of any kind, whereas the earnest must be part of the same thing or substance."[146]

> "Earnest" implies, besides the security of the believer's future inheritance, its identity in kind, though not in degree, with his present possessed enjoyment of the [S]pirit. Heaven perfected will continue heaven already begun in part (Rev.22:11 ff).[147]

Paul writes about a very similar thing in Rom.8:22-24:

> For we know that the whole creation groaneth and travaileth in pain together until now. And not only they, but ourselves also, which have the firstfruits of the Spirit, even we ourselves groan within ourselves, waiting for the adoption, to wit, the redemption of our body. For we are saved by hope: but hope that is seen is not hope: for what a man seeth, why doth he yet hope for?

In this chapter Paul has been telling us that the Spirit of God bears witness with our spirit that we are children of God, and therefore we are heirs of God and joint heirs with Christ (vv.16,17), there is glory ahead for us. How does the Spirit bear witness with our spirit? Firstly, it would be by means of the *new direction* in our lives; we walk according to the Spirit, mortifying the deeds of the flesh. Our lives have been changed and there is an internal drive and instinctive draw toward holiness which was never there before.

Secondly, the Spirit would bear witness by means of the *new desire* we have in our spirits, we have a connection with and a yearning for the Father (v.15); it is the Holy Spirit who gives us this consciousness.

---

[146] A. McShane, *2 Corinthians*, p.264.
[147] A. R. Fausset, *Bible Dictionary*, e-Sword.

Thirdly, it would be by means of the *new distress* we have; Paul says we suffer with Christ (v.17). This is not suffering for Christ, but something more fundamental than that, it is jointly suffering with Him in this world so that what is grieving to Him is grieving to us. The unregenerate enjoy the way the world is, they drink from the fountains of sin and live in rebellion against Christ. Paul says if we don't like the way the world is now then we will like the way it will be. The believer has longings for Christ to reign and it pains him that Christ is not enthroned in this world where He should be, and Paul says that if that is your attitude it means that when Christ is enthroned in this world you will actually reign with Him, and when He is glorified you will share in it.

This assurance gives Paul the hope and encouragement he needs as he endures *the sufferings of this present time* (v.18), he knows that this is not permanent and hopeless. The whole creation is groaning as a result of the fall of man, labouring under the burden of the curse and held in the bondage of corruption, longing for the relief and release that will be brought about when the Lord comes to reign. Because we are living in unredeemed bodies we are groaning and longing too, but we are not only longing in a negative way, i.e. longing for deliverance from sin's effects, but there is a positive aspect to it; we have blessings we are looking forward to enjoying in a way we cannot now in our unredeemed bodies. The guarantee and foretaste of these blessings is the Holy Spirit of God, and the phrase Paul uses here is that we *have the firstfruits of the Spirit*.

The firstfruit was the guarantee of a harvest to come, and Paul is saying here that the Spirit is the firstfruit. He is the guarantee of more to come, so while Paul knew the dark clouds of disappointment, sorrow and pain, he also could feel the beams of light from heaven breaking through, bringing the warmth of fellowship with God. The Holy Spirit was the proof that the clouds would clear, and that he, and every saint, would bask in the full blaze of the sunshine of God's presence.

We saw in our chapter on the Son of God that because He is our representative and became answerable for our sin, the only way we can be rejected is if the Son of God is rejected. In this section what we are learning is that because the Spirit of God is the pledge of our future inheritance then if we don't come into that inheritance we get to keep the pledge, so if we are ever lost then the Spirit is lost with us! This shows us how foundationally damaging and fundamentally blasphemous the denial of eternal security really is.[148] So, what I want you to take from this is that being indwelt by the Spirit of God is a promise and a preview of a wonderful future inheritance. It is guaranteed; we have the earnest of the Spirit.

> As believers, we have the Holy Spirit as the divine pledge of our inheritance, God's first instalment of His guarantee that the fullness of His promises will one day be completely fulfilled. We are assured with an absolute certainty only God can provide. The Holy Spirit is the church's irrevocable pledge, her divine engagement ring signifying that as Christ's bride, she will never be neglected or forsaken.[149]

> *"No separation"! – O my soul,*
> *'Tis God who speaks the word;*
> *So close the Spirit thee unites*
> *With Christ, thy risen Lord.*

> *"No separation"! – thou art His,*
> *And His for evermore;*
> *Upon the cross thy debt He paid,*
> *And all thy judgment bore.*

> *"No separation"! – precious word!*
> *In it, my soul, be glad;*
> *Loved with an everlasting love,*
> *And one with Jesus made.*

> *"No separation"! – Life nor death,*
> *Things present nor to come,*

---

[148] I am not saying that those who believe that Christians can lose their salvation are blasphemers, but what I am saying is that the teaching leads to blasphemous conclusions. It is only because adherents to the falling away doctrine are inconsistent with it and don't follow it through to its logical conclusion that they avoid being blasphemers.

[149] MacArthur. *Saved Without a Doubt*, p.26.

Can part thee from His precious care,
Or rob thee of thy home.

"No separation"! – Linked with Him,
His glory – all is thine;
Oh, wondrous love, that thus could plan
A union so divine!
(Albert Midlane)

Summary

What a God we have! Aren't you glad you aren't feverishly trying to merit acceptance with a make-believe, man-made god who can be bribed with good works and will give up on you if you don't please him enough. We have a perfect God who has done a perfect work and perfectly saves. God the Father has a purpose that cannot be thwarted and power that cannot be overcome. The Son of God's finished work needs no repetition and His unfinished work will never end until we are gathered safely home. The Spirit of God is the unbreakable seal of our salvation and indisputable earnest of our inheritance. God is for us, and if God is for us, who can be against us?

> Here then, most assuredly, we have final perseverance, and that moreover, not merely the perseverance of the saints, but of the Father, and of the Son, and of the Holy Ghost. Yes, dear friend, this is the way we would have you view the matter. It is the final perseverance of the Holy Trinity. It is the perseverance of the Holy Ghost in opening the ears of the sheep. It is the perseverance of the Son in receiving all whose ears are thus opened. And, finally, it is the perseverance of the Father in keeping through His own name, the blood-bought flock in the hollow of His everlasting hand. This is plain enough. We must either admit the truth – the consolatory and sustaining, truth of final perseverance, or succumb to the blasphemous proposition that the enemy of God and man can carry his point against the holy and eternal Trinity. We see no middle ground. "Salvation is of the Lord", from

first to last. It is free, unconditional, everlasting salvation. It reaches down to where the sinner is in all his guilt, ruin, and degradation, and bears him up to where God is, in all His holiness, truth, and righteousness, and it endures for ever. God the Father is its source, God the Son is its channel, and God the Holy Ghost is the power of application and enjoyment. It is all of God, from beginning to end, from foundation to top-stone, from everlasting to everlasting. If it were not so, it would be presumptuous folly to speak of final perseverance; but, seeing it is so, it would be presumptuous unbelief to think of aught else.[150]

---

[150] C. H. Mackintosh, *Final Perseverance, What is it? The Mackintosh Treasury*, Chapter Two, p.645, or http://www.stempublishing.com/authors/mackintosh/Bk1/PERSEVER.html.

Dealing with the Case
against Eternal Security

Any questions?

> If a believer may make shipwreck of the faith, then
> a man that believes now may be an unbeliever
> some time hence; yea, very possibly tomorrow;
> but if so, he who is a child of God to-day, may be
> a child of the devil tomorrow.[151]

Solomon tells us, *The one who states his case first seems right, until the other comes and examines him.*[152] I really hope that our consideration of the activity of the Triune God on our behalf has given Scriptural strength to your faith in eternal security. But we can't just leave it there. It is obvious that those who believe Christians can lose their salvation aren't just emoting. They really think they have a Biblical basis for their position and we have to listen to what they say and answer the questions they ask. We don't need to fear examining these passages or facing these questions. It is true that there are passages which, if we had nothing else to go on, would likely lead us to conclude salvation could be lost, but that's the thing, we do have something else to go on, a lot else to go on. We have looked at passages that explicitly and unequivocally teach eternal security; we have seen that a denial of eternal security has blasphemous ramifications that would literally and eternally sever the Godhead Itself! It really is that serious. Since we know that God's Word will not contradict itself, we proceed with openness on our journey, and we will see that none of the passages presented against eternal security undermine it at all if properly understood, rather they will harmonise with it.

---

[151] John Wesley, *Perseverance of the Saints* http://www.imarc.cc/esecurity/perseverance.html.
[152] Prov.18:17, ESV.

Getting away with murder?

One of the primary objections to the doctrine of eternal security isn't actually a text or passage but a concept. If eternal security is true, then it means that someone can be saved and then literally get away with murder, or any other sin they would care to commit because the grace of God covers it, surely that can't be right, can it?

What has Paul to say?

As we noticed in the section relating to the purpose of God, the doctrine of justification ought to lead people to ask that question, for when Paul had concluded that section of his letter to the Romans he anticipates the objection, "Shall we continue in sin, that grace may abound?" (Rom.6:1). Any gospel that doesn't make people say, "Well, then you can just live as you like!" isn't the gospel of the Bible, and Paul had strong words for those in the counterfeit gospel business:

> I marvel that ye are so soon removed from Him that called you into the grace of Christ unto another gospel: which is not another; but there be some that trouble you, and would pervert the gospel of Christ. But though we, or an angel from heaven, preach any other gospel unto you than that which we have preached unto you, let him be accursed. As we said before, so say I now again, If any man preach any other gospel unto you than that ye have received, let him be accursed. (Gal. 1:6-9)

Paul writes to the Galatians precisely because there was a teaching abroad that said that faith and works, law and grace are mingled and merged. Paul is unsparing with them:

> O foolish Galatians, who hath bewitched you, that ye should not obey the truth, before whose eyes Jesus Christ hath been evidently set forth, crucified among you?
> This only would I learn of you, Received ye the Spirit by the works of the law, or by the hearing

of faith? Are ye so foolish? having begun in the Spirit, are ye now made perfect by the flesh? Have ye suffered so many things in vain? if it be yet in vain.

He therefore that ministereth to you the Spirit, and worketh miracles among you, doeth he it by the works of the law, or by the hearing of faith?

Even as Abraham believed God, and it was accounted to him for righteousness.

Know ye therefore that they which are of faith, the same are the children of Abraham.

And the scripture, foreseeing that God would justify the heathen through faith, preached before the gospel unto Abraham, saying, In thee shall all nations be blessed.

So then they which be of faith are blessed with faithful Abraham.

For as many as are of the works of the law are under the curse: for it is written, Cursed is every one that continueth not in all things which are written in the book of the law to do them.

But that no man is justified by the law in the sight of God, it is evident: for, The just shall live by faith. And the law is not of faith: but, The man that doeth them shall live in them.

Christ hath redeemed us from the curse of the law, being made a curse for us: for it is written, Cursed is every one that hangeth on a tree: that the blessing of Abraham might come on the Gentiles through Jesus Christ; that we might receive the promise of the Spirit through faith. (Gal.3:1-14)

The point Paul makes here is that you can't have this mixture. If works are involved, if law is introduced, then perfect obedience is required, and the curse falls on all those who do not deliver the demanded perfection. But if we have put our faith in Christ then there is no curse, but rather the blessing of Abraham (i.e. justification).

It reminds me of a lady I spoke to who told me she was a Bible believer, but didn't believe that one could be saved now and sure of it. She said we have an obligation to walk as Christ walked. I asked her was she doing that. She stalled a bit and said, "By the grace of God, yes." Well, my eyes widened a bit, I said, "Oh, so you are good enough for God then?" She got defensive here and accused me of twisting her words and she said she was saying no such thing, so I explained to her I hadn't twisted her words but had asked her a question and would like to know what I'd missed. She said she did not believe that salvation was something someone could be sure of now because we had an obligation to walk as Christ walked (in order to be right with God and get to heaven), so why is it inappropriate for me to ask if she was doing that well enough? She told me the grace of God and the blood of Christ were available for her sins, but I pointed out to her that she had to be good enough to earn that grace and avail of that blood and she could be too bad to the extent that the grace of God could not reach her and the blood of Christ could not cleanse her. You can dress it up with whatever language you like; the lady believed in salvation by works, and the only people that qualify for grace are those that are good enough, and therefore have cause to boast.

If we are in Christ then there is nothing the law of God condemns about us that Christ has not atoned for, so there is no sin that a believer will ever commit that God will ever say, "Well, *that* sin hasn't been covered by the sacrifice of My Son!" But what about the objection then? Is the believer free to live whatever way he likes? Well, in a sense, yes, but the thing is this, when someone is born again the way *he likes to live* is transformed.

> "If it be so, then, will not people say, they may live as they like?" Well, how does a true Christian like to live? As like Christ as possible. If one had put this question to Paul, what would have been his answer? 2 Cor.5:14,15, and Phil.3:7-14, furnish the reply. It is to be feared that the persons who ask such questions know but little of Christ. We can quite understand a person getting entangled in the meshes of a one-sided theological system, and being perplexed by the conflicting dogmas of

> systematic divinity; but we believe that the man who draws a plea from the freedom, sovereignty, and eternal stability of the grace of God, to continue in sin, knows nothing of Christianity at all, has neither part nor lot in the matter, but is in a truly awful and dangerous condition.[153]

I was doing some literature distribution in our area on one occasion and could see at the other end of the street someone I suspected to be one of the so-called "Jehovah's Witnesses". Eventually we met at the bottom of a driveway and a conversation about salvation ensued. When I told him about the salvation I had and was enjoying he said, "Oh, so you can just go out and rape, murder and steal and still go to heaven?" I asked him if he would rape, murder and steal if he was guaranteed a place in heaven, and he got a bit tongue-tied at that. I tried to help him with an illustration and asked him if there was anything I could do that could stop me being a child of my parents. He said, no. So I asked him then would that lead to me mistreating, abusing or hurting my mother and father. Of course it wouldn't. I am in a loving relationship with them, they have done so much for me, and I don't want to do anything to hurt them, but I want to please them and live in the enjoyment of that relationship. So it is, except on a massively multiplied way, with salvation. I am in a loving relationship with God, He has done so much for me, and in the shadow of that cross I don't want to do anything to grieve the Lord. Added to that, I told him, upon trusting Christ to save me, I was indwelt with the Holy Spirit who gives me the desires and the power to live a holy life and enjoy the service of God. His reaction stunned me a bit; he said, "Huh! The Holy Spirit must be superhuman if you actually enjoy serving God!" I told him he was right, although the Holy Spirit is not merely superhuman, He is God.

There are times when Paul will refer to certain sins and say that the person who practises such sins shall not inherit the kingdom, or will bear the wrath of God (1 Cor.6:9-11; Eph.5:3-7; Col.3:5-11). This is not because these things disqualify a person from salvation, but because the person who engages in such sins as a habitual

---

[153] Mackintosh, *Final Perseverance, What is it? The Mackintosh Treasury*, p.646.

course of life is giving evidence that he is not indwelt by the Spirit of God.[154]

Harry Ironside says about the Christian:

> Turning to Christ he is born from above...and thus possesses a new nature. This new nature abominates sin, and henceforth dominates his desires and his thinking. Sin becomes detestable. He loathes himself for the follies and iniquities of his past, and he yearns after holiness. Energised by the Holy Spirit, his life trend is changed. He practises righteousness...His new nature finds joy in surrendering to Jesus as Lord, and so sin ceases to be characteristic of his life and character.[155]

This gives us another opportunity to consider the wisdom of God presented in the gospel. We have spent quite a bit of time already in this book looking at how the gospel deals with our legal problem; we stood condemned in God's courtroom needing justification and God provided that, we are free, but there is another need. Let's suppose a man is in court for a crime that was fuelled by his enslavement to alcohol. That man has two needs, firstly, there is a legal problem; he is guilty of breaking the law and needs freedom from the penalty for his crime. Secondly, there is a moral problem; he is a slave of sin and needs freedom from the power of sin in his life. If the man gets freedom from the penalty and not the power then he will just walk free to commit the very same crime. If the man gets freedom from the power and not the penalty then he will be locked away without any hope of living a useful life. We were in a very similar position to this man, legally guilty of sin and morally enslaved to sin, and God has met both needs. We are not only free from the penalty of sin but we have been set free from the power of sin. This is Paul's answer to the objection he anticipates in Rom.6:1:

> What shall we say then? Shall we continue in sin, that grace may abound? God forbid. How shall

---

[154] It should be noted that his warning not to be partakers with them in their sins is not because it would jeopardise their salvation but because it is totally foreign to what God has done and what He intends for His people.
[155] Ironside, *Full Assurance*, loc. 1004-1013.

we, that are dead to sin, live any longer therein?

Notice Paul does not say to the imaginary interlocutor, "No, you misunderstood; justification does depend on us living a good enough life!" or something similar. He speaks rather about something that God has done in us. In this chapter Paul speaks not of Christ's death for us (that frees us from the penalty of sin), but of our death with Christ. Sin is personified as a master and we are his slaves; when sin said, "Jump!" we said, "How high?" We were under his tyrannical dominion and cruel authority. We didn't work for sin 40 hours a week with weekends off; we were his property 24/7. The only way out of his clutches is by death. So, Paul says that in the death of Christ we have died. The Lord Jesus entered death as our representative and He died not only for us but as us, so that in identification with Him we are dead to sin; we have escaped his power and passed out of his ownership by death. There is a lot of talk in Christian circles about the need to die to sin, but the Bible tells us we have died to sin, it has happened and we are to live in the light of that, sin has no claim upon us, no right to us, no authority over us, we do not belong to him or work for him anymore, *For he who has died has been freed from sin* (Rom.6:7, NKJV).

But Christ not only died, He rose again, and we who are identified with Him can now walk in this new kind of life:

> Therefore we are buried with Him by baptism
> into death: that like as Christ was raised up from
> the dead by the glory of the Father, even so we
> also should walk in newness of life. (Rom.6:4)

So, we have been put in the place of death as regards sin. Because it is said that we are buried *with Him* it shows that this took place in the divine reckoning when Christ died and was buried, but in a symbolic way, it took place at baptism. It is evident that in experience this happened when we trusted Christ.[156] The life of

---

[156] It is evident this took place at conversion for two reasons. The first reason is contextual, Paul has launched into this argument on the back of his treatment of the fact that we are right with God by grace through faith, notice he says later in the chapter that we were freed from sin when we obeyed from the heart that form of doctrine to which we were delivered (v.17), baptism is illustrating and declaring what took place at that moment of conversion. The second reason is practical, many believers have never been baptised and yet have experienced liberation from sin's power, and those that have been baptised know that their baptism didn't free them from sin, conversion to Christ did.

the risen Christ is imparted to every believer and just as Christ lives unto God (v.10), so too should, and so too can, every believer.

> Likewise reckon ye also yourselves to be dead indeed unto sin, but alive unto God through Jesus Christ our Lord. (Rom.6:11)

So there is an appeal to the mind to reckon[157] ourselves to be dead to sin. There is then an appeal to the will to yield ourselves to God:

> Let not sin therefore reign in your mortal body, that ye should obey it in the lusts thereof. Neither yield ye your members as instruments of unrighteousness unto sin: but yield yourselves unto God, as those that are alive from the dead, and your members as instruments of righteousness unto God. (Rom.6:12,13)

Then there is an appeal to the emotions:

> What fruit had ye then in those things whereof ye are now ashamed? for the end of those things is death. But now being made free from sin, and become servants to God, ye have your fruit unto holiness, and the end everlasting life. For the wages of sin is death; but the gift of God is eternal life through Jesus Christ our Lord. (Rom.6:21-23)

Paul is telling them that their enslavement to sin brought shame. Why would they want to volunteer for such a cruel master in such a shameful service? As Paul looked at his relationship to God and his standing in regard to sin he viewed it this way: intellectually he should not serve sin; volitionally he would not serve sin; emotionally he could not serve sin.

The gospel does not call on people to strive for holiness in order to obtain or retain or maintain their salvation. In a way, that kind of a system makes true moral virtue very difficult if not impossible because we would only be doing good deeds for reward.

It seems to me that rules-based and works-based

---

[157] To reckon something to be so means to count it as a fact and live accordingly.

religious systems don't actually produce 'good' people. They instead produce people who **look** good. True goodness is a heart condition. It's a reflection of who we are when no one is looking. It's a reflection of our desire to do what's right, even when there is nothing in it for us. It's one thing to experience joy or satisfaction for doing what you know you ought to do; it's another thing to do something **only** because you are hoping to gain a prize. If we are only 'performing' because we are hoping to get the reward of 'salvation', we're merely trying to serve ourselves by earning a prize. On the other hand, if our hearts are so changed that we desire to behave morally even when the carrot of salvation is not dangling in front of us, then we can say that we truly are 'good' people.

If you are looking for a spiritual worldview in which truly good people are even possible, you are going to have to look for one that does not **require** good works. Now what religious worldview teaches that salvation is **not** the result of anything that you can do, but is instead the result of something that has already been done for you by God Himself? There is only one; it is called Christianity. The Christian worldview teaches that Jesus came to pay the price for every 'less than perfect' thing you ever did; every sin and crime you've ever committed. God doesn't judge us based on any good deed we might do, because our good deeds aren't all that impressive if you really think about it. Instead, God accepts us on the basis of who **Jesus** is and the price that he paid for us if we will only believe in Him and trust **Him** instead of ourselves. Good works are not **required** for salvation, even though they are typically the **result** of our transformation. True moral goodness comes when we live and love in response to what has already been done for us, and not because we are hoping to win a prize.[158]

The man who has been born again isn't saying, "I'd better not murder because that would jeopardise my salvation, and I'd better be good to ensure I get to heaven." He has seen sin in the shadow of the cross and doesn't want to grieve his Lord. God has anticipated all the objections and has not missed anything; He has given the believer the indwelling Holy Spirit, he is no longer "in the flesh" but "in the Spirit", and he no longer has "the mind of the flesh" but "the mind of the Spirit" (Rom.8:5-9), and is thus given a new attitude, new ability and new appetites. That means that believer will never again be truly happy or really at peace unless he is pursuing holiness and living in fellowship with God, and the person who manifests an attitude of rebellion against God, has no ability to live for God and no appetite for the things of God, is giving evidence that he does not have the Spirit of God (Rom.8:13).[159]

What has John to say?

John wrote his Gospel to tell us *how* we can have eternal life:

> And many other signs truly did Jesus in the presence of his disciples, which are not written in this book: but these are written, that ye might believe that Jesus is the Christ, the Son of God; and that believing ye might have life through His name. (Jn.20:30,31)

But he wrote his first epistle to tell us how we can *know* we have eternal life:

> These things have I written unto you that believe on the name of the Son of God; that ye may know that ye have eternal life... (1 Jn. 5:13)

John's point in this epistle is that talk is cheap and if someone really has eternal life it will manifest itself because eternal life is

---

[158] J. Warner Wallace, *A Wallet, a Dollar, and the Existence of God, Training Manual*, available at http://pleaseconvinceme.com/academy/.

[159] The change in pronoun from *we* in v.12 to *ye* in v.13 is significant. Paul has no doubt about his own salvation and the salvation of the majority of his readers, but in v.13 he is pointing out to any in the company that if their life gives no evidence of the Spirit's working then they have no reason to think they are saved; they are thus still in danger of divine judgment.

not merely a ticket to heaven or a fire escape from hell. He gives three main tests for life in the epistle: he tests us on our behaviour, our love and our beliefs, and he deals with this triumvirate three times, once in each of the three main sections of the book. A skeleton structure of the book with the three tests looks like this:

1.1-2.27 First cycle

>
> Test one – 1.5-2.6: behaviour
>
> Test two – 2.7-11: love
>
> Test three – 2.22-27: belief

2.28-4.6 Second cycle

>
> Test one – 2.28-3.10: behaviour
>
> Test two – 3.10-24: love
>
> Test three – 4.1-6: belief

4.7-5.21 Third cycle

>
> Test one – 4.7-21: love
>
> Test two – 5.1-13: belief
>
> Test three – 5.18,19: behaviour

Each cycle begins with a manifestation. The first cycle commences with the manifestation of the *life* of God:

> That which was from the beginning, which we have heard, which we have seen with our eyes, which we have looked upon, and our hands have handled, of the Word of life; (For the life was **manifested**, and we have seen it, and bear witness, and shew unto you that eternal life, which was with the Father, and was manifested unto us;)... (1:1,2, emphasis added)

The second cycle commences with the manifestation of the *Son* of God:

> And now, little children, abide in Him, that when He **appears**, we may have confidence and not be

ashamed before Him at His coming. If you know that He is righteous, you know that everyone who practises righteousness is born of Him.

Behold what manner of love the Father has bestowed on us, that we should be called children of God! Therefore the world does not know us, because it did not know Him. Beloved, now we are children of God; and it has not yet been revealed what we shall be, but we know that when He is *revealed*, we shall be like Him, for we shall see Him as He is. And everyone who has this hope in Him purifies himself, just as He is pure.

Whoever commits sin also commits lawlessness, and sin is lawlessness. And you know that He was *manifested* to take away our sins, and in Him there is no sin. Whoever abides in Him does not sin. Whoever sins has neither seen Him nor known Him.

Little children, let no one deceive you. He who practises righteousness is righteous, just as He is righteous. He who sins is of the devil, for the devil has sinned from the beginning. For this purpose the Son of God was *manifested*, that He might destroy the works of the devil. (2:28-3:8, NKJV, emphasis added.)

Then the third cycle commences with a manifestation of the *love* of God:

In this was *manifested* the love of God toward us, because that God sent His only begotten Son into the world, that we might live through Him. Herein is love, not that we loved God, but that He loved us, and sent His Son to be the propitiation for our sins. (4:9,10, emphasis added.)

The three manifestations capture the essence of the three tests: the manifestation of the life of God shows us what eternal life looks like and how it will be seen in our behaviour. The manifestation of the Son of God shows us who He really is and what our beliefs about Him ought to be. The manifestation of the love of God gives us a picture of the love that will be seen in the lives of those who are born of God.

In John 8 the Lord Jesus emphasises the indispensable importance of our beliefs, behaviour and love as proofs of the genuineness of our profession. Look at how essential it is to get our Christology right:

> I said therefore unto you, that ye shall die in your sins: for if ye believe not that I am [He], ye shall die in your sins. (8:24)

The Lord is telling us that someone cannot be saved who denies the deity of Christ. John will tell us that someone cannot be saved who denies the true humanity of Christ:

> Beloved, believe not every spirit, but try the spirits whether they are of God: because many false prophets are gone out into the world. Hereby know ye the Spirit of God: Every spirit that confesseth that Jesus Christ is come in the flesh is of God: and every spirit that confesseth not that Jesus Christ is come in the flesh is not of God: and this is that spirit of antichrist, whereof ye have heard that it should come; and even now already is it in the world. (1 Jn. 4:1-3)

So why is it so important to believe the right things about Jesus Christ? Is it not a bit petty to deny salvation to someone just because he got his theology a bit wrong? It might seem that way until we stop to think about why we need Christ. We do not stand in need of a good dose of wise teaching, but we stand in need of a Saviour who has the ability to pay for our sins and the authority to forgive our sins, and so if we have a Saviour who is not fully God and truly man then we have do not have a Saviour at all. This is not telling us that we need to be 100% accurate in every detail of Biblical truth, but we need to have a Saviour who is both human and divine. And even if these truths were not prominent in our minds before or at conversion, if someone is truly born again and thus indwelt by the Spirit of God then that person will bow to the truths relating to the person of Christ when he encounters them.

The Lord goes on in the chapter to show that salvation affects behaviour:

> As He spake these words, many believed on Him. Then said Jesus to those Jews which believed on Him, If ye continue in My word, then are ye My disciples indeed; and ye shall know the truth, and the truth shall make you free.
> They answered Him, We be Abraham's seed, and were never in bondage to any man: how sayest Thou, Ye shall be made free?
> Jesus answered them, Verily, verily, I say unto you, Whosoever committeth sin is the servant of sin. And the servant abideth not in the house for ever: but the Son abideth ever. If the Son therefore shall make you free, ye shall be free indeed.
> I know that ye are Abraham's seed; but ye seek to kill Me, because My word hath no place in you. I speak that which I have seen with My Father: and ye do that which ye have seen with your father.
> They answered and said unto Him, Abraham is our father. Jesus saith unto them, If ye were Abraham's children, ye would do the works of Abraham. But now ye seek to kill Me, a man that hath told you the truth, which I have heard of God: this did not Abraham.
> Ye do the deeds of your father. (Jn.8:30-41)

The teaching of the Lord had led many people to believe in Him (v.30), and then the Lord spoke to those Jews who had believed His teaching (v.31).[160] See how the Lord is telling them that salvation brings freedom from the bondage of sin in the life, just as Paul taught in Romans 6. If someone is enslaved to sin with no power over it or deliverance from it, it shows that he has never encountered the liberating power of the Son of God.

---

[160] There is no preposition in v. 31; John does not say the Jews believed in Him, but rather they believed Him, i.e. they were tracking with His teaching and going along with it.

Then the Lord shows how salvation will affect our love:

> Jesus said unto them, If God were your Father, ye
> would love Me: for I proceeded forth and came
> from God; neither came I of Myself, but He sent
> Me. (Jn.8:42)

Love for Christ is the inescapable result of being born again; if
God is our Father it is inevitable that we will love the Son of the
Father.

We see in John 8 the seeds that would blossom into the tests
of 1 John. These three tests also spring from the three main
themes of John's Gospel: life, light and love. Life has to do
with behaviour, light has to do with beliefs, and love has to do
with...well, love, obviously!

Now it is important to underscore that neither the Lord in John 8
nor John in his first epistle are telling us how we get this life. These
passages are showing us the indispensable marks of eternal life,
and one of those indispensable marks is a love for righteousness,
so if a person comes to John the apostle professing to have eternal
life but this person's life continues without change and he sins
without conscience, John's message to him is quite clear: *You are
a liar!*

> He that saith, I know Him, and keepeth not His
> commandments, is a liar, and the truth is not in
> him. (1 Jn.2:4)

John's purpose in writing is this: you know you've had the new
birth if you have the new life. If there is no new life then there has
been no new birth.

In 1 Jn.2:28-3:10 we have John's major section teaching that
righteousness is an indispensable part of a believer's life.

> And now, little children, abide in Him; that, when
> He shall appear, we may have confidence, and
> not be ashamed before Him at His coming.
> If ye know that He is righteous, ye know that
> every one that doeth righteousness is born of
> Him.

Behold, what manner of love the Father hath
bestowed upon us, that we should be called the
sons of God: therefore the world knoweth us not,
because it knew Him not.

Beloved, now are we the sons of God, and it doth
not yet appear what we shall be: but we know
that, when He shall appear, we shall be like Him;
for we shall see Him as He is. And every man that
hath this hope in Him purifieth himself, even as
He is pure.

Whosoever committeth sin transgresseth also the
law: for sin is the transgression of the law. And ye
know that He was manifested to take away our
sins; and in Him is no sin. Whosoever abideth
in Him sinneth not: whosoever sinneth hath not
seen Him, neither known Him.

Little children, let no man deceive you: he that
doeth righteousness is righteous, even as He is
righteous. He that committeth sin is of the devil;
for the devil sinneth from the beginning. For this
purpose the Son of God was manifested, that He
might destroy the works of the devil. Whosoever
is born of God doth not commit sin; for His seed
remaineth in him: and he cannot sin, because he
is born of God. In this the children of God are
manifest, and the children of the devil: whosoever
doeth not righteousness is not of God, neither he
that loveth not his brother.

It is a section in which there is a great *emphasis on righteousness*; the
only mention of the noun righteousness in 1 John is found here
three times (2:29; 3:7, 10). He is telling us that righteousness is an
inevitable feature of the life of one who has been born of God.

There are also great *encouragements to righteousness*. John uses the
future manifestation of Christ as an encouragement to righteous
living, by telling us negatively what we may be in 2:28, "And now
little children, abide in Him; that when He shall appear, we may
have confidence, and not be ashamed before Him at His coming."
And then he tells us positively what we shall be in 3:2, "...we

know that, when He shall appear, we shall be like Him..." He is exhorting us to live in light of the future, the Lord is coming, we are not here to stay, so let us live so we have nothing to be ashamed of, and let us live as closely as possible now to how we will live when we are made like Him.

John then uses the past manifestation of Christ as an encouragement to righteous living. He speaks about Christ's past manifestation in relation to sin in 3:5, "And ye know that He was manifested to take away our sins..." There is no time when sin looks so unappealing as when we are considering what it did to God's beloved Son. As we consider the immense, intense burden Christ bore we realise sin is no light matter. When we hear His cry, "My God, My God, why hast Thou forsaken Me?" we recognise sin is no laughing matter. What an encouragement to righteousness. There is another reference to His past manifestation in 3:8, "For this purpose the Son of God was manifested, that He might destroy the works of the devil." It is noticeable how John refers to the two persons in this verse. He refers to Satan as the devil, which conveys the idea of slander. The devil is the great twister, misrepresenting God, giving people wrong notions and false impressions about the true God. John says the Son of God was manifested to undo the works of the devil; he doesn't refer to Him as the Lord, or Christ, etc. but the Son of God. When we think of this expression we know that it does not mean the Lord Jesus was God's male child, but the expression "Son of" is a Hebrew idiom denoting character, telling us that the Lord Jesus is possessed of all the attributes of God. So the devil tells lies about God, but then one was manifested who fully expressed all that God is, and as we look at the Son of God we see God's righteous nature, it is a further encouragement to righteousness.

But it is all very well emphasising the importance of righteousness and giving encouragements to righteousness, but our sinful nature stands in the way of us actually practising righteousness. This is why John tells us about *empowerments to righteousness* in the passage. He speaks about us abiding in Christ:

> And now, little children, abide in Him; that, when
> He shall appear, we may have confidence, and

not be ashamed before Him at His coming. (2:28)

Whosoever abideth in Him sinneth not:
whosoever sinneth hath not seen Him, neither
known Him. (3:6)

In John's reckoning, abiding in Christ is drawing strength from
Him through fellowship and faith. We can't do that and practise
sin at the same time.

A second empowerment in this section is the Spirit abiding in us:

Whosoever is born of God doth not commit sin;
for His seed remaineth in him: and he cannot sin,
because he is born of God. (3:9)

The Spirit of God imparts to the believer the divine nature which
means there is no possibility of the believer continuing indefinitely
in known sin.

It will help us to see that the tense of the verb here
is what has been called the "present continuous."
It is not a question of occasional, or even of
frequent failure, bitterly lamented and grieved
over. It rather implies a course of behaviour that
is characteristic.[161]

The life that the Spirit of God imparts cannot die and so the one
who has been born again can never be settled and content in a life
of sin.

It is so important to notice exactly what John says here because
this passage has been used to support the view that a Christian
can forfeit his salvation, but it can mean no such thing. John does
not say that the person *who is a Christian* cannot continue in sin,
or the person *who is saved* cannot continue in sin. Had that been
his language then you could, on the strength of that statement,
justifiably say that a man stops being a Christian and loses
salvation if he continues in a course of sin, but John says *he that
has been born of God* doesn't continue in sin. He is not saying a life
of continual rebellion means you lose salvation, but rather a life of

---

[161] Ironside, *Full Assurance*, loc. 996

continual rebellion means you never had salvation; *you were never born again*. If a true Christian can lose his salvation then it means that one who has been born of God *can* continue in rebellion. I hope you see the force of this; according to those who believe you can be saved then lost, there are many people who were truly born of God who are now atheists and living in rebellion against God. John says that can't happen; the one who has been born of God in the past can't continue in sin, so rather than this verse implying a believer can lose salvation, it affirms he can't.

John tells us that as Christians our sins have been forgiven us for Christ's name's sake (1 Jn.2:12). This is an absolute and unqualified promise, so why then does the same writer in the same letter say that we need forgiveness?

> If we confess our sins He is faithful and just to forgive us our sins and to cleanse us from all unrighteousness. (1 Jn.1:9)

Does this imply our salvation is in jeopardy if we don't confess? Why does John say we are forgiven but then speak about our need for forgiveness? The answer is found in distinguishing who needs forgiveness, from whom, and in what capacity. You might say that there's no difference; in both 1 Jn. 2:12 and in 1:9 we need forgiveness from God, but that's not the whole story. In 1 Jn. 2:12 John is thinking of a legal forgiveness, we are guilty criminals before the Judge, the record is cleared and the penalty removed. That is a forgiveness that is for all sins for all time, and it is ours the moment we avail of the provision in Christ. However, in 1 Jn.1:9 it is not criminals needing forgiveness from a Judge but children needing forgiveness from a Father. John is picturing us as being in the family and, as we have said before, just as there is nothing I can do to stop myself being a child of my parents so there is nothing I can do to stop myself being a child of God. But in the same way that my behaviour affects my enjoyment of my relationship with my parents, the same applies in the family of God. If I disobey the Father, discipline will be required, and I won't enjoy the warmth of His fellowship until I confess my sins, that is, agree with God about them. Once I come to the Father in agreement with Him about my sins, they are forgiven and I can then enjoy that relationship again.

> It is quite certain that those whom Christ has washed in His precious blood need not make a confession of sin, as culprits or criminals, before God the Judge, for Christ has forever taken away all their sins in a legal sense, so that they no longer stand where they can be condemned, but are once for all accepted in the Beloved; but having become children, and offending as children, ought they not every day to go before their heavenly Father and confess their sin, and acknowledge their iniquity in that character? Nature teaches that it is the duty of erring children to make a confession to their earthly father, and the grace of God in the heart teaches us that we, as Christians, owe the same duty to our heavenly Father...If I have not sought forgiveness and been washed from these offences against my Father, I shall feel at a distance from Him; I shall doubt His love to me; I shall tremble at Him; I shall be afraid to pray to Him: I shall grow like the prodigal, who, although still a child, was yet far off from his father. But if, with a child's sorrow at offending so gracious and loving a Parent, I go to Him and tell Him all, and rest not till I realise that I am forgiven, then I shall feel a holy love to my Father, and shall go through my Christian career, not only as saved, but as one enjoying present peace with God through Jesus Christ my Lord. There is a wide distinction between confessing sin *as a culprit*, and confessing sin *as a child*. The Father's bosom is the place for penitent confessions. We have been cleansed once for all, but our feet still need to be washed from the defilement of our daily walk as children of God.[162]

---

[162] Spurgeon, *Morning and Evening,* Evening reading, 19th February.

So, can a Christian get away with murder? The Christian is capable of great wickedness and grievous sin, but what the Christian is incapable of is this, continuing in great wickedness and grievous sin with contentment and joy. That life within simply will not die and the Spirit just will not go away and leave him to sin in peace.

Lost at last? Matthew 7:21-23

I spoke to a young man one night after a meeting who was in terror of being one of the people referred to in this chilling passage:

> Not every one that saith unto Me, Lord, Lord, shall enter into the kingdom of heaven; but he that doeth the will of My Father which is in heaven.
> Many will say to Me in that day, Lord, Lord, have we not prophesied in Thy name? and in Thy name have cast out devils? and in Thy name done many wonderful works? And then will I profess unto them, I never knew you: depart from Me, ye that work iniquity.

The Lord Jesus is telling us that there are people who will get a rude awakening and an awful shock on a coming day when they are rejected by the Lord and told to depart. These people *seem* to have shown evidence in their lives of being sincere believers, but here they are locked out and cast away at the end. What is the answer?

> Such people then may have been very active in what is called Christian work – they have preached, they have cast out demons, that is, their influence has been such that men and women have found deliverance from satanic power through their ministrations in the name of Jesus, they have professed with their lips, they have accomplished many wonderful works, but they are found in that day among the lost, and when they plead their great activity and their earnestness in Christian testimony, the Lord says to them, "I never knew you." Notice, He does not say to them. "I used to know you, but you have

forfeited My favour and I do not know you any longer." He says, "I never knew you."[163]

Whatever this passage is teaching, it certainly cannot be teaching that a true believer can be lost. The Lord's words are perfectly clear, these are people who have never been brought into relationship with Him, they were never saved at all.

This incident comes in amongst some very challenging teaching from the Lord Jesus on the subject of separating the true from the false, the real from the fake. He speaks about two gates and two ways in vv.13,14:

> Enter ye in at the strait gate: for wide is the gate, and broad is the way, that leadeth to destruction, and many there be which go in thereat: because strait is the gate, and narrow is the way, which leadeth unto life, and few there be that find it.

These verses are often used by the gospel preacher in application to the whole human race, and everybody is on either the broad or narrow way. We start life on the broad way, having entered the gate at birth, and we need to get off it by conversion to Christ. It certainly is true that God divides the human race into two distinct categories, saved and lost, and everyone is travelling either down to destruction or up to life, but I don't think that is the Lord's point here. To be fair to the text we have to see that the "many" of v.13 make a choice to enter this gate. The Lord is addressing the matter of profession in this context. There are people with a spiritual interest, they have a desire to be right with God and welcomed into His kingdom. The Lord's challenge is to make sure you enter the right gate and you are on the right road. There is a gate that is broad and a road that is wide, you can enter that gate and travel that road and keep your religion, retain your self-righteousness, and hold on to your pride, but it ends in destruction.[164] Alternatively, there is a narrow gate that puts one

---

[163] Ironside, *The Eternal Security of the Believer*, p.7.
[164] This isn't to say that it's only those who have an empty profession that are on their way to destruction. Imagine if someone is mixed up with a cult; you would warn him that no matter what the cult promises, if he goes down that road it will end in hell. You aren't meaning to imply if he doesn't join the cult he won't end up in hell. It's a wake-up call to make sure people are on the right path.

on the path to life and to get through it we need to be stripped of all the robes of self-righteousness and accoutrements of pride.

The next contrast is in vv.15-20 and is between two trees:

> Beware of false prophets, which come to you in sheep's clothing, but inwardly they are ravening wolves. Ye shall know them by their fruits. Do men gather grapes of thorns, or figs of thistles? Even so every good tree bringeth forth good fruit; but a corrupt tree bringeth forth evil fruit. A good tree cannot bring forth evil fruit, neither can a corrupt tree bring forth good fruit. Every tree that bringeth not forth good fruit is hewn down, and cast into the fire. Wherefore by their fruits ye shall know them.

The Lord is teaching that entering the narrow gate will result in fruit in the life. What will that fruit be? Well, what can it be other than the fruit previously referred to in Matthew's Gospel?

> But when he saw many of the Pharisees and Sadducees come to his baptism, he said unto them, O generation of vipers, who hath warned you to flee from the wrath to come? Bring forth therefore fruits meet for repentance: and think not to say within yourselves, We have Abraham to our father: for I say unto you, that God is able of these stones to raise up children unto Abraham. And now also the axe is laid unto the root of the trees: therefore every tree which bringeth not forth good fruit is hewn down, and cast into the fire. (Matt.3:7-10)

John the Baptist sees these proud religious leaders coming to him and he tells them to stop the charade and show evidence of repentance. What would that "fruit" look like? It would mean they would no longer be boasting in and resting on their lineage ("We have Abraham to our father..."). It would involve an abandoning of their self-righteousness, a recognition of their own personal guilt and an attitude of contrition. The repentant soul may stumble and stray, but he won't take a light view of his sin or a low view of his Saviour. This is the fruit he was looking for, and since the Lord uses exactly the same language ("Every tree that bringeth not forth good fruit is hewn down and cast into the fire") we can conclude this is what He was talking about too. Let's make sure we understand and underline the point: repentance is a necessity. So much of what passes for gospel preaching is geared toward letting people feel good about themselves as they slide easily into salvation, but the tragedy is they are sliding through a wide gate onto a broad road. We hear testimonies of people who jauntily accept Jesus, not knowing the truth of repentance and certainly not showing the fruit of it.

It is at this stage that the Lord Jesus says, "Not everyone that saith unto Me, 'Lord, Lord,' shall enter into the kingdom of heaven". Who are these people then that will be rejected in a coming day? The man I spoke to after a meeting I took was so concerned he would be one of them. I asked him to look at the passage and tell me why these people thought they should be accepted into God's kingdom. The text is pretty clear, they thought they should be accepted because of what they had done. I asked the enquirer what he would say if he was seeking admission into the kingdom, would he point to all the wonderful things he had done? No, he told me, he would point to the Lord Jesus Christ and what He has done, and that's the vital difference.

The Lord then speaks about the two foundations in vv.24-27:

> Therefore whosoever heareth these sayings of Mine, and doeth them, I will liken him unto a wise man, which built his house upon a rock: and the rain descended, and the floods came, and the winds blew, and beat upon that house; and it fell not: for it was founded upon a rock.
> And every one that heareth these sayings of Mine, and doeth them not, shall be likened unto a foolish man, which built his house upon the sand: and the rain descended, and the floods came, and the winds blew, and beat upon that house; and it fell: and great was the fall of it.

The two houses both get constructed and as far as anyone could see both of them look the same, but the difference was in the foundation. The only rock solid foundation is the word of Christ Himself. He is teaching His listeners that they need to act on what He has been telling them. The challenge the Lord gives is not to keep your salvation but to make sure you really have it. Everyone needs to have entered in the narrow gate in the past, this will be demonstrated by the fruits of repentance in the present, and means we will not be rejected in the future.

Seeds, Weeds, Roots and Fruits, Matthew 13:3-9, 18-23
The parable of the sower is one of the Lord's most well-known teachings, and many have found it to be fertile soil and a fruitful field where the falling away doctrine can flourish.

> And He spake many things unto them in parables, saying, Behold, a sower went forth to sow; and when he sowed, some seeds fell by the way side, and the fowls came and devoured them up:
> Some fell upon stony places, where they had not much earth: and forthwith they sprung up, because they had no deepness of earth: and when the sun was up, they were scorched; and because they had no root, they withered away.
> And some fell among thorns; and the thorns sprung up, and choked them:
> But other fell into good ground, and brought forth fruit, some an hundredfold, some sixtyfold, some thirtyfold. Who hath ears to hear, let him hear.
> ...
> Hear ye therefore the parable of the sower.
> When any one heareth the word of the kingdom, and understandeth it not, then cometh the wicked one, and catcheth away that which was sown in his heart. This is he which received seed by the way side.
> But he that received the seed into stony places, the same is he that heareth the word, and anon with

> joy receiveth it; yet hath he not root in himself,
> but dureth for a while: for when tribulation or
> persecution ariseth because of the word, by and
> by he is offended.
> He also that received seed among the thorns is he
> that heareth the word; and the care of this world,
> and the deceitfulness of riches, choke the word,
> and he becometh unfruitful.
> But he that received seed into the good ground is
> he that heareth the word, and understandeth it;
> which also beareth fruit, and bringeth forth, some
> an hundredfold, some sixty, some thirty.

I'm sure you can see the issue here, there are two grounds in which there certainly seems to be life and growth, but then it shrivels up, withers away and dies off. Surely then we can conclude that people can have new life but lose it, can't we? I don't think so.

We will be helped greatly in our understanding of this parable if we bear in mind that the different types of people are represented by the different types of ground, not what the ground produces. What the ground produces is symbolic of what the person professes. If there is no actual fruit then the profession is an empty one.[165] So let's look at these different types of ground more closely.

The way side hearer

The fowls of the air snatch away the seed, speaking of the forces of the devil distracting people so that they never give the word any thought. The way side hearer doesn't make any profession at all; there is nothing to show, so he need not detain us any further.

The stony ground hearer

Let's put Mark's and Luke's accounts here too:

> And some fell on stony ground, where it had
> not much earth; and immediately it sprang up,
> because it had no depth of earth:

---

[165] Let's keep in mind the fruit desired is the fruit of repentance (Matt.3:8), i.e. fruit that comes from a repentant heart. If there is no fruit there is no repentance; if there is no repentance then there is no salvation.

> And these are they likewise which are sown on
> stony ground; who, when they have heard the
> word, immediately receive it with gladness; and
> have no root in themselves, and so endure but for
> a time: afterward, when affliction or persecution
> ariseth for the word's sake, immediately they are
> offended. (Mk.4:5,16,17)

> And some fell upon a rock; and as soon as it was
> sprung up, it withered away, because it lacked
> moisture.
> They on the rock are they, which, when they
> hear, receive the word with joy; and these have
> no root, which for a while believe, and in time of
> temptation fall away. (Lk.8:6,13)

The one that received the seed in the stony places is one who (note
the two key words here) *immediately* with *gladness* receives it. Here
is someone who has not considered the issues and has not felt
the impact of the message. He responds immediately and does
so with joy.[166] It is to be noticed then that when we read about
the good ground in Mark's account it is said that they "hear the
word, and receive it, and bring forth fruit..." (Mk.4:20). Surely
there is significance in the fact that there is no mention of joy. Now
certainly there is joy associated with receiving Christ as Saviour,
but the joy is preceded by the conviction of sin, the recognition
of our lost condition, the realisation of the danger we are in,[167] all
these features are sadly lacking in the case of the stony ground
hearer. The ground hasn't been worked and prepared by the
conviction of sin. Those stones of pride haven't been taken out.
The result is that his profession withers as quickly as it is made,
"immediately they are offended".

> The immediate reception of the word with joy,
> in the next case, tends rather to prove that the

---

[166] Indeed, his lack of depth is given as the reason for his immediate response. This is not implying
that people cannot be genuinely saved on their first hearing of the gospel, but it is to say this, if
there has only been a very shallow understanding of the issues then it is unlikely the person has
got the root of the matter. We have seen people affected at gospel meetings, wanting to become
Christians, but after speaking to them it has been clear they have not understood the message. One
could have pressed ahead and pushed for a profession, but it would not have stood the test of time.
[167] See for instance the case of Zacchaeus in Lk. 19:1-10, a man who was earnestly seeking, and the
Jews in Acts 2, a company who were "pricked in their heart".

heart will not retain it; for it is scarcely probable in such a case that the conscience was reached. A conscience touched by the word makes a man serious; he sees himself in the presence of God, which is always a serious thing whatever may be the attraction of His grace, or the hope inspired by His goodness. If the conscience has not been reached, there is no root. The word was received for the joy it imparted; when it brings tribulation, it is given up. When the conscience has been already exercised, the gospel brings at once joy; but when not, it awakens the conscience where there is a real work.[168]

The response in the stony ground hearer is a fleshly response, "Jesus offers peace, joy, satisfaction, a wonderful plan for my life? Sure, I'm up for that!" He "accepts Jesus into his heart", thinking life will be a great adventure with higher highs and greater fun than all the nights out he had before had ever provided. He then discovers that identifying himself with a rejected Christ brings reproach and mockery, and it doesn't bring all the fun he had hoped. Problems still occur, disasters still happen, sickness still comes, and tears still flow. What happens? He loses faith, as Luke puts it, he only "for a while" believes. Belief is a necessary condition for salvation, but it is belief in the right message and with the right motive. The stony ground hearer has not allowed the word to get down to his conscience, it is a surface-level understanding and a shallow kind of faith. He has believed a misunderstood message, and thus he thinks the message is false when it fails to deliver what he believed it would. Ray Comfort vividly illustrates this for us:

> Two men are seated on a plane. A stewardess gives the first man a parachute and instructs him to put it on because it will "improve his flight".
>
> Not understanding how a parachute could possibly improve his flight, the first passenger is

[168] J. N. Darby, *Synopsis of the Books of the Bible*, vol. 3, *Matthew-John*, Stow Hill Bible and Tract Depot, 1943, pp.68,69.

a little sceptical. Finally he decides to see if the claim is true. After strapping on the parachute, he notices its burdensome weight, and he has difficulty sitting upright. Consoling himself with the promise of a better flight, our first passenger decides to give it a little time.

Because he's the only one wearing a parachute, some of the other passengers begin smirking at him, which only adds to his humiliation. Unable to stand it any longer, our friend slumps in his seat, unstraps the parachute, and throws it to the floor. Disillusionment and bitterness fill his heart because as far as he is concerned, he was told a lie.

Another stewardess gives the second man a parachute, but listen to her instructions. She tells him to put it on because at any moment he will be jumping out of the plane at 25,000 feet.

Our second passenger gratefully straps the parachute on. He doesn't notice its weight upon his shoulders nor that he can't sit upright. His mind is consumed with the thought of what would happen to him if he jumped without it. When other passengers laugh at him, he thinks, "You won't be laughing when you're falling to the ground!"

Inoculated Backsliders

Let's now analyse the motive and the result of each passenger's experience.

The first man's motive for putting on the parachute was solely to improve his flight. As a result, he was humiliated by the passengers, disillusioned by an unkept promise, and embittered against the stewardess who gave it to him. As far as he is concerned, he will never put one of those things on his back again.

The second man put the parachute on to escape the danger of the coming jump. Because he knew what would happen to him without it, he had a deep-rooted joy and peace in his heart. Knowing he was saved from certain death gave him the ability to withstand the mockery of the other passengers. His attitude toward the stewardess who gave him the parachute was one of heartfelt gratitude.

Now listen to what the contemporary gospel says: "Put on the Lord Jesus Christ; He will give you love, joy, peace, and fulfilment." In other words, He will improve your flight. In an experimental fashion, the sinner puts on the Saviour to see if these claims are so.

What does he get? Temptation, tribulation, and persecution. The other passengers mock his decision. So what does he do? He takes off the Lord Jesus Christ; he is offended for the Word's sake; he is disillusioned and embittered, and quite rightly so.

He was promised peace, joy, fulfilment, and all he got were trials and humiliation. His bitterness is directed at those who gave him the "good news." His latter end is worse than the first – another inoculated, bitter backslider![169]

Anyone who actually thinks that one could be saved with a shallow reception of the word and without having any "root" to his profession needs to examine his evangelistic foundations. The message has to reach the heart and conscience. It is clear that this profession was never genuine because it's not that the root was plucked up, there never was any root.

The New Testament does not lack examples of people who

---

[169] Ray Comfort, *Hell's Best Kept Secret*, http://www.christiananswers.net/evangelism/methods/law.html.

"believed" without being saved. Let's look at a few examples:

> Now when He was in Jerusalem at the passover,
> in the feast day, many believed in His name, when
> they saw the miracles which He did. But Jesus did
> not commit Himself unto them, because He knew
> all men, and needed not that any should testify of
> man: for He knew what was in man. (Jn.2:23-25)

This example is very much akin to what we see in the shallow, stony ground believer. Please notice that the people in these verses in John 2 haven't believed then lost faith; they haven't believed then embarked on a course of open, deliberate sin; they haven't believed then apostatised. They haven't fulfilled any of the criteria that saved-and-lost advocates say must be done to lose your salvation; their "belief" never changed. They believe, but the Lord did not commit Himself to them. Why not? Because He could see into their heart and knew their motives, and was aware that, while they believed He was who He claimed to be, they did not believe *they were what He claimed them to be.*[170] What I mean by that is this, it is one thing to believe that Jesus is the Son of God; it's quite another thing to believe that I am a sinner, lost, helpless and in need of Him to save me. That's why it's so unfortunate that the chapter division comes in here, because in John chapter 3 we are introduced to a man who was impressed and convinced by the miracles of Christ, but he needed to be convinced of something more: "Except a man be born again, he cannot see the kingdom of God...That which is born of the flesh is flesh...Ye must be born again" (Jn.3:3,5,7). The people who "believed in His name when they saw the miracles which He did" had yet to believe that they were in need of a new birth, thus their believing did not result in salvation.[171] So it is with the stony ground; the issue is not *whether* they believe, but *what* they believe and *why* they believe. Do they believe not only that Jesus is the Son of God, but that they are hell-deserving sinners, and that His sacrifice is both necessary and

---

[170] In Jn.1.10 we see that Christ was not recognised ("the world knew Him not"); in v.11 He was not received ("His own received Him not"). In v.12 we see the converse: "But as many as received Him [in contrast to v.11]...even to them that believe on His name [in contrast to v.10]". Thus believing in His name is the recognition of who He is.

[171] In Jn.1:12,13 we see that believing in His name is to be accompanied by receiving Him, and that results in new birth. Obviously if someone doesn't believe he needs to be born again then he is not believing in Christ *to that end* and will not receive Christ for that purpose.

sufficient for their salvation? If not, then their faith is an empty faith that will result in no fruit.

John has another example to give us of unbelieving believers in a section we have looked at before:

> As He spake these words, many believed on Him. Then said Jesus to those Jews which believed on Him, If ye continue in My word, then are ye My disciples indeed; and ye shall know the truth, and the truth shall make you free.
>
> They answered Him, We be Abraham's seed, and were never in bondage to any man: how sayest Thou, Ye shall be made free?
>
> Jesus answered them, Verily, verily, I say unto you, Whosoever committeth sin is the servant of sin. And the servant abideth not in the house for ever: but the Son abideth ever. If the Son therefore shall make you free, ye shall be free indeed.
>
> I know that ye are Abraham's seed; but ye seek to kill Me, because My word hath no place in you. I speak that which I have seen with My Father: and ye do that which ye have seen with your father.
>
> They answered and said unto Him, Abraham is our father. Jesus saith unto them, If ye were Abraham's children, ye would do the works of Abraham. But now ye seek to kill Me, a man that hath told you the truth, which I have heard of God: this did not Abraham.
>
> Ye do the deeds of your father. Then said they to Him, We be not born of fornication; we have one Father, even God.
>
> Jesus said unto them, If God were your Father, ye would love Me: for I proceeded forth and came from God; neither came I of Myself, but He sent Me. Why do ye not understand My speech? even because ye cannot hear My word. Ye are of your father the devil, and the lusts of your father ye will do. He was a murderer from the beginning, and abode not in the truth, because there is no

truth in him. When he speaketh a lie, he speaketh of his own: for he is a liar, and the father of it. And because I tell you the truth, ye believe Me not. Which of you convinceth Me of sin? And if I say the truth, why do ye not believe Me? He that is of God heareth God's words: ye therefore hear them not, because ye are not of God.

Then answered the Jews, and said unto him, Say we not well that Thou art a Samaritan, and hast a devil?

Jesus answered, I have not a devil; but I honour My Father, and ye do dishonour Me. And I seek not Mine own glory: there is one that seeketh and judgeth. Verily, verily, I say unto you, If a man keep My saying, he shall never see death.

Then said the Jews unto him, Now we know that Thou hast a devil. Abraham is dead, and the prophets; and Thou sayest, If a man keep My saying, he shall never taste of death. Art Thou greater than our father Abraham, which is dead? and the prophets are dead: whom makest Thou Thyself?

Jesus answered, If I honour Myself, My honour is nothing: it is My Father that honoureth Me; of whom ye say, that He is your God: Yet ye have not known Him; but I know Him: and if I should say, I know Him not, I shall be a liar like unto you: but I know Him, and keep His saying. Your father Abraham rejoiced to see My day: and he saw it, and was glad.

Then said the Jews unto Him, Thou art not yet fifty years old, and hast Thou seen Abraham? Jesus said unto them, Verily, verily, I say unto you, Before Abraham was, I am.

Then took they up stones to cast at Him: but Jesus hid Himself, and went out of the temple, going through the midst of them, and so passed by. (Jn.8:30-59)

What can we conclude from this passage? Well, like John 2, it is inconceivable to think that these people were saved in vv.30,31 and then lost by the end of the chapter.[172] We are told clearly in the passage that they didn't understand (vv.27,43), they didn't know the truth (v.32), they had never been made free (v.36), God was not their Father (v.42), they were of the devil (v.44), they were unbelievers (vv.45,46), and were not of God (v.47). Yet, it is said they believed, so in what sense? They were clearly swayed by the authoritative preaching of the Lord Jesus, and believed His authority was indeed God-given, perhaps even to the point of believing Him to be the promised Christ, but that is not saving faith, and the Lord, who in this chapter refers to Himself as the Light of the world, shines the light into their hearts and upon Himself to show their faith was shallow and false.

> This tells me that there is believing, and believing. It tells me there is a certain superficial consent to the facts regarding the person of Christ, without a deep reliance on Him for salvation. They believed, but they were of their father, the devil.[173]

We have to remember what James says:

> You believe that there is one God. You do well. Even the demons believe – and tremble! (Jms.2:19, NKJV)

Saving faith, as we have already noticed, involves not merely belief of propositional statements, but it involves actual, active trust in the divine Son of God to save us. That necessitates we believe Him with regard to what we are and who He really is. These people did not believe they were slaves of sin, their words are soaked and dripping with self-righteousness, these are not examples of people who had trusted Christ for salvation then apostatised, they never saw themselves as needing salvation at all. Neither did they bow to the truth of Christ's deity, but rather when He revealed Himself as the "I Am", they picked up stones

---

[172] John may well intend us to make a distinction between the believers of v. 30 and the believers of v. 31. In v. 30 it is said that many "believed on Him", while in v.31 there is no preposition in the original, and thus the Lord addresses those that believed Him. They believed what they heard on that occasion, but it was not an act of trust in Him as Saviour.
[173] Paul Grieve, *Christ All-Sufficient*, CMML, 1999, p.62.

to stone Him, believing Him to be demon possessed. They had not changed their minds on this issue; they had never believed Him to be the Son of God. By denying they were slaves of sin they denied their need of a Saviour, and by denying His deity they denied His capability of being a Saviour. Thus, their belief withered because they never had the root of the matter.[174]

We'll take one more example, this time from Acts 8:

> Then Philip went down to the city of Samaria, and preached Christ unto them. And the people with one accord gave heed unto those things which Philip spake, hearing and seeing the miracles which he did. For unclean spirits, crying with loud voice, came out of many that were possessed with them: and many taken with palsies, and that were lame, were healed. And there was great joy in that city.
>
> But there was a certain man, called Simon, which beforetime in the same city used sorcery, and bewitched the people of Samaria, giving out that himself was some great one: to whom they all gave heed, from the least to the greatest, saying, This man is the great power of God. And to him they had regard, because that of long time he had bewitched them with sorceries. But when they believed Philip preaching the things concerning the kingdom of God, and the name of Jesus Christ, they were baptized, both men and women. Then Simon himself believed also: and when he was baptized, he continued with Philip, and wondered, beholding the miracles and signs which were done.
>
> Now when the apostles which were at Jerusalem heard that Samaria had received the word of God, they sent unto them Peter and John: who, when they were come down, prayed for them,

---

[174] Current examples can be cited of this kind of thing: people hear the gospel and it sounds great and they do believe it, as they understand it, but when they really get an accurate understanding and are clearly shown the implications they hastily back away.

that they might receive the Holy Ghost: (for as yet he was fallen upon none of them: only they were baptized in the name of the Lord Jesus.) Then laid they their hands on them, and they received the Holy Ghost.

And when Simon saw that through laying on of the apostles' hands the Holy Ghost was given, he offered them money, saying, Give me also this power, that on whomsoever I lay hands, he may receive the Holy Ghost.

But Peter said unto him, Thy money perish with thee, because thou hast thought that the gift of God may be purchased with money. Thou hast neither part nor lot in this matter: for thy heart is not right in the sight of God. Repent therefore of this thy wickedness, and pray God, if perhaps the thought of thine heart may be forgiven thee. For I perceive that thou art in the gall of bitterness, and in the bond of iniquity.

Then answered Simon, and said, Pray ye to the Lord for me, that none of these things which ye have spoken come upon me. (vv.5-24)

Simon the sorcerer no doubt heard the preaching of Philip, but the thing that is prominent in the passage is that he saw the miracles and signs which were done. Simon was touted as "the great power of God", but then he sees the greater powers that this preacher has.[175] These are powers that excel and exceed his, and he wants in on the action. He believes, he really does, he knows this isn't trickery or illusion; he is convinced it is real. However, he's not convinced about his need of salvation. He wants the temporal benefits he believes the gospel will give him, but that is a stony ground response, and let us all take care that we don't feed this desire in our gospel outreach. Christians may, generally speaking, be happier, more content and have stronger marriages, etc.,

---

[175] The AV doesn't convey the point terribly clearly here. In v.13 it has left untranslated the word *megas*, which means *great*. It is the same word used in vv.9,10, "giving out that he himself was some great one...This man is the *great* power of God". And it has translated as *miracles* the word which is translated in v.10 *power*. So Simon's reputation was that he was the great power of God, but he sees Philip demonstrating great power, indeed, in v.10 in reference to Simon the words *great power* are singular, while in v.13 the words are plural.

than the societal norm, but if that *alone* is what draws someone to Christ then be prepared to witness the withering process of a stony ground hearer before your eyes when the time of testing comes. People need to recognise that it is in light of eternity they need salvation, not in light of their bank balance or blood pressure. Their problem is their sin and estrangement from God, not their low self-esteem or estrangement from their families. If someone never gets to the root of the problem then they will never get the real thing. This is why Peter had such harsh words and strong warnings for Simon the sorcerer; his heart was not right in the sight of God. Simon, like many others, wanted a salvation that would improve his me-first life but not a salvation that would end his me-first life.

The stony ground hearer looked the part, but there was never actually any fruit. The reason there was no fruit is because there was no root, that is, there were no fruits of repentance because repentance had never taken place: there had never been a genuine change of attitude towards self, sin and the Saviour. You might be wondering if your faith is a saving faith or a shallow, stony ground faith. Can you be sure? Ask yourself the following, *Do I believe what God says about my sin?* Do you agree that your sins are hell-deserving and hateful? *Do I believe what God says about myself?* Do you agree that you are entirely helpless to save yourself? Have you abandoned all self-righteous thoughts? *Do I believe what God says about His Son?* Do you accept that His sacrifice is both necessary and sufficient to pay for your sin? Do you acknowledge Him as God, own Him as Lord, and trust Him as Saviour? These are the marks of true saving faith.

Paul tells us in Romans 5 that the tribulations of life can give us assurance as well:

> Therefore, having been justified by faith, we have peace with God through our Lord Jesus Christ, through whom also we have obtained our introduction by faith into this grace in which we stand; and we exult in hope of the glory of God. And not only this, but we also exult in our tribulations, knowing that tribulation brings

about perseverance; and perseverance, proven character; and proven character, hope; and hope does not disappoint, because the love of God has been poured out within our hearts through the Holy Spirit who was given to us. (Rom.5:1-5, NASB)

Paul is saying that in the trials of life we prove the reality of God and the reality of our salvation. The fact that we continue to love God despite the troubles prove that we have the root of the matter; our faith is not shallow, it is not the case that we are trusting the Lord to smooth the road and remove the obstacles.

This is why Paul was so relieved to get a positive report from Timothy when he came back from Thessalonica. Paul had to leave the fledgling assembly there in the midst of persecution. He wondered how they were getting on and so he sent Timothy back:

Wherefore when we could no longer forbear, we thought it good to be left at Athens alone; and sent Timotheus, our brother, and minister of God, and our fellowlabourer in the gospel of Christ, to establish you, and to comfort you concerning your faith: that no man should be moved by these afflictions: for yourselves know that we are appointed thereunto. For verily, when we were with you, we told you before that we should suffer tribulation; even as it came to pass, and ye know. For this cause, when I could no longer forbear, I sent to know your faith, lest by some means the tempter have tempted you, and our labour be in vain.

But now when Timotheus came from you unto us, and brought us good tidings of your faith and charity, and that ye have good remembrance of us always, desiring greatly to see us, as we also to see you: therefore, brethren, we were comforted over you in all our affliction and distress by your faith: for now we live, if ye stand fast in the Lord. (1 Thess.3:1-8)

The fact that they were going on and growing up in the midst of such circumstances proved to Paul the reality of their faith because nothing but a work of God could have survived the onslaught from satanic forces there at Thessalonica.

As we move on then, what are the lessons? Till the ground, talk is cheap and time will tell.[176]

The seed amongst the thorns
Again, let's put the accounts from Mark and Luke here:

> And some fell among thorns, and the thorns grew up, and choked it, and it yielded no fruit.
> And these are they which are sown among thorns; such as hear the word, and the cares of this world, and the deceitfulness of riches, and the lusts of other things entering in, choke the word, and it becometh unfruitful (Mk.4:7,18,19)

> And some fell among thorns; and the thorns sprang up with it, and choked it.
> And that which fell among thorns are they, which, when they have heard, go forth, and are choked with cares and riches and pleasures of this life, and bring no fruit to perfection. (Lk.8:7,14)

We have seen with the wayside hearer that the devil is against the gospel. In the stony ground hearer we learn that the flesh is against the gospel. Here we have the third of our enemies, the world. The picture here is not someone who is saved then loses his salvation, but rather someone who hears the word, shows interest in it, but this world chokes the interest out of them and the goal is never reached, i.e. the person never repents, and the word "proves unfruitful" (Mk.4:19, ESV).

Let's just spend a moment looking at the things that cause the word to be unfruitful. First of all, the word is choked by the cares of this world: perhaps the thought is a person's poverty may keep him back from salvation. We have seen people whose lives are in

---

[176] This is not meant to encourage a cynical attitude toward any who profess salvation. It can be very off-putting for a new convert not to be believed. We can take people at their word unless and until there are clear indications to the contrary.

such a mess that when they have been faced with the gospel their response is something like, "I've got enough problems" or, "I've too much on my mind at the moment." Many think this life is all the hell there is. I have met many people who are brought down to the gutter and they would love to be lifted, but they are occupied with the symptoms of the problem (e.g. the drink, drugs, etc.) rather than the root (i.e. sin). They are concerned with just making it through the day, getting enough to get by, rather than the great forever that seems so far off. The cares of this world choke the seed.

The second thorn bush is the deceitfulness of riches. The problem here is not a person's poverty but rather a person's riches. These people think this life is all the heaven there is, so they want to get the most out of it. They have the attitude of the Laodiceans: "I am rich, and increased with goods, and have need of nothing" (Rev.3:17), and because this life is so comfortable they never give any thought to the next one.[177] Is this why Agur prayed "Give me neither poverty nor riches; feed me with food convenient for me: lest I be full and deny Thee, and say, 'Who is the Lord?' Or lest I be poor, and steal, and take the name of my God in vain." (Prov.30:8,9)?

The third hindrance is the desire for other things, just chasing whatever this world has to offer. Whether people like it or not, we are made by God and made for God, and will never be truly satisfied unless and until we are in a right relationship with God. However, since most people don't like that, they seek that elusive satisfaction and peace in any amount of other things. Solomon had been there and done that long before them, and has this to say, "All the rivers run into the sea; yet the sea is not full...the eye is not satisfied with seeing, nor the ear filled with hearing" (Eccl.1:7,8). The human heart is too big for the world to fill, but man chases the rainbow seeking the pot of gold, and the result is no fruit.

The way Luke puts it is that they bring no fruit to perfection. That is not to say that there was fruit produced, rather it means no fruit was produced. It looked like it was going to bear fruit but something came in and interfered, meaning that the seed never

---

[177] See two examples of this in Lk.12:16-21 and 16:19-31.

reached its intended goal. So when we keep in mind that soil is the person, and the fruit is that which evidences reality, we have to conclude that where there is no fruit it means there is no salvation. With the way side hearer there is no profession whatever, in the stony ground and thorny ground hearer there is profession, but no reality; these hearers are interested, but something keeps them back. Anyone who wants to see a saved and lost doctrine in this parable has to accept then that people can be saved without bearing any fruit of it in their lives whatsoever, because it is not the case that grounds two and three produced less fruit than ground four, it produced no fruit at all, and this is the point. The intended distinction is not between the first ground and the last three, the only difference there is between profession and no profession. The intended distinction is between the first three grounds and the last one, with the difference being the fourth ground produced fruit and the previous three yielded none, thus showing there was no reality.

Endurance Test? Matthew 10:22; 24:13
There is an expression used a couple of times in Matthew's Gospel that demands our attention. In the Lord's discourse in Matthew 10 we read the following:

> Behold, I send you forth as sheep in the midst of wolves: be ye therefore wise as serpents, and harmless as doves. But beware of men: for they will deliver you up to the councils, and they will scourge you in their synagogues; and ye shall be brought before governors and kings for my sake, for a testimony against them and the Gentiles.
> But when they deliver you up, take no thought how or what ye shall speak: for it shall be given you in that same hour what ye shall speak. For it is not ye that speak, but the Spirit of your Father which speaketh in you.
> And the brother shall deliver up the brother to death, and the father the child: and the children shall rise up against their parents, and cause them to be put to death. And ye shall be hated of

> all men for My name's sake: but he that endureth
> to the end shall be saved.
> But when they persecute you in this city, flee ye
> into another: for verily I say unto you, Ye shall
> not have gone over the cities of Israel, till the Son
> of man be come. (vv.16-23)

And in chapter 24:

> Then shall they deliver you up to be afflicted,
> and shall kill you: and ye shall be hated of all
> nations for My name's sake. And then shall many
> be offended, and shall betray one another, and
> shall hate one another. And many false prophets
> shall rise, and shall deceive many. And because
> iniquity shall abound, the love of many shall
> wax cold. But he that shall endure unto the end,
> the same shall be saved. And this gospel of the
> kingdom shall be preached in all the world for a
> witness unto all nations; and then shall the end
> come. (vv.9-14)

Do these passages put the believer's security in jeopardy? Not at all! Let's outline a few key thoughts and then fill in with a bit more detail.

1. These passages are not talking about believers of this present age, so, at worst, based on these passages it is only threatening believers during the Tribulation period.

2. The word *saved* is not univocal, and it may well be that *saved* in this context is not salvation from the penalty of sin, but salvation in a more physical sense.

3. The words of the Lord are indicatives not imperatives, He is not saying what one must do to be saved, but rather He is saying what one who is saved will do.

1. The believers in that future Tribulation period will be dealt with on the same grounds as believers in the Old Testament. The blessings of being sealed by the Spirit and having a Great High Priest representing us appear to be blessings unique to

this age of grace, so even if this passage were teaching that a believer could be lost through a loss of faith, it does not at all impinge on the security of believers in this present age. We have the assurance of our Great High Priest praying for the maintenance of our faith, He is our Representative before God, and His Spirit is the guarantee of our full salvation. That being said, I don't think a believer in Old Testament times or in Tribulation times can be lost, and we'll see that when I expand on point 3.

2. Many expositors think that the salvation referred to in this verse is not salvation from the penalty of sin, but rather a physical salvation brought about at the end of the Tribulation period. There are indications in the text that lend some support to this view, for example, in regard to "the end", note the following references in the immediate context:

> And ye shall hear of wars and rumours of wars: see that ye be not troubled: for all these things must come to pass, but *the end* is not yet. (Matt.24:6, emphasis added.)

> And this gospel of the kingdom shall be preached in all the world for a witness unto all nations; and then shall *the end* come. (Matt.24:14, emphasis added.)

The end, therefore does not mean the end of life, but it is speaking specifically about the end of the Tribulation period. Look too at how the word *saved* is used in the discourse:

> For then shall be great tribulation, such as was not since the beginning of the world to this time, no, nor ever shall be. And except those days should be shortened, there should no flesh be *saved*: but for the elect's sake those days shall be shortened. (Matt.24:21,22, emphasis added.)

It is clear that being saved in this setting is a physical salvation from death, not a spiritual salvation from hell. The Lord is saying that if there was not a limitation put on the days of Tribulation no one would survive.

So then, if we take these contextually justifiable thoughts of *the end* and being *saved* back into the phrase in question it looks like this: "The person who makes it to the end of the Tribulation will be delivered from death." An extended quote from Thomas Ice will be helpful in setting out the case:

> The exact meaning and implications of "the one who endures to the end, he shall be saved," is a hotly debated passage. Some use this passage to teach a Christian doctrine known as the perseverance of the saints. While others believe that it refers to a physical deliverance. I hold to the latter position, primarily because it is the only view that makes sense in this specific context.
>
> The first issue that must be dealt with in this matter is the meaning of the term "saved." Because the word "saved" is used in the New Testament to refer to the time when one becomes a Christian...many just plug that meaning into this passage. The leading Greek lexicon of our days says that the basic meaning of this word is "save, keep from harm, preserve, rescue."[178] This word can be used in relation to the doctrine of salvation (Matt.1:21; Acts 16:31; 1 Cor.1:18; Eph.2:8-9; Phil.1:19; Titus 3:5, etc.), or it can simply refer to physical deliverance or rescue (Matt.8:25; 14:30; 27:49; Acts 27:31; Heb.5:7; Jude 5, etc.). The exact nuance is determined by its context. "The problem begins with the superficial hermeneutic of giving 'saved' the same meaning in every context, which is not true of any word," declares Glasscock. "Words have no specific meaning apart from context. Here, 'saved' (*sozo*) means basically to 'deliver' or to 'rescue' – from what and in what manner is dependent upon the context."[179]

[178] William F. Arndt and F. W. Gingrich, *A Greek-English Lexicon of the New Testament*, Chicago: University of Chicago Press, 1957, p.805.
[179] Ed Glasscock, *Moody Gospel Commentary: Matthew*, Chicago: Moody Press, 1997, p.466.

Many commentaries on this passage fail to consider the contextual factors before they start sermonising on endurance in the Christian life. They make this into a passage that teaches the Christian doctrine of endurance, even though it is not supported by the specific factors in the text. Truly, there is a Christian doctrine of endurance taught in the Epistles (Rom.12:12; 1 Cor.13:7; 2 Tim.2:10,12; Heb.12:3,7; Jms.1:12; 5:11; 1 Pet.2:20). This doctrine teaches that one of the many character qualities that the believer is to have is endurance. Why is this so? It is true because endurance under suffering produces character (Rom.5:3,4). Yet, none of those references to the Christian doctrine of endurance speaks of "enduring to the end". Instead, passages that speak of enduring to the end all occur within the same context – the tribulation (Matt.10:22; 24:13; Mk.13:13; Lk.21:19; Rev.13:10; 14:12). John Walvoord explains:

> The age in general, climaxing with the second coming of Christ, has the promise that those that endure to the end (Matt.24:13), that is, survive the tribulation and are still alive, will be saved, or delivered, by Christ at His second coming. This is not a reference to salvation from sin, but rather the deliverance of survivors at the end of the age as stated, for instance, in Rom.11:26, where the Deliverer will save the nation Israel from its persecutors.[180]

Specifically this section is referring to the Jewish remnant, who, if they endure to the end, will be physically rescued by Christ at His second advent

---

[180] John F. Walvoord, *Matthew: Thy Kingdom Come*, Chicago: Moody Press, 1974, p.184.

and they will go into the millennial kingdom in their mortal bodies (Matt.25:21,34). William Kelly explains: "It is evident that the language is only applicable in its full force to Jews – believing ones, no doubt, but still Jews in the midst of a nation judicially chastised for their apostasy from God and rejection of their own Messiah...Thus there is a certain, defined period of endurance – an end to come, as truly as there was a beginning of sorrows."[181]

Parallel Passages

There are a number of parallel passages to Matt.24:13 that support my understanding of this text. First, Dan.12:1 says, "Now at that time Michael, the great prince who stands guard over the sons of your people, will arise. And there will be a time of distress such as never occurred since there was a nation until that time; and at that time your people, everyone who is found written in the book, will be rescued." Michael tells Daniel that this will be the time of tribulation in which the elect Jews will be rescued, which is the Hebrew word for saved.

Second, Mk.13:13, a direct parallel passage to Matt.24:13 and says, "And you will be hated by all on account of My name, but the one who endures to the end, he shall be saved." The first half of Mk.13:13 is a summary statement of Matt.24:9-12, which is followed by the endurance statement in both passages. Lk.21:18,19, also parallel, says, "Yet not a hair of your head will perish. By your endurance you will gain your lives." This is the clearest of all when it reads: "you will gain your lives." "Lives" is the normal word for physical life.

Third, Matt.10:22, also within the context of the future tribulation says, "And you will be hated

---

[181] William Kelly, *Lectures on The Gospel of Matthew*, Sunbury, PA: Believers Bookshelf, 1971 [1868], p.484.

by all on account of My name, but it is the one who has endured to the end who will be saved." Once again we see an emphasis upon the physical deliverance of Jews during the tribulation after a time of persecution.

Finally, Rev.13:10 and 14:12 which speak of the "perseverance of the saints," also are references to physical deliverance. Both references are clearly within a tribulational context and speak of physical deliverance when one endures to the end.[182]

Now some might object at this point because they smell a bit of tautology lurking around. Surely it is redundant to say that the person who makes it to the end of the Tribulation will be delivered from physical death, who would have thought otherwise? I think that is a valid point, but not insurmountable. This discourse got started by the Lord's stunning statement about the total destruction of the temple in Jerusalem (vv.1,2). This made the disciples somewhat curious to say the least and they began to ask the Lord about His coming and the end of the age. The Lord then begins to give a very bleak picture of what lies ahead: wars, rumours of wars, famines, pestilences and earthquakes, and He tells them that these are only the beginning of sorrows! There will be affliction, hatred and betrayal. Things will get worse and worse, and then at the end the Son of man will come in power and great glory. This coming will be one of judgment, but the comfort is it will not be indiscriminate judgment, there will be a separation that will take place:

And then shall appear the sign of the Son of man in heaven: and then shall all the tribes of the earth mourn, and they shall see the Son of man coming in the clouds of heaven with power and great glory. And He shall send His angels with a great sound of a trumpet, and they shall gather together His elect from the four winds, from one end of heaven to the other. (Matt.24:30,31)

---

[182] Thomas Ice, *An Interpretation of Matthew 24-25*, part XI, https://www.raptureready.com/featured/ice/AnInterpretationofMatthew24_25_11.html.

The Lord is showing that His coming, although bringing disaster and judgment for many, will bring deliverance for His own, and thus the believer that gets to the end of the Tribulation will be saved.

3. But let's say for the sake of argument that the Lord is indeed saying that the salvation here is salvation from sin's punishment, what follows from that? It is completely in keeping with all that we have gleaned from Scripture so far to say that the true believer will endure, if we understand endurance to mean continue to believe the truth of the gospel. Indeed, the Lord Jesus Christ affirms that this is the case, and affirms the impossibility of the believer losing his faith. Let me show you.

In this Tribulation era in which there will be diabolical deception and horrendous persecution on a global scale. Those who had previously rejected the truth will "believe the lie" and ultimately be damned,[183] many will exhibit that they were only stony ground, shallow-hearted believers.[184] And what will be the proof that someone is genuine? In such days of betrayal and apostasy, talk is cheap. It is the one that keeps going despite all the pressure and persecution who is genuinely saved. Now, notice how He teaches that the true believer cannot but endure to the end.

> Then if any man shall say unto you, Lo, here is Christ, or there; believe it not. For there shall arise false Christs, and false prophets, and shall shew great signs and wonders; insomuch that, *if it were possible*, they shall deceive the very elect. (Matt.24:23,24, emphasis added.)

See how the Lord introduces the thought of divine purpose here; He calls believers the elect ones.[185] He says that the

---

[183] 2 Thess.2:8-12. This passage has, as a hinge, one time marker – the removal of the Restrainer and the revelation of the wicked one. The Restrainer is undoubtedly the Holy Spirit, and at the rapture He will be removed in the same sense in which He came at Pentecost. The way is then open for the revelation of the man of sin. The use of aorist tenses to describe the rejection of the gospel in vv.10 and 12 show that Paul is pointing back prior to that time marker of the rapture, those who received not and believed not the truth before the rapture will believe the lie after the rapture.
[184] See previous section, Matt.3:5,20,21.
[185] The word is in the plural. It is evident that the elect in Matthew 24 is not the nation as a whole, because many of them will be deceived.

deception will ensnare everyone except these elect ones, and it is impossible that they will be taken in. Thus the Lord is teaching that people endure because they are saved; they are not saved because they endure. And the reason they are saved and do endure is because of a work of God.

At the end of that period of Tribulation the Son of man will come and send His angels to gather together His elect ones, showing that not one of them has been lost.

I think enough has been done, not only to show that this phrase does not teach a believer can lose his salvation, but also to show that contextually the passage actually teaches that a believer cannot lose his salvation.

Burning branches, John 15:1-6

I am the true vine, and My Father is the husbandman.
Every branch in Me that beareth not fruit He taketh away: and every branch that beareth fruit, He purgeth it, that it may bring forth more fruit.
Now ye are clean through the word which I have spoken unto you.
Abide in Me, and I in you. As the branch cannot bear fruit of itself, except it abide in the vine; no more can ye, except ye abide in Me.
I am the vine, ye are the branches: He that abideth in Me, and I in him, the same bringeth forth much fruit: for without Me ye can do nothing.
If a man abide not in Me, he is cast forth as a branch, and is withered; and men gather them, and cast them into the fire, and they are burned.

A Christian could be forgiven for breaking into a bit of a sweat as he reads this passage. There are a couple of striking phrases that cannot be avoided if this book is to serve its purpose. How does a believer in eternal security handle the threat of branches in the Lord being taken away, or how do we deal with the warning about branches being cast into the fire? We deal with it by keeping calm and going not just to the text but to the context.

Some take the view that what is in view here is not branches being taken away but branches being lifted up. It is true that the word translated *taketh away* can have the idea of lift up[186] and so it is suggested that what the Lord is indicating here is that the branch which is getting too close to the earth, trailing in the mud, wallowing in the mire, is lifted up, picturing for us the restoring ministry of the Lord Jesus Christ. Then further down, when it says that anyone not abiding in the Lord is cast forth as a branch and burned, we are told that it is not the husbandman that casts them into the fire, but just men, and thus it is not picturing a soul being lost, but a life and testimony being lost, a bit like what Paul feared in 1 Cor.9:27 or what Lot experienced in Genesis 19. Now this is a noble interpretation and cannot be quickly dismissed, but in fairness to the passage I don't think it is sustainable. I don't think the word translated *taketh away* can justifiably be understood in the sense of lifting up here. Firstly, although the word can be translated as lift up, it seems to always have the connotation of lift up and carry. It would appear to me that another word would be required to give us the idea of lift up and support. Secondly, if lifting up was the idea then I find it hard to believe it would not say something like, "Every branch in Me that beareth not fruit He *lifteth up that it may bring forth fruit*: and every branch that beareth fruit, He purgeth it, that it may bring forth more fruit." It is understandable that we would want to render the word "lifts up" but it just can't bear all the weight and do all the work that interpretation demands of it.[187] As regards the man in v.6 being a believer who loses his testimony, well, it seems a bit forced. It is true that the verse doesn't say that the husbandman casts the branch into the fire, but that is hardly convincing because surely the Lord is just continuing the metaphor, and presumably someone other than the husbandman would gather up the branches he has cast forth. Furthermore, we really can't make much capital out of the point that it says "men gather them" because there is no word for *men* in the text, it is literally, "they gather them". This has led

---

[186] e.g. Matt.4:6; 9:6
[187] I'm not going to take issue with the idea that the burning pictures a ruined life, I think that could (possibly) be the case, and it is entirely compatible with the view I take. Apostasy inevitably leads to moral ruin as well as spiritual ruin. See the contempt that was shown for Judas by the chief priests and elders in Matt.27:3-5, and is confirmed by the teaching of Peter in 2 Peter 2.

a number of translations to render the statement something like this, *the branches are gathered, thrown into the fire, and burned.*[188]

A similar but slightly different approach sees the burning as a reference to the loss of reward at the Judgment Seat of Christ, in line with Paul's teaching in 1 Cor.3:12-15:

> Now if any man build upon this foundation gold, silver, precious stones, wood, hay, stubble; every man's work shall be made manifest: for the day shall declare it, because it shall be revealed by fire; and the fire shall try every man's work of what sort it is.
> If any man's work abide which he hath built thereupon, he shall receive a reward.
> If any man's work shall be burned, he shall suffer loss: but he himself shall be saved; yet so as by fire.

This view is set forth in the notes of the NKJV Study Bible as follows:

> Not abiding in Christ has serious consequences: (1) The person is cast out as a branch, indicating the loss of fellowship; (2) the person is withered, indicating a loss of vitality; (3) the person is burned, indicating a loss of reward.[189]

This is really a lot more problematic. It entails not only that we see true believers being cast forth by God, but that we see them being burned! Any correspondence with 1 Corinthians 3 is extremely tenuous, because at the Judgment Seat it is not the believer that is burned (thankfully) but his works of wood, hay and stubble.

> It is vain and mischievous to distinguish between the person and the work, as theologians and others do who reason on either side of the equation of truth. The Calvinist fears to compromise his doctrines of grace; the Arminian is anxious to push his advantage on the side of

---

[188] See, for example, ESV, NET Bible.
[189] Nelson's NKJV Study Bible, 1997.

falling away. Hence the former is apt to evade the solemn warning of personal ruin and final judgment conveyed here, as the latter argues that the passage implies that a saved soul may be lost after all. They both confound the figure of the vine with the body in Ephesians 2-4, and hence are alike wrong, and of course unable to expound these Scriptures satisfactorily, so as to hold all the truth without sacrificing one part to another.[190]

We can safely say that v.6 has nothing to do with the Judgment Seat of Christ.

Another interpretation worth considering is that the branch not bearing fruit in v.2 is a carnal believer, and he is taken away in judgment as per 1 Cor.11:30-32:

> For this cause many are weak and sickly among you, and many sleep. For if we would judge ourselves, we should not be judged. But when we are judged, we are chastened of the Lord, that we should not be condemned with the world.

Those holding this view point out, quite rightly, that the picture of the vine and the branches is not the same as the picture of the church as the body of Christ, from which no member can be lost, nor is it the picture of the church as the building from which no stone can be dislodged. These are pictures that are not illustrating something merely true of believers in the world, because saints who have gone to heaven are still in the body and in the building. The metaphor of the vine is full of significance. A vine is something that grows out of the earth, and is intended to produce fruit. The use of this illustration is intended to communicate the thought of testimony on earth. It is suggested then that a believer who is not bearing fruit may be taken away in discipline, still in the dispensational church, but not in the vine. The person mentioned in v.6 however is a different category. This is evident by the change of pronouns from v.5 to v.6. In v.5 the Lord says, "I am

---

[190] William Kelly, *An Exposition of the Gospel of John*, available at http://www.stempublishing.com/authors/kelly/2Newtest/John_pt3.html.

the vine, *ye* are the branches...for without Me *ye* can do nothing" (emphasis added). Then in v.7 He says again, "If *ye* abide in Me, and My words abide in *you*, *ye* shall ask what *ye* will, and it shall be done unto you" (emphasis added). But in between there is this stark switch, "If *a man* abide not in Me, *he* is cast forth as a branch and is withered; and men gather *them*, and cast them into the fire, and *they* are burned" (emphasis added). The Lord doesn't say, "If ye abide not in Me..." The unspoken but plain implication is that what He was speaking about in v.6 was something that would not, and could not, befall the men He was addressing.[191] We can look at Matt.18:7-9 to see a contrast in how the Lord gave warnings when Judas was present:

> Woe unto the world because of offences! for it must needs be that offences come; but woe to that man by whom the offence cometh!
> Wherefore if thy hand or thy foot offend thee, cut them off, and cast them from thee: it is better for thee to enter into life halt or maimed, rather than having two hands or two feet to be cast into everlasting fire. And if thine eye offend thee, pluck it out, and cast it from thee: it is better for thee to enter into life with one eye, rather than having two eyes to be cast into hell fire.

Judas was among the disciples at this stage, and so the Lord doesn't do here what He does in John 15, and speak in the third person about "a man", He speaks in the second person singular, and warns "if thy hand or foot offend thee..."[192] But in John 15 there was no one present to whom the warning applied, for each of them had come to Him in true faith, and thus they could never be cast forth or cast into the fire, for they had the promise of the Lord Himself, "him that cometh to Me *I will in no wise cast out*."[193]

So, according to this view we have the three types of people Paul mentions in 1 Cor.2:14-3:4: the natural man (v.6 – taken as a branch

---

[191] "Only in v.6 it changes to 'a man,' and speaks of destruction, which could not be of a true disciple in Christ." J. N. Darby, *On the Gospel according to John*, available at http://stempublishing.com/authors/darby/EXPOSIT/25027E_B.html.
[192] Noticeably it's not the second person plural. It seems He had Judas specifically in mind.
[193] Jn.6:37, emphasis added.

and burned), the carnal man (v.2 – the fruitless branch), and the spiritual man (v.2 – the branch bearing fruit).

I am on board with seeing the natural man in v.6, but there are, in my opinion, a couple of problems with this interpretation that the fruitless branch in v.2 is a carnal Christian. The first problem I have is this, is there really any true believer who does not bear fruit? As far as I can see in Scripture, if there's no fruit there's no life.

> There is no such thing as a fruitless Christian. Everyone bears some fruit. You may have to look hard to find even a small grape, but if you look close enough, you will find something.
> Since all Christians bear fruit, it is clear that the fruitless branches in John 15 cannot refer to them. In fact, the fruitless branches had to be eliminated and thrown into the fire. Yet Jesus referred to the fruitless branches as those who are in Him (v.2). Doesn't that imply they are genuine believers?
> Not necessarily. Externally they may be attached, but no life flows through them. Other passages in Scripture show it is possible to be a parasite on the vine, seemingly a part of it, but only in appearance. In Rom.9:6 for example, Paul said, "They are not all Israel who are descended from Israel." It was possible for a person to be part of the nation of Israel, yet not be a true Israelite. Likewise it is possible to be a branch without living connected to the true vine.[194]

It is important to notice that fruit in this context is not success in service or seeing souls saved, it is manifesting the life of the vine, that is, manifesting eternal life.

> ...one must remember that for John, to have life at all is to bear fruit, while one who does not bear fruit shows that he does not have the life...[195]

---

[194] MacArthur. *Saved Without A Doubt*, pp.38,39.
[195] NET Bible study note, John 15:6.

Bearing more fruit and much fruit is living out our eternal life in every aspect of life, it is Christ being seen in us. That doesn't mean the believer will necessarily always be abounding in fruit, but there will be evidence in the life that someone has been born again. Yet here, it seems that the Lord is speaking here of continual fruitlessness. The answer to that may be that this is talking about a sustained period of fruitlessness; it's not saying he never bore fruit, but he is going through a period in which there is none.

While some might not see the above objections as insurmountable they are certainly big enough to cause me to look for another explanation, and the context does provide one.

Let's first of all see how some versions render v.2:

> He cuts off every branch that does not produce fruit in Me, and He cuts back every branch that does produce fruit, so that it might produce more fruit.[196]

> He takes away every branch that does not bear fruit in Me. He prunes every branch that bears fruit so that it will bear more fruit.[197]

These translations confirm what was said by Matthew Henry:

> It is here intimated that there are many who pass for *branches* in Christ who yet do *not bear fruit.* Were they really united to Christ by faith, they would bear fruit; but being only tied to him by the thread of an outward profession, though they seem to be branches, they will soon be seen to be dry ones. Unfruitful professors are unfaithful professors; professors, and no more. It might be read, *Every branch that beareth not fruit in Me,* and it comes much to one; for those that do not bear fruit in Christ, and in his Spirit and grace, are as if they bore no fruit at all, Hos.10:1. It is here threatened that they shall be *taken away,* in justice to them and in kindness to the rest of the

---

[196] International Standard Version.
[197] NET Bible.

> branches. From him that has not real union with
> Christ, and fruit produced thereby, *shall be taken*
> *away even that which he seemed to have,* Lk. 8:18.
> Some think this refers primarily to Judas.[198]

This removes any difficulty there may be with the branch being said to be "in Me". The Lord is in effect saying that if someone does not bear fruit in communion with Him it shows there has never been any vital union in Him.

> [S]o the disciples of Christ may be spiritually
> fruitful or the reverse, according as they are
> *vitally* and *spiritually connected* with Christ, or but
> *externally* and *mechanically attached* to Him.[199]

> Those who make a profession, who attach
> themselves to Christ in order to follow Him, will,
> if there is life, be cleansed; if not, that which they
> have will be taken away.[200]

The teaching then is that a mere external attachment to Christ is not sufficient, there has to be life flowing in and showing through the branch to demonstrate reality. When we look at the context of the wider discourse which takes in chapters 13-17 I think it will inform and confirm our understanding of what the Lord meant when He spoke about these fruitless branches, because there is a very definite structure.

The discourse commences with the incident about the foot-washing. The Lord and His disciples have made their way to this upper room, they find everything furnished and prepared. They have everything they need, except a servant to wait on them. The basin, water and towel are all there but who is going to do the menial task of taking dusty feet into his hands and washing them. The disciples just flop onto the couches; they're prepared to forget about the foot-washing. They would rather have dusty feet than stoop to do the slave's job. Supper gets underway, no one has volunteered for the job. It is then that the disciples see the Lord rise from supper, lay aside the outer garment and take the

---

[198] Matthew Henry, *Commentary on the Whole Bible*, Hendrickson, 2000, vol.5, *Matthew to John*, p.906.
[199] Jamieson, Fausset and Brown, e-Sword.
[200] Darby, *Synopsis*, vol.3, p.374.

servant's towel. As He silently stands, tying this towel around His waist, the disciples sit stunned. Then He gets the basin and kneels and washes their feet. No doubt their jaws dropped, and likely their cheeks reddened. He comes to Peter, who takes his foot away from the Lord's hands (and, as usual, went and put that foot in his mouth!) He tells the Lord, "Thou shalt never wash my feet." The Lord's response was, "If I wash thee not, thou hast no part with Me." The Lord is saying there can be no fellowship with Me unless this happens, so then Peter, whose heart was in the right place, goes completely in the other direction and says in effect, *Well, if this is about communion with Christ then I want as much as possible, Lord, wash my hands and my head too!*

Peter hasn't got the point, and who could blame him? How could he have known the Lord was giving a living parable of the ministry He would undertake for them when He returned to the Father? The Lord tells Peter that the one who has been bathed all over only needs to have his feet washed. I'm sure this brought puzzled looks and questioning glances from the disciples, but from our vantage point the picture is clear and beautiful.

It is evident that the Spirit of God is seeking to create a real atmosphere as we join the Lord and His disciples in the upper room. The chapter commences by emphasising that the Lord was going home:

> Now before the feast of the passover, when Jesus knew that His hour was come that He should depart out of this world unto the Father, having loved His own which were in the world, He loved them unto the end. And supper being ended, the devil having now put into the heart of Judas Iscariot, Simon's son, to betray Him; Jesus knowing that the Father had given all things into His hands, and that He was come from God, and went to God; He riseth from supper, and laid aside His garments; and took a towel, and girded Himself. (Jn.13:1-4)

So for us, the readers, we are to take all that happens here as being closely connected with the Lord's return to heaven. A bit of Old

Testament background will help us understand the picture. When the priests of Israel were consecrated they were ceremonially bathed.[201] This all-over ceremonial washing was done once, and never repeated. It pictures conversion, or what Paul calls the washing of regeneration (Titus 3:5). However, the priests still had to visit the laver, not to wash themselves all over, but to wash their hands and feet as they performed their priestly duties. If they did not go to the laver then they could not minister to the Lord:

> And the LORD spake unto Moses, saying, Thou shalt also make a laver of brass, and his foot also of brass, to wash withal: and thou shalt put it between the tabernacle of the congregation and the altar, and thou shalt put water therein.
>
> For Aaron and his sons shall wash their hands and their feet thereat: when they go into the tabernacle of the congregation, they shall wash with water, that they die not; or when they come near to the altar to minister, to burn offering made by fire unto the LORD: so they shall wash their hands and their feet, that they die not: and it shall be a statute for ever to them, even to him and to his seed throughout their generations. (Ex.30:17-21)

When Peter asked to be washed from head to foot he was spoiling the picture and the Lord tells him he's had that washing and doesn't need it again; he is "clean every whit." He just needs the washing of the feet.[202] The Lord is the answer to the laver of the Old Testament, and as we move through this defiling world we are defiled, and we need continual recourse to the Lord, not for the washing of regeneration, but for the practical cleansing from the defilement we pick up along life's pathway.

When the Lord told Peter that the person who has been bathed only needs his feet washed, He points out that the disciples had experienced this once-for-all bathing because He says, "and ye

---

[201] Ex.29:4; Lev.8:6
[202] Why does the Lord not mention the hands needing washed here? The priests needed their hands washed because they were handling the sacrifices, but the Lord offered one sacrifice for sins forever.

are clean," but then He adds these ominous words, "but not all." John explains, "For He knew who should betray Him; therefore said He, 'Ye are not all clean'" (vv.10,11). The Lord is telling them, *There's one in here who, although identified with Me, is not actually saved.* This faker amongst them would soon be evicted:

> When Jesus had thus said, He was troubled in spirit, and testified, and said, Verily, verily, I say unto you, that one of you shall betray Me. Then the disciples looked one on another, doubting of whom He spake. Now there was leaning on Jesus' bosom one of His disciples, whom Jesus loved.
>
> Simon Peter therefore beckoned to him, that he should ask who it should be of whom He spake.
>
> He then lying on Jesus' breast saith unto Him, Lord, who is it?
>
> Jesus answered, He it is, to whom I shall give a sop, when I have dipped it. And when He had dipped the sop, He gave it to Judas Iscariot, the son of Simon.
>
> And after the sop Satan entered into him. Then said Jesus unto him, That thou doest, do quickly. Now no man at the table knew for what intent He spake this unto him. For some of them thought, because Judas had the bag, that Jesus had said unto him, Buy those things that we have need of against the feast; or, that he should give something to the poor.
>
> He then having received the sop went immediately out: and it was night. (Jn.13:21-30)

Where are we going with this? This is all designed to help us understand the first six verses of John 15 because this passage in chapter 13 is set in parallel with chapter 15. Let me try to show how. This last discourse of the Lord to His disciples is in two sections: chapters 13 and 14 form the first, and conclude with the Lord saying, "Arise, let us go hence" (14:31). Whether they immediately left the upper room at that point or not is irrelevant, the pertinent point is there is a break here, and chapters 15 and 16 form the second section. In keeping with the word of the Lord to leave the upper room, these two chapters have an "outside feel" about them; the warm, homely atmosphere of the upper room is exchanged for the cold, hostile atmosphere of a sinful world. The Lord speaks at length about the world's hatred, about the persecution they will experience, about the need to bear testimony to Him, and the tribulation they would endure. In the first section the Lord deals with the ministry of the Holy Spirit in the realm of their fellowship with the Father and the Son, while in chapters 15 and 16 He deals with the ministry of the Holy Spirit in relation to the world and our testimony. With that division in our minds, let's briefly see how the parallelism is developed.

Chapters 13 and 15 mirror each other. There is the thought of cleansing (13:1-11; 15:2,3); there is the statement of the Lord, "The servant is not greater than his lord" (13:16; 15:20); there is the Lord's choice of His own (13:18; 15:19); and there is the thought that the treachery of Judas and the hatred of the world are both in fulfilment of Scripture (13:18; 15:25), and these two verses contain the only two Old Testament quotations in the discourse.

Chapters 14 and 16 likewise complement each other. We have the teaching of the Lord on asking in His name (14:13,14; 16:23-26); the Holy Spirit is spoken of as the Spirit of truth (14:17; 16:13) and the Comforter (14:26; 16:7) in these two chapters; the statement "a little while" occurs in these two chapters (14:18; 16:16-19); and He tells them how it is beneficial that "I go away": it is beneficial for Him (14:28) and for them (16:7). More details could be given, but I think it is clear there is definitely an intention in chapters 15 and 16 to repeat and enlarge upon teaching given in chapter 13 and 14.[203]

The key thing to notice for our study is that each section starts with the need for a cleansing and the affirmation that they are clean. As we have noticed, the Lord tells His disciples their feet need to be washed if they are to have any part with Him, then He tells them, "ye are clean". In chapter 15 the Lord says that every branch that bears fruit is purged by the Father that it might bear more fruit. That verb *purged* means *cleansed*, and the adjectival form of

---

[203] For a more thorough look at the parallelism in this discourse see Gooding's *In the School of Christ*.

the word appears in v.3, "Now [i.e. *already*] ye are clean through the word which I have spoken unto you." This expression, ye are clean, is exactly the same as in 13:10. It is clear then that we are to see a link here. In chapter 15 the Lord doesn't add the words, "But not all", because the false professor had been removed.

It seems apparent then that we are to see Judas as a branch that bore no fruit and has been taken away. Those disciples who walked no more with Him in chapter 6 would also be examples of this teaching. They had an association with Him, but He knew they weren't genuine, so by His teaching He takes them away, they drop off, fall back, and show that there was no real link with Christ.[204] It ought to be the case in the local assembly that the Word of God and the devotion of the Lord's people will be used by the Lord to take away the false. Surely, if believers are bearing fruit as they ought, the lifeless can't abide long amongst them.

This is something John never forgot and it served him well when he put pen to paper to write his first epistle. He writes about antichrists, who by their teaching deny fundamental truths regarding the Son, and therefore they deny the Father too. John says:

> They went out from us, but they were not of us;
> for if they had been of us, they would no doubt
> have continued with us: but they went out, that
> they might be made manifest that they were not
> all of us. (1 Jn.2:19)

Does this not strike you as very similar to the Lord's teaching in John 15? There is an association, (*They went out from us*), but there was no vital union, they were not saved. How can we be so certain? Because John says so! With apostolic authority, in God-breathed words, John says that if these antichrists *had been of us* (i.e. saved) then they would *have continued with us*. That word *continued* is the same word translated in John 15 as *abide*. The true believer abides in the vine, he will never disassociate himself from the Lord as revealed in Scripture. So someone who is saved, according to

---

[204] In v.6 we see that the Lord taking the unfruitful branch away is stated in terms of the person's own action, "If a man abide not in Me". So the taking away need not be premature death or judgment, but the person disassociating himself from the Lord.

1 Jn.2:19 will not and cannot apostatise. Those who left the apostolic doctrine of Christ were giving evidence, not that they had lost salvation, but that they had never been saved at all.

So, does the Lord's teaching in John 15 indicate that someone can lose his salvation? Only if you extract it from the immediate context of the Lord's discourse and divorce it from the wider context of John's writings, failing to see how he understood and applied the concept in his epistle. However, if you read contextually and interpret consistently you will come to the conclusion that the Lord is speaking about those who only have a visible association with the Lord, not a vital union.

Broken branches, Romans 11:16-24

> For if the firstfruit be holy, the lump is also holy: and if the root be holy, so are the branches. And if some of the branches be broken off, and thou, being a wild olive tree, wert graffed in among them, and with them partakest of the root and fatness of the olive tree; boast not against the branches. But if thou boast, thou bearest not the root, but the root thee.
> Thou wilt say then, The branches were broken off, that I might be graffed in. Well; because of unbelief they were broken off, and thou standest by faith. Be not highminded, but fear: for if God spared not the natural branches, take heed lest He also spare not thee. Behold therefore the goodness and severity of God: on them which fell, severity; but toward thee, goodness, if thou continue in His goodness: otherwise thou also shalt be cut off.
> And they also, if they abide not still in unbelief, shall be graffed in: for God is able to graff them in again. For if thou wert cut out of the olive tree which is wild by nature, and wert graffed contrary to nature into a good olive tree: how much more shall these, which be the natural branches, be graffed into their own olive tree?

Some have wondered why chapters 9 to 11 come in to the epistle to the Romans, because they seem (to them) to be a relatively insignificant parenthesis. The answer is actually very relevant to our subject. In Romans 8, as we have noticed, Paul is seeking to assure us regarding our security. He speaks about our sonship and glory (8:15,18,23); he tells us we were foreknown and called (8:29,30); he assures us of God's love for us. But the question then naturally arises, *What about the nation of Israel?* They had a national sonship and an earthly glory (9:4); they were foreknown (11:2) and called (9:7); they were loved (9:13). But where are they now? The promises and purpose of God for them seem to have been shattered into a million pieces and would shortly be buried by the rubble of AD 70. That is why these three chapters are so vital to the epistle and so important in regard to our eternal security. If God's promises to Israel can fail then His promises to us can too; if God's purpose for Israel can be derailed then His purpose for us can too. We need to be sure about the integrity of His promises and the immutability of His purpose, and Paul proves to us in these chapters that we can be sure. But in this particular section we are introduced to olive trees and branches that get grafted in then those very same branches get cut off. What is this all about?

I think we will be greatly helped in seeing what this passage is teaching if we ascertain who these first branches which were broken off represent. It is clear that these broken branches represent Jews. They are described as holy, but it is evident that the word is not intended to convey the thought of moral and spiritual purity but rather separation to a sphere of privilege.[205] The nation of Israel was in a position of special favour and blessing. It was a nation that was intended to be a testimony for God and to give light to the nations.[206] But many in the nation rejected their Messiah and they were cut off from the tree, that is, they were no longer in that special place of favour and that particular position of testimony. These branches do not represent people who were saved then lost, but those who failed in their responsibility and rejected

---

[205] If the meaning was that they were morally and spiritually pure then they would not have been cut off. It is completely legitimate to understand the word in a relative sense, i.e. they are separate, marked off, singled out, e.g. 1 Cor.7:14.
[206] This is why the figure of an olive tree is used: it gives light; it was the first choice of the trees when they wanted a king in Jotham's fable, Judg.9:8.

their opportunity. It will help us greatly if we carry this thought through.[207] Because of the cutting off of the natural branches (i.e. unbelieving Jews), the nations were brought into a sphere of blessing and special favour.

> It is no question of saving grace here but of earthly responsibility according to the respective testimony, first of Israel, next of Christendom.[208]

If we think this through we will see that it makes no sense to import the loss of salvation into the passage. Look again at v.19:

> Thou wilt say then, The branches were broken off, that I might be graffed in.

If being cut off equals the loss of salvation and being grafted in equals the obtaining of salvation, why would a saved Gentile think a Jew losing his salvation had anything to do with him obtaining his? The gospel didn't go out to the Gentiles because saved Jews apostatised, did it? The gospel went out to the Gentiles because the nation rejected it. This really closes the case and shows us that the falling away doctrine is not in Romans 11. In fact, Romans 11 teaches that "the gifts and calling of God are without repentance" (v.29). The word translated *gifts* occurs several times in the book of Romans, but one mention will suffice to make a point: Paul says in 6:23, "the gift of God is eternal life through Jesus Christ our Lord." God has granted eternal life to all who receive Christ, and that gift He has given is a gift He will never recall, for the gifts of God are without repentance. The word translated *calling* is found in its adjectival form in 8:28, in which Paul says, "And we know that all things work together for good to them that love God, to them who are the called according to His purpose." We have been called according to the purpose of a sovereign God, and that calling will never be revoked; He will see His purpose through to its glorious conclusion when we are fully conformed to the image of God's Son, because the calling of God is without repentance. So rather than Romans 11 overthrowing eternal security, it actually

---

[207] The natural branches were marked by unbelief, and the Gentiles were warned about being highminded. These two thoughts seem to stand in opposition to the two requirements of Rom. 10:9; confessing Jesus as Lord stands in contrast to being highminded; believing in one's heart that God raised Him from the dead stands in contrast to unbelief.

[208] Kelly, *Notes on the Epistle to the Romans*, p.228.

establishes it.

Let's just clarify in our minds then what Paul meant when he spoke about these branches being cut off. Paul addresses himself to the Gentiles as Gentiles, not as saints, and he engages in a dialogue with a Gentile for illustrative purposes, he is not speaking to the Christians here.[209] Following the rejection of the gospel by the Jewish nation, the centre of testimony for God in the world was shifting from the nation to the nations, from the Jew to the Gentiles.[210] Consequently many Gentile nations were brought into a position of great opportunity. They had come to see the emptiness of idolatry, the reality of the one true God, and the power of the living Christ. People in such an environment have a weighty responsibility to respond appropriately to the light they have, that they might bear that light to others, and Paul tells us what this appropriate response is: he says the Gentile is to continue in God's goodness (v.22). Now, it is not without significance that the last place where Paul speaks about God's goodness is in 2:4:

> Or despisest thou the riches of His goodness and
> forbearance and longsuffering; not knowing that
> the goodness of God leadeth thee to repentance?

In this passage Paul is having a 'conversation' with an upright, moralising Gentile. This Gentile has great privilege but is not acting on it. The privilege isn't intended to make him smug; it is intended to bring him to repentance. God's goodness was leading him to that place of repentance, but he wasn't continuing in it, he was pulling back and not going on. That, I suggest, is similar to what is going on in chapter 11.[211] The loss of light and privilege is what is involved in being cut off, and a study of the last 2,000 years would show us nations that have been greatly blessed with gospel light but have despised their privilege and lost their place as light-bearing nations.[212]

---

[209] Just as he wasn't speaking to any Christian in 2:1-29.
[210] The period in which the gospel was "to the Jew first" (1:16) seems to span the whole book of Acts, and during this period the nation turning to the Lord was held out as a possibility, but that terminates at the end of the Acts, see Acts 28:25-28.
[211] In chapter 2 the Gentile Paul is addressing is looking down on the heathen, while in chapter 11 the Gentile Paul is addressing is looking down on the Jew.
[212] Take note UK and USA.

So we have seen what the cutting off of branches cannot represent, and what it does represent. We can relax and move on to our next section, our security is not the least bit threatened by Romans 11, in fact, it is protected.

Castaway? 1 Corinthians 9:24-27

> Know ye not that they which run in a race run all, but one receiveth the prize? So run, that ye may obtain.
> And every man that striveth for the mastery is temperate in all things. Now they do it to obtain a corruptible crown; but we an incorruptible.
> I therefore so run, not as uncertainly; so fight I, not as one that beateth the air: but I keep under my body, and bring it into subjection: lest that by any means, when I have preached to others, I myself should be a castaway.

This passage has been unfairly pressed into service in the efforts of some to teach a Christian can be lost. It ought to be clear that no such meaning was intended by Paul, but let us delve into the passage to prove that conclusively.

Paul is drawing on the Isthmian games which were held in Corinth every two years.

> The Isthmian games, in which the foot race was a leading one, were of course well known, and a subject of patriotic pride to the Corinthians, who lived in the immediate neighbourhood. These periodical games were to the Greeks rather a passion than a mere amusement: hence their suitableness as an image of Christian earnestness.[213]

Paul is speaking here about the self-control that is essential in the service of God. Just like the athlete exercises discipline, sets goals, makes sacrifices, denies self, so too must the Christian. There is a judgment seat before which the Christian must stand and at

---

[213] Jamieson, Fausset and Brown, e-Sword.

which his life of service will be made manifest. Paul is exhorting us to put the same effort into living for God that the athlete puts into his competing at the games.

It is clear that Paul does not have salvation in view in this passage because no Christian believes that we obtain salvation by our striving and our temperance. How could salvation (which is not of works) ever be likened to competing in an athletic contest (which most certainly is of works). Salvation is not a prize to be won but a gift to be received, but if Paul is fearing the loss of it here then it means that it is his devotion, his discipline, his striving and efforts which have kept him on the road to heaven, and if he breasts the tape, crosses the line and lands in heaven, he wins the crown, he gets the glory; he got to heaven by his works.

Remember to whom Paul was writing; he was writing to an assembly splintering with division and stained with defilement. They had not been marked by *temperance in all things*. Paul says to them quite bluntly in 1 Cor.3:3, "For ye are yet carnal", but at the end of that same chapter he says, "...ye are Christ's" (v.23). It was certainly and sadly the case that they were carnal, but it was also certainly the case that they were Christ's. Their carnality did not sever them from the Saviour.

So, when Paul spoke of the possibility of being castaway (the word really is *disapproved*) we have to see it against this background of these games. There was a need to abide by the rules, and if one was found to have broken the rules he would not get the prize, he would be disapproved. Paul recognised that there was within him the potential for catastrophic failure that would result in him being disapproved for public service on earth and would mean loss of reward at the judgment seat of Christ. It is importing error into the text rather than exporting truth from the text to introduce any thought of the loss of salvation here.

Falling from grace, Galatians 5:1-4

> Stand fast therefore in the liberty wherewith Christ hath made us free, and be not entangled again with the yoke of bondage.
> Behold, I Paul say unto you, that if ye be

circumcised, Christ shall profit you nothing.
For I testify again to every man that is circumcised,
that he is a debtor to do the whole law. Christ is
become of no effect unto you, whosoever of you
are justified by the law; ye are fallen from grace.

It certainly appears on first blush that this passage could provide some support for the falling-away doctrine since the expression is (near enough) in the text, but even Scriptural expressions can take on a meaning over time that is far removed from the original, divine intention. We have to go back to the text and back to the context to see if we are using the phrase in a Scriptural way.

Something very important to be pointed out is that this statement is not found in a context in which Paul is warning of gross immorality or backsliding. This statement is given in a context in which Paul is warning his readers about adding to faith and seeking to be justified by works. The importance of this is twofold: first, this phrase *fallen from grace* is almost never used in this specific context by those who believe a Christian can be lost. They will use the phrase in relation to people who have fallen into some moral sin, but that is not in this passage. Second, if this passage did teach that a Christian could lose his salvation, the ones who are in danger of falling foul of it are those who bandy the phrase about most and say if you aren't holy enough you'll be lost. Paul is saying that the people who fall from grace are those who seek acceptance with God based on their own performance. That sounds very like the message that we hear from those who say a Christian can lose his salvation.

The letter to the Galatians is a tightly argued defence of the gospel from a Jewish Christian (Paul) to Gentiles who had professed salvation. These Gentiles were under attack from Judaising teachers who said that Christ was not sufficient for salvation, law-keeping was essential. Paul sees the Galatians being threatened with this error and wants them to know that there can be no mixing of law and grace, no mingling of faith and works, and no merging of Christ and self; if someone is not depending on Christ alone for salvation then that individual is not saved. He is not therefore addressing his letter to a company of people whose salvation was assumed, he is addressing his letter to companies of professing Christians, and he is quite upfront about the fact that they were giving him serious cause for concern about the reality of their profession. He says in 4:20, "I stand in doubt of you".[214]

Verse one of chapter five shouldn't be severed from the last verse of chapter four. Paul has said in 4:31 that we are not children of the bondwoman but children of the free; chapter five commences with a note of triumph and an exhortation: "For freedom did Christ set us free: stand fast therefore, and be not entangled again in a yoke of bondage" (ASV). Paul is exhorting them to enjoy the liberty that Christ has given them, and not let any "false brethren" (2:4) take it from them. How could this happen? Well, it could happen if they believed that the Christian is under obligation to keep the law to maintain his relationship with God.[215] This would lead him into bondage to a system of law-keeping that would mean in practical effect that Christ profits him nothing; he is striving to maintain his relationship with God in the very same way a Christ-rejecting Jew is striving to make his relationship with God, and thus he is fallen from grace; he is not living in the good of the grace of God.

F. B. Hole has this to say:

> The words "fallen from grace" are sometimes wrongly used as though they meant that a believer who once stood in the grace of God has now been ejected from it by God because of his bad behaviour. The point of the passage is rather that anyone who has once taken up his position before God in grace, as these Galatians had, and then abandons it *in his own mind and consciousness* for law has had a bad fall. To step off the grace platform on to the law platform – if we may so speak – involves a descent that amounts to a fall, for the one is far lower than the other. In the case

---

[214] One of the keys to a proper understanding of the letter is keeping track of the pronouns Paul uses and making sure we understand to whom Paul is referring. This can, admittedly, be quite difficult. Sometimes Paul's use of *we, us* and *our* is intended to denote Paul and those who were with him when he preached (1:9). Sometimes it is intended to be taken as "we Jews" (2:15), sometimes it refers to Paul and the Galatians (4:31). A careful look at the context will help determine the meaning.
[215] Although the ordinance of circumcision preceded the giving of the law, it was part and parcel of the ceremonial law, and as such was something the Judaisers enjoined upon the Gentiles to bring them under the demands of the Mosaic law.

of a true believer being entangled thus, the fall, we repeat, is in his own mind and consciousness. God's grace and the relationship established by grace remain the same, for "the gifts and calling of God are without repentance" (Rom.11:29).[216]

Lewis Sperry Chafer agrees:

> His departure from grace is only in the sphere of his own contemplation of his responsibility as a saved person. He may thus sacrifice his joy and peace, but there is no intimation that his salvation is sacrificed.[217]

Paul is, in this passage, seeking to show the Galatians the ramifications of the erroneous path on which they were embarking; he tells them that by putting themselves under the yoke of the law they are seeking to be justified by law. Now the effect this would have on those who are genuinely saved is that they would recoil from such a thought and reject any such teaching that they could ever be justified by law. Those amongst them who continued in this legalism are giving evidence that they have never learnt their own depravity and Christ's sufficiency. We have observed this many times as we have seen people who professed to be saved subsequently swim the Tiber and become Roman Catholic. If the convert to Rome fully grasps the implications of the 'gospel' of Roman Catholicism and accepts those implications, then the only conclusion we could come to is that they never actually believed what once they professed.[218] If someone thinks that his penance is able to "recover the grace of his justification",[219] or his suffering in purgatory is required to satisfy "God's holiness and justice" and can make expiation for his sins,[220] or that the mass "is truly propitiatory",[221] it makes "reparation for the sins of the living and the dead",[222] and in observing it "the work of our redemption is

---

[216] F. B. Hole, *Notes on Galatians*, taken from Scripture Truth, Volume 18, 1926, p.8, available at http://www.stempublishing.com/authors/hole/Art/Notes_on_Galatians.html.

[217] Chafer, *Systematic Theology*, vol.3, p.311.

[218] There is no doubt there are true believers in the Roman Catholic church, but that is because they are ignorant of, and inconsistent with, the teachings of Roman Catholicism and don't adhere to the doctrines of that system.

[219] *Catechism of the Catholic Church*, paragraph 1446.

[220] See *The Second Vatican Council*, p.63, or *Catechism of the Catholic Church*, paragraph 1030.

[221] *Catechism of the Catholic Church*, paragraph 1367.

[222] Ibid., paragraph 1414.

accomplished",[223] then such a person has never appreciated the true gospel that really saves, and therefore has never been born again.

So Paul is making it plain to the Galatians, this is what bowing to these Judaisers implies; it is a denial of the sufficiency of the work of Christ, and it is an undertaking to keep the whole law. Those who were truly saved would shake their head in disgust at such blasphemous thoughts and repent, while those who weren't truly saved would nod their head in agreement and keep on going.

Iffy verses, 1 Corinthians 15:2; Colossians 1:23

There are a couple of verses that guarantee salvation to us if certain conditions are fulfilled. So do these *ifs* make salvation a bit iffy? Are they verses that should cause doubt or give assurance? Before having a look at them, let's notice something that I think is quite important. Those who would use these verses to combat the doctrine of eternal security are actually not denying that once people are saved they are always saved, they are denying that people can be saved now. They are looking at salvation as a process which has begun but can stop somewhere along the way. If these verses are holding out salvation as a consequence of continuing right to the end then it means that no one has salvation on earth. I hope our journey thus far in the book has convinced you that this runs roughshod over far too many clear verses, conclusive passages and well established truths for us to begin to believe it so there must be some other way of understanding these verses that does not deny the possibility of one knowing now that he is saved.

We will take a look at Paul's words to the Corinthians in 1 Cor.15:1-8:

> Moreover, brethren, I declare unto you the gospel which I preached unto you, which also ye have received, and wherein ye stand; by which also ye are saved, if ye keep in memory what I preached unto you, unless ye have believed in vain.
> For I delivered unto you first of all that which I

[223] Ibid., paragraph 1068.

also received, how that Christ died for our sins according to the scriptures; and that He was buried, and that He rose again the third day according to the scriptures: and that He was seen of Cephas, then of the twelve: after that, He was seen of above five hundred brethren at once; of whom the greater part remain unto this present, but some are fallen asleep. After that, He was seen of James; then of all the apostles. And last of all He was seen of me also, as of one born out of due time.

Paul sets about to deal with a most serious doctrinal error threatening the assembly at Corinth: there were some who were denying or doubting the physical resurrection of the dead. Paul shows that the error is one that strikes right at the heart of the gospel and undermines its foundation, and so to combat the error he takes the Corinthians back to the gospel that he preached, the gospel by which they were being saved, if they held fast to the message he preached, unless they believed in vain.

There are three things that demand our attention here, first, Paul states the Corinthians are being saved; second, this present salvation seems to be contingent on them holding fast what Paul had preached; and third, Paul speaks about the possibility they have believed in vain.

The first issue need not detain us too much. The Bible speaks about salvation in a three-fold way: we *have been* saved:

> For by grace you have been saved through faith... (Eph.2:8, NKJV)

> Who has saved us and called us with a holy calling... (2 Tim.1:9, NKJV)

These are a couple of examples of salvation being viewed as something complete, and that is because it is to do with the penalty of sin. As regards the punishment we deserve for our sins against God, we have been saved, and we will never become any more saved than we were the moment we trusted the Lord Jesus to be our Saviour, *There is therefore now no condemnation to them which are in Christ Jesus* (Rom.8:1).

But the Bible also tells us we *shall be* saved:

> Much more then, being now justified by His blood, we shall be saved from wrath through Him. For if, when we were enemies, we were reconciled to God by the death of His Son, much more, being reconciled, we shall be saved by His life. (Rom.5:9, 10)

> And that, knowing the time, that now it is high time to awake out of sleep: for now is our salvation nearer than when we believed (Rom.13:11)

This has to do with the ultimate, complete salvation from the very presence of sin. This will take place at the coming of the Lord, and it is then that we will enter into the enjoyment of salvation in all its fulness.

And then there are verses (such as the one we are currently considering) that tell us we are being saved:

> For the message of the cross is foolishness to those who are perishing, but to us who are being saved it is the power of God. (1 Cor.1:18, NKJV)

This has to do with salvation from the power of sin. At the moment of conversion we were set free from the dominion of sin and Satan, but we are still in the realm where sin's influence and Satan's power are known, so the Lord by His power keeps us from Satan's evil clutches and sin's dark dominion, as is evident from John's words in 1 Jn.5:18:

> We know that whosoever is born of God sinneth not; but he that is begotten of God keepeth himself, and that wicked one toucheth him not.

The three aspects of salvation are seen together in the words of 1 Pet.1:3-5:

> Blessed be the God and Father of our Lord Jesus Christ, who according to His abundant mercy has begotten us again [past salvation] unto a living

hope through the resurrection of Jesus Christ from the dead, to an inheritance incorruptible and undefiled and that does not fade away, reserved in heaven for you, who are kept by the power of God through faith [present salvation] for salvation ready to be revealed in the last time [future salvation]. (NKJV)

So when Paul speaks here about the Corinthians being saved in the present it doesn't make their salvation provisional or probationary or anything like that, it is just a statement of the fact that they aren't home yet, but their arrival is guaranteed because, as Paul said elsewhere, and as we have previously noted, He who has begun a good work in you will complete it until the day of Jesus Christ.[224] It is like the sheep on the shoulders of the shepherd in Luke 15. The moment the shepherd lifts the sheep it is saved, but on the journey home it is being saved; no enemy can touch it, then when home is reached it is fully saved, not even in enemy territory any more.

But this ongoing salvation is conditional on something: the Corinthians have to hold fast the message that Paul preached. Paul is not saying that they were saved provided they lived a good enough life or anything of the sort; he is saying they were saved if they held fast to the truth of the gospel, the truth of the death and resurrection of Christ. In a book like this we are dipping into various texts, but we need to always take notice of context, and if we do we will see that the emphasis isn't on them holding fast, but the emphasis is on them holding fast *to the word Paul preached*. As we have intimated, there was aberrant doctrine being preached at Corinth and Paul is telling them that the only message that saves is the message he preached, and a true Christian will not abandon it for anything. A Christian is one who has received and rests upon (wherein ye stand) the death and resurrection of the Lord Jesus Christ, it is all his boast and his only plea. He may backslide, fall and fail; his heart may go hard and grow cold, but if you asked him what hope he had for acceptance with God his answer would only and ever be the death and resurrection of Christ.

---

[224] Phil.1:6, NKJV.

Although the problem threatening Corinth was different than that which threatened Galatia[225] there is a principle that applies to both cases; if professing Christians are faced with the ramifications of error regarding the person or work of Christ and they embrace it nonetheless then it shows they never had true saving faith. Those who were genuinely saved would hold fast to the apostolic gospel even in the face of false teaching.

So this is nothing other than what we have already looked at; the Bible teaches that there can be a false faith, a shallow faith that does not endure. However, one of the indispensable marks of one who has been born again is that he *believes,* and that he will believe the right things about the Lord Jesus. As we have said, and hopefully shown, the presence of the indwelling Holy Spirit and the activity of an interceding Great High Priest ensure that saving faith can never be lost.

This brings us to the third point, the point about them perhaps believing in vain. What does this mean? It may be the case that Paul is saying that if their faith doesn't endure then they have believed in vain:

> Holding fast to the apostle's doctrine would demonstrate the reality of faith...The other possibility that Paul visualises is "unless ye have believed in vain". There is no salvation here. A mere mental assent to the preaching is contemplated, an assent taken lightly and rashly to no purpose without plan or course. Such an effect is dangerously possible in gospel efforts which rely upon a mixture of the Spirit's power and techniques which appeal to the emotions.[226]

Many other respected commentators take this view, but I don't think that is what is taught here. It seems to me that the phrase unless ye have believed in vain would be redundant if that were the case. Paul would be saying, *You are saved if you hold to the message I preached unless you don't hold to it and your faith isn't genuine.* Here's what I think Paul is saying to these Corinthians:

[225] The Galatian error came from Judaism, the Corinthian error from Greek philosophy.
[226] John Heading, *First & Second Corinthians*, John Ritchie Ltd, 1995, p.224.

You are saved provided you hold to the message I preached, unless you have believed in something that is empty and powerless. Now I delivered the message to you as I got it, and it centred on a Christ who died for our sins and was buried, but He was raised from the dead and actually appeared. That is what I preached, that is what the other apostles preached (v.11), a physical resurrection, now if you are saying there is no physical resurrection then that implies Christ did not rise, and that implies your faith in Christ is useless, <u>you have believed in vain</u>, there is no Saviour for us; all hope is lost.

Paul is speaking about their faith being vain because of its object rather than its subject.

> First, he reminds them of that which he had preached among them as the gospel, that Christ died for our sins according to the Scriptures, and was raised again according to the Scriptures. This then was the means of their salvation, if they continued in it, unless they had believed in vain. Here at least was a very solid foundation for his argument: their salvation (unless all that they had believed was but a profitless fable) depended on the fact of the resurrection, and was bound up with it. But if the dead rose not, Christ was not risen, for He had died. The apostle begins therefore by establishing this fact through the most complete and positive testimonies, including his own testimony, since he had himself seen the Lord. Five hundred persons had seen Him at once, the greater part of whom were still alive to bear witness of it.[227]

> You will be saved by it, if you adhere to it, unless it shall turn out that it was vain to believe, and that the doctrine was false. That it was "not" false, he proceeds to demonstrate.[228]

> If Christ be not risen, the gospel message would be worthless or valueless, like a promissory note

[227] Darby, *Synopsis*, vol.4, pp.194,195.
[228] Albert Barnes, *Notes on the Bible*, e-Sword.

of no value.[229]

> As this denial of resurrection undermines the
> gospel, the apostle first reminds these believers
> of the gospel which he had preached, which they
> had received, wherein they had their standing
> in blessing before God, and by which they were
> saved. But he adds the words, "unless ye have
> believed in vain", for if there is no resurrection
> they had evidently believed in a myth. However,
> the apostle shows in a parenthetical remark that
> the reality of their faith would be proved by
> holding fast the word that he had announced to
> them in the glad tidings.[230]

So to summarise, Paul says they are being saved *if...unless...* The *if*
is to do with the content of their faith; is it in the right message?
They are being saved if they hold to the message of the death and
resurrection of Christ, there is no other message that can save.
The *unless* is to do with the reality of that message, if Christ has
not been raised then it doesn't matter if they are holding to the
message of His death and resurrection, they have believed in vain,
to no purpose, for no benefit. Paul then proceeds to show them
this was no empty message; the resurrection of Christ is a rock
solid reality; the risen Christ was witnessed beforehand by the
prophetic Scriptures and witnessed afterwards by a vast number
of eyewitnesses; it is impossible then that they had believed in
vain.

This passage doesn't pose any problem to the doctrine of eternal
security. There was false teaching abroad; the genuine would be
marked out by holding fast to the truth, just as John said:

> We [apostles] are of God: he that knoweth God
> heareth us; he that is not of God heareth not us.
> Hereby know we the spirit of truth, and the spirit
> of error. (1 Jn.4:6)

---

[229] Davies, *The Epistles to the Corinthians*, p.130.
[230] Hamilton Smith, *The First Epistle to the Corinthians*, available at http://www.stempublishing.com/authors/smith/CORINTH1.html.

Those who are genuinely born of God will hear and heed the apostolic witness. The Spirit of God indwelling His people guarantees that they will not be deceived by fundamental error[231] and that there will always be faithful testimony to the truth of the person and work of Christ.

The same is true of Col.1:23. Let's have a look at the context in which the verse is found:

> And you, that were sometime alienated and enemies in your mind by wicked works, yet now hath He reconciled in the body of His flesh through death, to present you holy and unblameable and unreproveable in his sight: if ye continue in the faith grounded and settled, and be not moved away from the hope of the gospel, which ye have heard, and which was preached to every creature which is under heaven; whereof I Paul am made a minister... (Col.1:21-23)

The details of the doctrinal error that was trying to make inroads into Colosse were different from the Corinthian problem, but the way of addressing the threat to eternal security is exactly the same.

Discerning what the error was is a bit like trying to gather the sense of a telephone conversation when you are only listening to one side of it. It seems that the error was one that involved robbing Christ of true deity and real humanity, kind of making Him a stepping stone between God and men (not touching either) rather than Him being a bridge (connected to both). Paul shows in the epistle in no uncertain fashion that the Lord Jesus is possessed of true deity and perfect humanity. He is not a stepping stone to God, but He is the one who has reconciled us to God; He has brought us all the way to Him because He is both God and man.

You can see that this was no petty squabble about some obscure detail of eschatology; this was a key salvation issue, and as we have said before, a true believer will not budge on it. A Christian will not seek to strip His Saviour of His essential and eternal Godhood

---

[231] Remember the Lord's words, in another context though relevant here, "insomuch that, if it were possible, they shall deceive the very elect" (Matt.24:24).

or rob Him of His real and holy manhood. For that reason Paul sees this error as a gust of wind that would separate the wheat from the chaff, those who were truly saved would continue in the faith.

It is important again to underscore what Paul is and is not saying here. He is not saying that you will be presented unblameable and unreproveable before God if you continue in obedience or in holiness. None of us has done that continually and completely (and anyone who thinks he has just has no idea of how holy God really is.) Nor is Paul saying that the condition is continuing in the apostles' doctrine; that is the condition for fellowship in the local assembly (Acts 2:42), but not the condition for a place in heaven. The apostles' doctrine (although in embryo in Acts 2) has been revealed and consists of all the truth of the New Testament relating to ecclesiology and eschatology as well as soteriology. There are many Christians who are not continuing in the apostles' doctrine and vast numbers of churches which are constitutionally unscriptural, but they are continuing in the faith. The faith is that body of doctrine that every Christian believes, and to deny any part of the faith is to show oneself not to be a Christian. This is the test Paul gives the Colossians. Look at what these false teachers are saying; if you can see that for what it is and embrace it then it proves you have never been saved.

Warning! The letter to the Hebrews
No section of the Bible has provided more grist to the mill of deniers of eternal security than the book of Hebrews. It contains some striking statements and strong warnings that have given more than a few believers some sleepless nights.

Some scholars and commentators have suggested that the letter is more of a sermon that has been transcribed. D. Edmond Hiebert comments, "The stately sentence with which it begins does not create the impression of opening an epistle but rather resembles the carefully worded introduction to an eloquent oration."[232] He then goes on to quote T. Rees, "Hebrews begins like an essay,

---

[232] D. Edmond Hiebert, *An Introduction to the New Testament, Volume Three*, Moody Press, 1981, p.68.

proceeds like a sermon, and ends like a letter." The author calls his message a "word of exhortation" (13:22), and so we are listening to the appeal of an earnest preacher. Like any wise preacher, he recognises that in any sizeable assembly there is a real possibility that there are some who are mere professors and not genuinely saved, thus the warnings sprinkled throughout his message. And it also explains why the first person plural "we" is used in some of the warnings; like any considerate preacher, he doesn't hammer his hearers continually with 'you'. He will press the truth home to them pointedly, but along the way he will include himself in the warning to show he wasn't putting himself above them and preaching down to them; it was a call for everyone, including himself, to examine themselves. As J. M. Davies points out:

> Five times the pronoun 'we' occurs in these verses, and 'us' once. It is to be understood in the same way as Peter used it when he and John were before the Sanhedrin... He charged them with having been the builders who had rejected the stone which is become the head of the corner. Neither is there salvation in any other, for there is none other name under heaven given among men whereby we must be saved.[233]

There is no question that Peter was already saved, so his use of the pronoun *'we'* doesn't indicate that he himself stood in need of salvation. It is simply a more winsome and less abrasive way of preaching.

We will look at the particular warning passages and look at the unique features of each, but to save myself being repetitive (and you becoming bored) I will point out some features that we need to bear in mind for all of these warning passages.

There is a unique people being considered in Hebrews

The letter to the Hebrews is a letter to...Hebrews. You may not be stunned by that insight, but it is important to bear in mind. The warnings of the letter are in regard to reverting back to a defunct system of sacrifices, going back to an old covenant that had served

---

[233] J. M. Davies, *Let us go on to Perfection*, Gospel Literature Service, 1978, p.13.

its purpose and reached its end. I'm not saying that there is no relevance to Gentiles but we have to make sure we filter any application to Gentiles through the specific Jewish context of this epistle.

To be specific then, when we read about sinning wilfully (10:26); we must not decontextualise and generalise that to mean any old sin; a very specific sin is in view. When we read about "brethren" (e.g. 3:12) we aren't to jump to the conclusion that he means Christian brethren and the people addressed are therefore saved; some occurrences of the designation refer to Hebrew brethren. Similarly with the expression "His people" in 10:30: we could easily assume this is a reference to all who are truly born again, but we must remember to read the epistle with our Hebrew spectacles on.[234] If we don the Hebrew spectacles we will see His people as the nation of Israel rather than the church, and many other knots in the epistle will come undone relatively easily as well.

There is a unique period being considered in Hebrews

The writing of this letter precedes the destruction of the temple in Jerusalem in AD 70 while sacrifices were still being offered (10:11). Had the temple been destroyed that would have been an overwhelming confirmation of the position the writer was advancing. Rather than the old covenant having vanished away the writer says it is ready to vanish away (8:13). It was written to people who had seen the miraculous signs that God gave to the nation of Israel (6:4-6). God always gave signs to confirm new revelation, and this letter was written (or this sermon was preached) to those who had been eyewitness of the powers of the age to come (6:5). They had been given the foretaste of the Messianic kingdom in the miracles that were performed, and it was to these people the warning is given. If you turn away from this there is nothing that will bring you back. It is very close to the unpardonable sin the Lord spoke about in His ministry:

> Then one was brought to Him who was demon-
> possessed, blind and mute; and He healed him,
> so that the blind and mute man both spoke and

---

[234] An expression the late Mr J. M. Flanigan was fond of using.

saw. And all the multitudes were amazed and said, "Could this be the Son of David?"

Now when the Pharisees heard it they said, "This fellow does not cast out demons except by Beelzebub, the ruler of the demons."

But Jesus knew their thoughts, and said to them: "Every kingdom divided against itself is brought to desolation, and every city or house divided against itself will not stand. If Satan casts out Satan, he is divided against himself. How then will his kingdom stand? And if I cast out demons by Beelzebub, by whom do your sons cast them out? Therefore they shall be your judges. But if I cast out demons by the Spirit of God, surely the kingdom of God has come upon you. Or how can one enter a strong man's house and plunder his goods, unless he first binds the strong man? And then he will plunder his house. He who is not with Me is against Me, and he who does not gather with Me scatters abroad.

"Therefore I say to you, every sin and blasphemy will be forgiven men, but the blasphemy against the Spirit will not be forgiven men. Anyone who speaks a word against the Son of Man, it will be forgiven him; but whoever speaks against the Holy Spirit, it will not be forgiven him, either in this age or in the age to come." (Matt.12:22-32, NKJV)

The people had seen the miraculous power of the Spirit of God in the ministry of the Lord Jesus Christ that proved His Messianic credentials, yet such was the stubbornness of their hearts, the darkness of their minds and the rebellion of their wills, they put such activity down to the activity of Satan. They saw the work of God and attributed it to the devil. The Lord says such an action cuts one off from the possibility of forgiveness, after all, what else can be shown? What more can be done? And if the Holy Spirit is resisted and blasphemed in such a fashion, such that He ceases to strive with and convict the sinner, then nothing else will ever bring him to repentance.

> As the Saviour had earlier taught another man,
> one of themselves, a Pharisee named Nicodemus,
> only the Spirit of God could effect new spiritual
> birth in a man, and if a man blasphemously
> rejected the ministry of the Spirit this was a
> rejection of the only means of salvation. There
> could be no forgiveness for that man. Obviously,
> in this particular context the unpardonable sin
> could only be committed in that day of miracles,
> but the principle must still obtain that rejection
> of the gracious ministry of the Holy Spirit is
> a rejection of the only means of salvation. It is
> impossible to bring a man to repentance who
> has so despised that divine Person who alone
> can produce a work of grace in the heart of the
> sinner.[235]

Thus this "unpardonable sin" seems, strictly speaking, to be
specific to this period when the miraculous ministry of the Lord
and His apostles was taking place.[236] The warnings in Hebrews
ought to be read with that context very much in mind as well.

Let's get into the specifics. We'll start with the first warning of the
epistle.

Hebrews 2:1-4

> Therefore we ought to give the more earnest heed
> to the things which we have heard, lest at any time
> we should let them slip. For if the word spoken
> by angels was stedfast, and every transgression
> and disobedience received a just recompence of
> reward; how shall we escape, if we neglect so
> great salvation; which at the first began to be
> spoken by the Lord, and was confirmed unto us

---

[235] J. M. Flanigan, *Behold Your King*, John Ritchie Ltd. 2002, p.74.
[236] The reference the Lord makes in Matt.12:32 to "the age to come" ought not to be understood as this sin won't be forgiven on earth or in eternity, as if some sins could be forgiven in eternity. No, the age to come is the future period of tribulation on earth when men will commit a similar kind of sin that seals their doom: not then attributing the work of God to the devil, but attributing the work of the devil to God (2 Thess.2:8-12).

> by them that heard Him; God also bearing them
> witness, both with signs and wonders, and with
> divers miracles, and gifts of the Holy Ghost,
> according to His own will?

The writer is sounding an alarm here and alerting his readers to the danger of drifting away from the things which they had heard. We need to observe that the AV rendering here doesn't really convey the image the writer is communicating. The warning is not that the things which we have heard may slip, but rather that *we* may drift.[237] The image is of the current carrying us away from salvation.

> Here the metaphor is that "of being swept along
> past the sure anchorage which is within reach"
> (Westcott), a vivid picture of peril for all.[238]

The question then is this: can the current carry away those that had salvation? It will not surprise you that I'm going to answer *No* to that question, but I'd better give you some justification for that.

This nautical imagery is used elsewhere in the epistle, in a section we have already considered, but we'd better have it before us again:

> And we desire that every one of you do shew the
> same diligence to the full assurance of hope unto
> the end: that ye be not slothful, but followers of
> them who through faith and patience inherit the
> promises.
> For when God made promise to Abraham,
> because He could swear by no greater, He sware
> by Himself, saying, Surely blessing I will bless
> thee, and multiplying I will multiply thee. And
> so, after he had patiently endured, he obtained
> the promise.
> For men verily swear by the greater: and an oath
> for confirmation is to them an end of all strife.
> Wherein God, willing more abundantly to shew
> unto the heirs of promise the immutability of

---

[237] See e.g. Darby's rendering, "lest in any way we should slip away", or NKJV "lest we drift away".
[238] A. T. Robertson, *Word Pictures in the New Testament*, e-Sword.

> His counsel, confirmed it by an oath: that by two immutable things, in which it was impossible for God to lie, we might have a strong consolation, who have fled for refuge to lay hold upon the hope set before us: which hope we have as an anchor of the soul, both sure and stedfast, and which entereth into that within the veil; whither the forerunner is for us entered, even Jesus, made an high priest for ever after the order of Melchisedec. (Heb.6:11-20)

This passage tells us that those who have salvation (see v.9) have their anchor grounded not in the shifting ground of their fluctuating emotions, or in the sinking sands of their own merit, but it is beyond the reach of any adversary, within the veil. No storms of temptation, waves of adversity, clouds of doubt, gales of fear or rocks of damnation can ever threaten our salvation. Nothing can ever intrude beyond that veil and dislodge that anchor. This ensures the security of the child of God, we can never drift away.

> In calm weather a boat can sit idly by the quayside in the harbour for hours without being properly tied up. But let bad weather come, and the boat can drift away and be lost, all because it was never actually moored.[239]

The challenge of 2:1-4 is to make sure they are anchored. When the sea is dead calm it is possible for a ship to remain close to the gospel harbour. It is when the waters get rough and the tempest strong that the test comes, because then it is only those who are actually anchored that will remain. So we have to let the challenge of Heb.2:1-4 reach our own hearts; have we taken the message of the gospel seriously? Have we humbly bowed to its claims? Have we honestly accepted its verdict on our guilt and helplessness? Have we truly trusted the glorious Saviour it presents?

J. N. Darby points out:

> [I]t is not of union with Christ of which the

[239] Gooding, *An Unshakeable Kingdom*, p.86.

apostle speaks here, responsibility is pressed; continual "ifs" and warnings flow from this. These warnings do not one whit touch the final perseverance of the saints, as the doctrine is called; though I would rather say, the perseverance of God, His faithfulness, for He it is who keeps us to the end.[240]

Let's move on now to the next warning.

Hebrews 3:7-19

> Wherefore (as the Holy Ghost saith, Today if ye will hear his voice, harden not your hearts, as in the provocation, in the day of temptation in the wilderness: when your fathers tempted Me, proved Me, and saw My works forty years.
>
> Wherefore I was grieved with that generation, and said, They do alway err in their heart; and they have not known My ways.
>
> So I sware in My wrath, They shall not enter into My rest.)
>
> Take heed, brethren, lest there be in any of you an evil heart of unbelief, in departing from the living God. But exhort one another daily, while it is called Today; lest any of you be hardened through the deceitfulness of sin.
>
> For we are made partakers of Christ, if we hold the beginning of our confidence stedfast unto the end; while it is said, Today if ye will hear His voice, harden not your hearts, as in the provocation.
>
> For some, when they had heard, did provoke: howbeit not all that came out of Egypt by Moses. But with whom was He grieved forty years? was it not with them that had sinned, whose carcases fell in the wilderness? And to whom sware He that they should not enter into his rest, but to them that believed not? So we see that they could not enter in because of unbelief.

[240] Darby, *Notes on the Epistle to the Hebrews*, pp.9,10.

This is the second of the warning passages in Hebrews, and it is one from which worrying conclusions may be drawn if we are not careful. For instance, we will be told that these people are addressed as brethren, implying they are saved, yet a warning is given about an evil heart of unbelief and the possibility of departing from the living God. The need for steadfastness to the end is enjoined on them, which could lead to the conclusion that their security was conditional and questionable. The example of the Israelites in the wilderness is used as a warning to them, and, we are told, there were those who were redeemed by blood but they never made it to the Promised Land, which shows (it is alleged) that it is possible to have known redemption but to never make it to heaven.

Well, a couple of these issues have already been addressed. The fact that the readers are addressed here as brethren is not proof positive that the writer is assuming they are saved. As we have pointed out, he is writing to his fellow Hebrews and it is as Hebrews he calls them brethren. This is similar to Peter's preaching:

> Men and brethren, let me freely speak unto you of the patriarch David... (Acts 2:29)

> And now, brethren, I wot that through ignorance ye did it... (Acts 3:17)

And Stephen's:

> And he said, "Men, brethren, and fathers, hearken..." (Acts 7:2)

And Paul's:

> Men and brethren, children of the stock of Abraham, and whosoever among you feareth God, to you is the word of this salvation sent. (Acts 13:26)

Needless to say, that on none of these occasions was the salvation of the hearers assumed or implied.[241] So the writer is making this appeal based on the experience of the Israelites in the wilderness

---

[241] Earlier in the chapter, when the writer wants to make clear he is speaking to the genuine, he will give an additional designation, "Wherefore, *holy* brethren, partakers of the heavenly calling..." (Heb.3:1, emphasis added).

that it is possible to be amongst God's people, to be exposed to immense privilege, to witness the miraculous, and yet not to exercise faith in the Word of God, believe His promise and enter into His provision. This ought to have been an arrow to the conscience of some who would have heard this letter. Sitting amongst the congregation were those who had been exposed to immense privilege; they had heard the message of the gospel, they had seen the confirming signs and wonders that God gave to validate that new revelation, and yet they had not a living, personal faith in the Word of God, and when the testing time comes they would go back.

There is a subtle but significant change in the quotation in Hebrews 3 from the source in Psalm 95. In Psalm 95 the Lord says He was grieved with them 40 years, but note the change here: it says that they "saw My works forty years." What is the significance?

> Forty years! Should there not have been, to these Hebrew readers, something ominously prophetic in these words? Forty years! Would not the thoughtful among them realise that it was now almost forty years since the commencement of the Lord's ministry? The shadows of AD 70 were now looming large. Forty years of unbelief had passed since Jesus had appeared among them with the glad tidings. Were the earlier forty years now being duplicated? The pending judgment of AD 70 would indeed be a righteous judgment on the nation. How solemn if among them there were those whose hearts were not right.[242]

The Lord in His ministry, and His apostles as they preached to the nation, performed signs and wonders to show that the message preached had divine approval and authority.[243] It was coming up on 40 years at the time of writing; still there were so many in the nation of Israel, a majority in fact, who had not believed. The writer is sounding the alarm for all to search their own hearts to see if they were amongst them, "Take heed..."

[242] J. M. Flanigan, *What the Bible Teaches, Hebrews*, p.69.
[243] This was required for those who had prior revelation that was being superseded. Because new revelation ceased with the apostles so too did the miraculous gifts.

He then introduces a phrase that initially may seem troublesome: "For we are made partakers of Christ, if we hold the beginning of our confidence stedfast unto the end" (v.14). We can sympathise with those who look at this phrase and take from it that becoming a partaker of Christ is dependent on holding fast unto the end, but that is not at all what is being taught here.[244] Let me give you the text again with the tenses more accurately expressed:

> For we *have become* partakers of Christ if we hold
> the beginning of our confidence steadfast to the
> end... (NKJV, emphasis added)

Notice the tense of the verb: it is a perfect tense, meaning that becoming a partaker of Christ is an event that has happened in the past with results continuing. The text cannot then be saying that holding fast makes one a partaker of Christ – that would be, *For we* **will become** *partakers of Christ...*, but it can only be saying that holding fast proves that you have already become a partaker of Christ. Becoming partakers of Christ cannot be dependent on us holding our confidence to the end, but rather it is the other way around, holding our confidence to the end is dependent on us having become partakers of Christ. This is in full agreement with all that we have previously dealt with regarding the intercessory work of Christ to maintain the believer's faith.

Some have tried to make the point from this passage that many people who came out of Egypt, having been redeemed by the blood of the lamb, perished under God's judgment in the wilderness, thus showing that it is possible to be saved and then lost. This is confused on a couple of counts. Firstly, the redemption from Egypt by the blood of the lamb was a literal deliverance from Egypt but only a pictorial deliverance from sin. No one was actually saved from his sins by the blood of the lamb being applied to the door, and thus, there is no reason to think that any who were saved from death on the passover night could not perish in the wilderness. But secondly, those who perished in the wilderness were not those who were sheltered by the blood of the

---

[244] Notice by the way, if the verse were saying that one becomes a partaker of Christ by holding fast to the end then it wouldn't teach that one could be saved and lost, it would be teaching that none are saved until they reach the end. Thus salvation could never be lost because it could never be found until one goes out to meet God.

lamb! Those who were sheltered were the firstborn in the home, not the adults in the home, but it was the generation of adults (with the exception of Joshua and Caleb) that were destroyed in the desert. It was indeed only those who had been sheltered by the blood of the lamb who ever entered Canaan. So once again, a passage that people have used to teach the falling away doctrine actually teaches the opposite.

We will now look at the stronghold of the falling away advocates.

Hebrews 6:1-8

> Therefore leaving the principles of the doctrine of Christ, let us go on unto perfection; not laying again the foundation of repentance from dead works, and of faith toward God, of the doctrine of baptisms, and of laying on of hands, and of resurrection of the dead, and of eternal judgment. And this will we do, if God permit.
> For it is impossible for those who were once enlightened, and have tasted of the heavenly gift, and were made partakers of the Holy Ghost, and have tasted the good word of God, and the powers of the world to come, if they shall fall away, to renew them again unto repentance; seeing they crucify to themselves the Son of God afresh, and put Him to an open shame.
> For the earth which drinketh in the rain that cometh oft upon it, and bringeth forth herbs meet for them by whom it is dressed, receiveth blessing from God: but that which beareth thorns and briers is rejected, and is nigh unto cursing; whose end is to be burned.

Hebrews 6 is a passage that has caused great concern to many believers, but I want us to see first of all, before coming to the details, that if this passage really did teach that it's possible to be saved and lost, it really proves far more than most adherents to that view actually want it to teach.

I will let Harry Ironside explain the difficulty:

Watch this carefully. See if I read it correctly. "For it is *quite* possible for those who were once enlightened, and have tasted of the heavenly gift, and were made partakers of the Holy Ghost, and have tasted the good word of God, and the powers of the world to come, if they shall fall away, to renew them again unto repentance; seeing they crucify to themselves the Son of God afresh, and put Him to an open shame." Is that what it says? You believe that a man can be once enlightened, made a partaker of the Holy Ghost, can taste the good word of God and the powers of the world to come, but fall away and then repent; don't you? That is what all the folk believe who do not believe in the eternal security of the believer. What are you going to do with your backslider? If backsliding and apostasy are the same, don't you see this passage is the worst possible passage in all the Bible for their favourite doctrine?

If those who hold that a man can be saved over and over again will ponder this passage I am sure they will see how fatally it knifes their theory. This is the way it reads: "For it is *impossible* for those who were once enlightened, and have tasted of the heavenly gift, and were made partakers of the Holy Ghost, and have tasted of the good word of God, and the powers of the world to come, if they shall fall away to renew them again unto repentance; seeing they crucify to themselves the Son of God afresh, and put Him to an open shame." If this passage teaches that a man once saved can be lost again, then it also teaches that if that man is lost again, he can never repent and be saved. In other words, if that passage teaches that a man once saved can be lost again, it teaches that if you have ever been saved and you are now lost, you have a through ticket for hell, and there is no turning back. You are checked right through.[245]

If anyone wants to use this passage to refute eternal security then he has to bite the bullet and accept that there is no way back for those who do indeed lose their salvation; it is impossible for anyone who "used to be a Christian" to become one again, but typically that is not what "falling away" advocates believe.

I want to point out another thing before we try to explain the verses, and this (I think) fairly conclusively explodes any possibility that the people described in vv.4-6 were actually saved. Look at what v.9 says:

> But, beloved, we are persuaded better things of you, and *things that accompany salvation*, though we thus speak. (Emphasis added.)

The writer is stating that, although he has given this warning, he does not really believe they were in such danger, why? *Because he was persuaded of their salvation!* What that shows us is that the people described in vv.4-6 are people who did not have salvation, not people that had it and lost it. The writer is saying it is possible to be so close but not actually possess salvation and turn away from it, but he doesn't think that is actually the case with his hearers, he believes they are possessors, not professors. He can see in them the things that accompany salvation, the marks of the genuine.[246]

Now that we have got that settled we can breathe a sigh of relief and go to the text knowing that it doesn't hold any threat for those who have salvation.

The chapter commences with an exhortation to go on to perfection and we have to ask what exactly the writer means. He has just spoken about how they are babies on the milk and should be full grown and on the meat. We need to make sure we don't incorporate Paul's teaching in 1 Corinthians 3 or Peter's teaching in 1 Peter 2 into this passage. In 1 Corinthians 3 Paul admonishes the Corinthian Christians for their immaturity in Christian growth.

---

[245] Ironside, *The Eternal Security of the Believer*, pp.33,34.
[246] J. M. Davies points out that the things that accompany salvation "are a manifestation of the three cardinal graces: faith, hope and love, referred to in their reverse order in vv.8-12." *Let us go on to Perfection*, p.40.

> And I, brethren, could not speak unto you as
> unto spiritual, but as unto carnal, even as unto
> babes in Christ. I have fed you with milk, and not
> with meat: for hitherto ye were not able to bear it,
> neither yet now are ye able. For ye are yet carnal:
> for whereas there is among you envying, and
> strife, and divisions, are ye not carnal, and walk
> as men? (1 Cor.3:1-3)

In terms of their moral development they were still at the baby
stage, acting like men of the world. That's not what is in view
here. In 1 Peter 2 Peter is encouraging his readers to have that
same appetite for the Word of God that newborn babies have for
milk.

> Wherefore laying aside all malice, and all
> guile, and hypocrisies, and envies, and all evil
> speakings, as newborn babes, desire the sincere
> milk of the word, that ye may grow thereby...
> (1 Pet.2:1,2)

But in Hebrews something entirely different is in view. The writer
here is talking about them as babies dispensationally. The age of
law was an age of infancy, full of object lessons. The most godly
saint under law was, dispensationally speaking, a baby. In this age
of grace we are brought to dispensational maturity. The shadows
have withdrawn, the types fulfilled, the tangible set aside; we have
reached reality. This is something Paul brings out in Galatians:

> But before faith came, we were kept under the law,
> shut up unto the faith which should afterwards
> be revealed.
> Wherefore the law was our schoolmaster to bring
> us unto Christ, that we might be justified by faith.
> But after that faith is come, we are no longer
> under a schoolmaster.
> For ye are all the children [sons] of God by faith
> in Christ Jesus.
> For as many of you as have been baptized into
> Christ have put on Christ. There is neither Jew
> nor Greek, there is neither bond nor free, there

> is neither male nor female: for ye are all one in
> Christ Jesus.
> And if ye be Christ's, then are ye Abraham's seed,
> and heirs according to the promise.
> Now I say, That the heir, as long as he is a child,
> differeth nothing from a servant, though he be
> lord of all; but is under tutors and governors until
> the time appointed of the father.
> Even so we, when we were children, were in
> bondage under the elements of the world: but
> when the fulness of the time was come, God sent
> forth His Son, made of a woman, made under the
> law, to redeem them that were under the law, that
> we might receive the adoption of sons.
> And because ye are sons, God hath sent forth the
> Spirit of His Son into your hearts, crying, Abba,
> Father.
> Wherefore thou art no more a servant, but a son;
> and if a son, then an heir of God through Christ.
> (Gal.3:23-4:7)

The point Paul is making here is that before the Christian faith came,[247] saints were under the law like children under a tutor, but then God sent His Son to redeem from the law and then sent His Spirit to indwell the believer, and this brings them out from the state of infancy into a position of sonship.

Carry that thought in your mind as you read about milk and meat, babes and those of full age, in Hebrews. So when he is exhorting them to go on to perfection, it is an exhortation to go on to Christian ground and not to stay with Judaism. This is confirmed by looking at how the thought of perfection is used in the epistle. A few examples will suffice.

> For the law made nothing perfect, but the
> bringing in of a better hope [did]; by the which
> we draw nigh unto God. (Heb.7:19)

> Which was a figure for the time then present, in

---

[247] The definite article is in the Greek text in Gal.3:23 giving the following sense: "But before *the* faith came..."

> which were offered both gifts and sacrifices, that could not make him that did the service perfect, as pertaining to the conscience... (Heb.9:9)

> For the law having a shadow of good things to come, and not the very image of the things, can never with those sacrifices which they offered year by year continually make the comers thereunto perfect. (Heb.10:1)

> For by one offering He hath perfected for ever them that are sanctified. (Heb.10:14)

The situation that pertained under law was not God's end in view. The law made nothing perfect or complete. It was an ongoing, never-ending, unsatisfying system. The gifts and sacrifices could not satisfy the throne of God or soothe the conscience of the sinner. By contrast, we are now in a dispensation of completion, fulfilment and divine satisfaction. A sacrifice has been offered that fully meets God's demands and our need; nothing more is required. The sinner needs nothing more than Christ at God's right hand.

C. H. Mackintosh says:

> Neither the Levitical priesthood nor the Levitical sacrifices could yield perfection. Insufficiency was stamped on the latter, infirmity on the former, imperfection on both. An imperfect man could not be a perfect priest; nor could an imperfect sacrifice give a perfect conscience.[248]

The writer then is appealing to his readers not to stick with a system that cannot meet their need, but to recognise God never intended it to be permanent; He had a goal in view, which has now arrived. They need to move on too. Staying with the doctrines laid out in vv.1,2 will not suffice; they need the completed sacrifice, the finished work, the exalted Christ on the other side of death.

Thus, the warnings issued here are not warnings to Christians, but are warnings to those who, in the full blaze of Christian revelation, choose to stick with Judaism.

---

[248] C. H. Mackintosh, *Notes on the Pentateuch*, Loizeaux Brothers, 1972, p.380.

I hope you can see then that both before and after the frightening warning are very clear indications that true Christians are not in view at all; the text will not allow a saved and lost doctrine to stand.

What this passage is telling us then is that there could have been those in the company who had been enlightened, their sinfulness had been exposed, and they saw the evidence that Jesus is the Messiah and the answer to their need, but this is not salvation. John tells us that the coming of Christ into the world has brought light to everyone (Jn.1:9). It is a serious thing to reject Christ in the light. The Lord prayed for forgiveness for those who knew not what they were doing (Lk.23:34), and Paul received mercy because he was doing what he was doing in ignorance (1Tim.1:13). Now these passages aren't saying that these people weren't culpable for their ignorance, or that their ignorance meant they deserved a chance at salvation. Rather it is saying that because of their ignorance there was still hope of them receiving mercy if and when the truth dawned upon them. Imagine if Saul of Tarsus knew that Jesus was the Son of God while he was persecuting the Christians: the revelation on the Damascus Road would have been no revelation; he would not have bowed his heart and yielded his will, because he already knew he was opposing the Son of God. So the issue is most solemn: the writer is saying to those who stood at the fork in the road, "Look, if you take the turn for Christ-rejecting Judaism, there's nothing I can say that will bring you back – you know you're rejecting the Son of God, there's nothing more I can tell you." Such a person cannot be renewed to repentance, i.e. they will never be brought back to that fork in the road, they have made their choice and chosen their course.

The following phrases look to present more of a difficulty, but a bit of digging will uncover the meaning. They had tasted of the heavenly gift, they were made partakers of the Holy Spirit, had tasted the good Word of God and the powers of the world to come. How can these things be said of non-Christians? It isn't as tricky as it might first appear. Let's start at the end and see that it is said that they tasted the powers of the world to come. What does that mean?

The powers of the world to come were those miracles that were wrought by Christ and His apostles to give a preview, a *taste*, of what the coming kingdom would be like. So what miracles were performed? Well, the sick were healed – Christ's kingdom will be one in which there is physical healing. The storms were calmed – Christ's kingdom will be one in which there are no natural disasters. The hungry were fed – Christ's kingdom will be one in which there will be no famines. The dead were raised – Christ's kingdom will be one in which death is the exception rather than the rule.[249] So what does it mean that they tasted these powers? It means they really, actually had experience of these things; they were eyewitnesses of them, and received something of the benefit of them.[250] Likewise then they had experience of the heavenly gift. This heavenly gift could be Christ Himself or the gospel, but it seems preferable to see it as a reference to the Holy Spirit. The word is used four times in the book of Acts and refers to the Holy Spirit on each occasion.[251] Remember that the message of this epistle was directed to those who heard the apostles and saw their miracles (2:3,4). So when the Spirit came at Pentecost the Jews certainly tasted of that gift, they heard the gospel in their very own dialect as the gift of tongues was given to the apostles – a sign of God's judgment upon them.[252] In that way then they were made partakers of the Holy Spirit, they partook of His ministry, and they heard the Word of God preached in His power. All that was a powerful vindication of who Jesus was, and a mighty validation of the message the apostles preached. However, it wasn't salvation. If one experienced that ministry of the Holy Spirit through the apostles, knew that Jesus is Lord and Christ, then rejected Christ, then there is no other means of reaching him; there will be no repentance,[253] he is crucifying the Son of God afresh, and there is no refuge.[254]

---

[249] See Isaiah 35 – these miracles marked the Lord out as being the coming King.

[250] That's the meaning of taste both here and in Heb.2:9. It is experiencing the flavour of the thing in question. Whether what is tasted is spat out or imbibed is another question.

[251] Acts 2:38; 8:20; 10:45; 11:17.

[252] See 1 Cor.14:21,22.

[253] David Gooding's point is worth quoting here: "He does not say that it is impossible for God to forgive them. God will forgive anyone who truly repents and believes. But these people will not repent; and there can be no forgiveness without repentance." *An Unshakeable Kingdom*, p.145.

[254] The cities of refuge were for manslayers not murderers. That may be in the background in this chapter.

There is one final passage from this epistle that needs to be considered:

Hebrews 10:26-31

> For if we sin wilfully after that we have received the knowledge of the truth, there remaineth no more sacrifice for sins, but a certain fearful looking for of judgment and fiery indignation, which shall devour the adversaries.
> He that despised Moses' law died without mercy under two or three witnesses: of how much sorer punishment, suppose ye, shall he be thought worthy, who hath trodden under foot the Son of God, and hath counted the blood of the covenant, wherewith he was sanctified, an unholy thing, and hath done despite unto the Spirit of grace?
> For we know him that hath said, Vengeance belongeth unto me, I will recompense, saith the Lord. And again, The Lord shall judge his people. It is a fearful thing to fall into the hands of the living God.

This passage on its own is quite intimidating, but before we face it we need to remember that this passage does not stand alone. It comes in a chapter that is full of unequivocal assurance to the believer that he can never be lost.[255] Nothing that we encounter here can be allowed to rob us of the assurance we received only a few verses earlier.

Also, if people are wanting to rip this verse from its context and wield it like a weapon to threaten Christians with eternal damnation they had better watch they don't kill themselves with it because this passage divorced from its setting leaves all of us in trouble. Look at how it commences: *For if we sin wilfully after that we have received the knowledge of the truth...* Let me ask a question to any Christian who has been saved more than a few days, *Have you ever sinned on purpose since you were saved?* Now be honest! As you think back on your Christian life can you honestly say that there

---

[255] See section on *The Finished Work of Christ*.

was never a time you sinned willingly? Never told a lie? Never passed on something you knew should have stopped with you? Never fed the flesh? etc. etc. I think if any Christian claims never to have sinned wilfully he has a massively inflated view of his own holiness and a massively deflated view of God's. The point I'm making is this, if we fail to see this verse set in its very specific setting then all of us are out of the family and off the reservation with no way back and nothing but the fire of God's judgment to look forward to. The fact of the matter is that every Christian has sinned by an act of his own will, and yet we know we are still regenerate, the Holy Spirit who indwells us has brought us under conviction and unto repentance, and we enjoyed restoration. When we look at the chapter as a whole and the verse in isolation we recognise that there is obviously something else going on.

The sin in question is a very specific sin, akin to what we were looking at in the previous Hebrews passages.

> This text has been the occasion of great distress to some gracious souls; they have been ready to conclude that every wilful sin, after conviction and against knowledge, is the unpardonable sin: but this has been their infirmity and error. The sin here mentioned is a total and final apostasy, when men with a full and fixed will and resolution despise and reject Christ, the only Saviour, despise and resist the Spirit, the only sanctifier, and despise and renounce the gospel, the only way of salvation, and the words of eternal life; and all this after they have known, owned, and professed, the Christian religion, and continue to do so obstinately and maliciously.[256]

It is to turn back to the sacrificial system of Judaism and reject the sufficiency and finality of the sacrifice of Christ. "The wilful sin is the abandonment of Christianity for Judaism,"[257] again, "The wilful sin in this passage is the definite rejection of His atoning sacrifice."[258]

---

[256] Matthew Henry, *Commentary on the Whole Bible*, vol.6, p.753.
[257] M. R. Vincent, *Vincent's Word Studies*, on e-Sword.
[258] H. A. Ironside, *Hebrews*, Loizeaux, 1997, p.94.

> The awful sin here referred to is not moral sin. It is neither the trespass which overtakes a man, as in Gal.6:1, nor the grievous sin which required the ultimate discipline as in 1 Cor.5:9-13. It is the sin of apostasy. It is the crime of rejecting revealed truth in a wilful, coldly-intelligent manner, and this though there may have been an earlier mental assent to it, and a certain sympathy with it, even a profession of adherence to it.[259]

Here is a man who has been convinced by the work of the Holy Spirit that Jesus is the Christ, the Son of God, but knowing that to be true he refuses to abandon the Levitical sacrifice. The passage is telling us that he is turning to, and sticking with, a system that offers him no hope because those sacrifices "can never take away sins" (v.11). "Where could a sacrifice for sins be found for the apostate? God had rejected the sacrifices of Judaism. The apostate had rejected the sacrifice of Christ."[260] This is not a temporary slip in a moment of weakness; the tense of the verb gives this force, "For if we go on sinning deliberately after receiving the knowledge of the truth..." (ESV)

To say that someone indwelt by the Holy Spirit could become an adversary, tread underfoot the Son of God, count His blood unholy, insult the Spirit of grace, and do it continually, is to deny all that we have proven about the unfinished work of Christ for the believer and the ministry of the Holy Spirit in the believer. He may wobble, but the Spirit of God would not permit him to continue in such a course.

Furthermore, to sin wilfully means that judgment awaits. However, the Lord Jesus said in Jn.5:24:

> Verily, verily, I say to you, He that heareth My word, and believeth on Him that sent Me, hath everlasting life, and shall not come into condemnation; but is passed from death to life.

The word translated *condemnation* in Jn.5:24 is the same word

---

[259] Flanigan, *Hebrews*, p.216.
[260] Ibid. p.217.

translated *judgment* in Heb.10:27. Now in Jn.5:24 the Lord Jesus gives a promise and states a fact. The promise is that the believer shall not come into judgment and the fact is that the believer has already passed from death to life. Only by admitting to a contradiction in the Bible can we have Heb.10:27 describing someone who was a genuine Christian.

At this point the observant antagonist will be saying I have evaded the key clause; v.29 speaks about the apostate counting the blood of the covenant *wherewith he was sanctified* an unholy thing. How can the implication be avoided that the person in question was indeed saved once upon a time?

We can explore a few options, but before doing so, let us admit that an option must be found, because v.14 of this very chapter says that through the offering of Christ He has perfected forever them that are sanctified; so, unless we are going to have the writer flatly contradicting what he has already said, we cannot have v.29 saying that a Christian is not perfected forever.

Let's look at some alternative views. Firstly, there is the possibility that the writer is taking the apostate up on his profession and is saying in effect, *Look, you are claiming to have been sanctified by the blood of Christ but you are counting it as something common and worthless.* In that regard it would be a bit like John's method in his writings; he takes people at their word but exposes that they are false. For example:

> We know that we have passed from death to life, because we love the brethren. He that loveth not his brother abideth in death.
> Whoever hateth his brother is a murderer: and ye know that no murderer hath eternal life abiding in him. (1 Jn.3:14,15)

John is saying if a man doesn't love his brother then he isn't actually a brother. The point is the person is claiming to be in the family, claiming that Christians are his brethren, but if there is no love for those he calls his brethren then he obviously is not in the family, he does not have eternal life. So, in order to understand John's statement we have to put quotes round the word 'brother', or insert the words, 'so called' before it, and there can be then no objection to the same thing being done in Hebrews 10: the blood wherewith he was "sanctified"...

Secondly, there could be a sense in which this apostate was sanctified, or set apart, in a practical way. He was amongst the Christians, in a position of privilege and light. Paul speaks about that kind of thing in 1 Cor.7:14:

> For the unbelieving husband is sanctified by the wife, and the unbelieving wife is sanctified by the husband: else were your children unclean; but now are they holy.

The unbeliever who lives in the same home as a believer is in a place of special favour. It is suggested that this is what is going on here.

> The person envisioned here is one who professed faith in Christ and came, as it were, under the shadow of the cross and was outwardly identified with the Christian community. He was associated in the public eye with those set apart by Christ. He was identified with "the blood of the covenant." He professed to be sanctified. But it was not real. He has turned his back on all that now. One step more and he would have truly been covered by the blood and saved forevermore, but now he has wilfully refused God's salvation.[261]

Some might object and say that 1 Corinthians 7 specifically says the unbelieving spouse is sanctified by the believing spouse, but here the person is said to be sanctified by the blood of the covenant. Surely that cannot be a relative sanctification, can it? Well, perhaps it can. In Heb.13:12 we read:

> Wherefore Jesus also, that He might sanctify the people with His own blood, suffered without the gate.

The blood of the Lord Jesus was intended to separate people from

---

[261] John Phillips, *Exploring Hebrews*, Kregel Publications, 1998, p.134.

defunct, ritualistic Judaism. The apostate was one who had taken his stand with the Christians "outside the camp" of Judaism. He had professed that the sacrifice of Christ brought to an end all the sacrifices of the Levitical system. In that sense he had been set apart / sanctified, but now was going back. In going back he was saying in effect, *Actually, the blood of Christ, that blood which He said inaugurated the new covenant, really is worthless. Nothing has changed. We need to continue with the blood of bulls and goats.* And he goes back inside the camp, and does not actually depend on the value of the blood of Christ and enter into the blessings of the new covenant.[262]

A third option is that the nation of Israel was set apart in a particular way by the blood of the covenant. Rom.9:4 states that the covenants are to that nation. They are set apart from all the nations in a very special position of privilege. Jer.31:31 prophesied a new covenant made with the house of Israel and the house of Judah, and in that generation following the death and resurrection of Christ, recorded in Acts, we see the Jews in a place of favour; the gospel was "to the Jew first" (Rom.1:16), but by rejecting Christ and His sacrifice, the apostate severs himself from the possibility of entering into the blessings of that covenant.

A fourth option is that the *he* in v.29 actually refers to Christ Himself. It would be saying that the blood of the covenant sets Christ apart as High Priest and Mediator. There are expositors of some worth and expositions of some weight that come down in support of this view. Let me cite a few here:

After giving the option of a relative sanctification, John Gill writes:

> [O]r rather the Son of God Himself is meant, who was sanctified, set apart, hallowed, and consecrated, as Aaron and his sons were sanctified by the sacrifices of slain beasts, to minister in the priest's office: so Christ, when He had offered Himself, and shed His precious blood, by which the covenant of grace was ratified, by the same

---

[262] Thus, being sanctified by the blood of Christ would be different from being sanctified by the offering of the body of Christ (v.10). The sanctification by the offering of the body involves actual vital union with Christ.

blood He was brought again from the dead, and declared to be the Son of God with power; and being set down at God's right hand, He ever lives to make intercession, which is the other part of His priestly office He is sanctified by His own blood to accomplish.[263]

Matthew Henry says this about the blood of the covenant:

[T]hat is, the blood of Christ, with which the covenant was purchased and sealed, and wherewith Christ Himself was consecrated.[264]

John Owen states the possibility that the verse is referring to that practical, relative sanctification mentioned above (option two), but then says:

But the design of the apostle in the context leads plainly to another application of these words. It is Christ Himself that is spoken of, who was sanctified and dedicated unto God to be an eternal high priest, by the blood of the covenant which He offered unto God, as I have showed before...That precious blood of Christ, wherein or whereby He was sanctified, and dedicated unto God as the eternal high priest of the church, this they esteemed "an unholy thing;" that is, such as would have no such effect as to consecrate Him unto God and His office.[265]

William Lincoln comments:

By the cross, Jesus was set apart (Jn.17:19), taking a new place up there, from which He calls a people into association with Himself.[266]

Admittedly, this is not the most natural reading of the text, but there are a couple of things that can be said in its favour, the first of which is that the nearest antecedent is the Son of God. Certainly

[263] *John Gill's Exposition of the Entire Bible*, e-Sword.
[264] Henry, *Commentary on the Whole Bible*, Vol.6, p.753.
[265] John Owen, *An Exposition of the Epistle to the Hebrews*, Vol.6, pp.545,546.
[266] William Lincoln, *Note of Lectures on the Epistle to the Hebrews*, http://www.plymouthbrethren.org/article/4215.

this is not conclusive, but there is more. In the ceremony in which Aaron and his sons were set apart from the people as priests, blood was sprinkled upon them, and it was by means of that blood they were sanctified:

> And thou shalt take of the blood that is upon the altar, and of the anointing oil, and sprinkle it upon Aaron, and upon his garments, and upon his sons, and upon the garments of his sons with him: and he shall be hallowed, and his garments, and his sons, and his sons' garments with him. (Ex.29:21)

In the Greek Old Testament (the Septuagint), which is used so much in Hebrews, the word translated *hallowed* in this verse is the very same word translated *sanctified* in Heb.10:29. Thus these priests were sanctified by blood. Could the same thing be true of Christ? Look at Heb.9:11-15:

> But Christ being come an high priest of good things to come, by a greater and more perfect tabernacle, not made with hands, that is to say, not of this building; neither by the blood of goats and calves, but **by His own blood** He entered in once into the holy place, having obtained eternal redemption [for us].
> For if the blood of bulls and of goats, and the ashes of an heifer sprinkling the unclean, sanctifieth to the purifying of the flesh: how much more shall the blood of Christ, who through the eternal Spirit offered Himself without spot to God, purge your conscience from dead works to serve the living God?
> **And for this cause** He is the mediator of the new testament, that by means of death, for the redemption of the transgressions that were under the first testament, they which are called might receive the promise of eternal inheritance. (Emphases added.)

Do you see how the writer speaks about Christ entering into the holy place by His own blood? Again, reference is made to His blood and offering, then we read, "for this cause He is the mediator of the new testament..." The teaching is that Christ was set apart by the blood He shed to be the Great High Priest and the Mediator, and it could be argued that this is what is in view in 10:29.

One more Scripture that may be brought in to support this view is Heb.13:20:

> Now the God of peace, that brought again from the dead our Lord Jesus, that great shepherd of the sheep, through the blood of the everlasting covenant,

The Lord Jesus was raised from the dead in virtue of the blood He shed. It was by His resurrection that He was "separated from sinners."[267] He is in glory and by His endless life He is able to be to us all that we need (see Heb.7:23-28). Thus, it is said, it was by the blood of the covenant He was set apart for us.

So there are four options, each one with quite a bit going for it, which means we are not forced by Heb.10:29 to believe something the very chapter forbids us to believe: that a true Christian can ever be lost.

The not so great escape, 2 Peter 2:20-22

> For if after they have escaped the pollutions of the world through the knowledge of the Lord and Saviour Jesus Christ, they are again entangled therein, and overcome, the latter end is worse with them than the beginning. For it had been better for them not to have known the way of righteousness, than, after they have known it, to turn from the holy commandment delivered unto them.
> But it is happened unto them according to the true proverb, The dog is turned to his own vomit again; and the sow that was washed to her wallowing in the mire.

---

[267] Heb.7:26, as in ASV, ESV, JND.

In Peter's second epistle he is dealing with very different issues than he was in his first. In the first letter the attack is coming from the outside, the saints are being persecuted. In the second letter the danger is coming from the inside; there were false teachers seeking to introduce error amongst God's people. In the first chapter he emphasises the need for godly living (vv.1-11), and the supreme authority of the Word of God (vv.12-21). These were the targets at which these false teachers were taking aim. They wanted to corrupt the Lord's people (as per chapter 2) and they wanted to undermine their faith in the Word of God (as per chapter 3).

The issue is that it is said of these false teachers that they previously escaped the pollutions of the world through the knowledge of the Lord and Saviour Jesus Christ. Earlier in the chapter it says these people have been bought by the Lord (v.1). Are these not indications that they were saved? There is no need to conclude that, and there are indications in the passage that this cannot be the case. As regards the statement that the Lord bought them, this is a reference to the work of Christ on the cross, and it casts the mind back to Peter's words in 1 Pet.1:18,19:

> Forasmuch as ye know that ye were not redeemed
> with corruptible things, as silver and gold, from
> your vain conversation received by tradition
> from your fathers; but with the precious blood of
> Christ, as of a lamb without blemish and without
> spot...

In this passage Peter speaks about Christians having been redeemed, but in 2 Pet.2:1 he doesn't say that the false teachers had been redeemed, he says they were bought. The difference is significant. The Lord told a parable about a man who bought a field in order to get the treasure in that field (Matt 13:44). In virtue of the infinite value of Christ's precious blood He has bought the world, all men are His by purchase, but only those who have trusted Christ are His by redemption.

> 1 Jn.2:2 asserts that Christ's death provided a
> propitiation for the sins of the whole world. His
> atoning work rendered all men saveable, but His
> redemptive work is effective only in those who

exercise a living faith in the Redeemer.[268]

But what about them escaping the pollutions of the world through the knowledge of the Lord and Saviour Jesus Christ? Did you notice that Peter doesn't say they escaped through the knowledge of *their* Lord and Saviour? Three times in this letter when Peter speaks about Christ as Saviour he uses a possessive pronoun,[269] but here he doesn't. It is a pointer to the fact that these men had no personal relationship or living link with the Lord.

Furthermore, it should be of no surprise that these people had escaped the pollutions of the world and that this had something to do with knowledge of Jesus as Lord and Saviour, because, after all, these people were professing Christians. They didn't start out as apostates, they started out as making a profession of faith in Christ and their lives were, for a time and to a degree, changed. If they had started off repudiating Christ and living a debauched life then they never would have had any place among the Christians and never would have got a hearing from them.

> Who can deny that while Judas walked with Jesus and the other eleven disciples he largely escaped the pollutions of the world? But he was never saved.[270]

These were people who were not genuinely born again, and so they could not sustain that outward change because there was no inward reality. This led to them overthrowing Biblical standards of morality.[271]

Peter says, in language so reminiscent of his Lord that he surely intends us to make the connection, that their latter end is worse than the first. The Lord Jesus had spoken about an unclean spirit going out of a man, and the "house"[272] is swept and adorned, but unoccupied. He then takes seven spirits worse than himself and the last state of the man is worse than the first (Mt.12:43-45). This

---

[268] D. Edmond Hiebert, *Second Peter and Jude*, Universal Publications, 1989, p.90.

[269] 1:1,11; 3:18.

[270] Kendall, *Once Saved, Always Saved*, Loc. 2248.

[271] How relevant this is today with so called evangelicals seeking to justify and sanitise homosexuality. There are organised projects to introduce "gay-affirming" theology into churches. As the pressure from a godless society increases, many professing Christians will capitulate and sign up and buy in to this movement.

[272] i.e. the man, the place where the unclean spirit had dwelt.

is doubtless the state of the people Peter is describing. There had been an eviction of evil from the life, but the Spirit of God had never taken up His abode within, they had never received eternal life and so there was no power to keep the evil out. Thus Peter describes them as dogs returning to their vomit and pigs going back to the mire. The dog had rejected something from its system, but then it goes back to it. The pig had been washed, but it was still a pig and only had the nature of a pig, and so it is inevitable it will go back to the mud. Believers are never pictured as dogs or pigs; these are unregenerate people in view here.

Is that a threat or a promise? Revelation 3:5

> He that overcometh, the same shall be clothed in white raiment; and I will not blot out his name out of the book of life, but I will confess his name before My Father, and before His angels.

This passage is addressed to the assembly in Sardis. This is an assembly that was marked by cold formality and dead routine. The Lord said to them, "I know thy works, that thou hast a name that thou livest, and art dead" (v.1). The majority in the company were drifting like deadwood, and the Lord is calling them to reality and to repentance.

The Lord Jesus then gives a promise to those who overcome: He will not blot their names out of the book of life. We will get into the meaning of this presently, but let us see first of all that these words are a promise not a threat. There is a formal logical fallacy known as affirming the consequent. Here's an example:

- If it's Christmas then it's December
- It's not Christmas
- Therefore it's not December

You can see the problem, and let's see how it applies to this text.

- If you overcome then your name won't be blotted out of the book of life
- You didn't overcome

- Therefore your name will be blotted out of the book of life

The argument isn't valid. What this means is that this text cannot be used to say that anyone will have his name blotted out of the book of life.

Someone will say, *OK, so the text isn't definitively stating that if you don't overcome you will have your name blotted out, but is it not fair enough to infer that?* I don't think so. "Scripture is perfectly clear on the eternal security of a New Testament believer so that there is no possibility of a name being blotted out of the register of heaven. Christ is not threatening the removal of a name but is encouraging the overcomer."[273]

> Absolute security is seen in the expression "I will not blot out his name out of the book of life". This does not mean that believers can be blotted out, rather the secure consolation that this can never be.[274]

The next bit we need to chew on is this, *Who are these overcomers, because even if this is just a promise and not a threat, certainly the promise can only be claimed by overcomers.* Are these overcomers super spiritual saints?

To find the answer to this question we need to go to John's first epistle.

> Whosoever believeth that Jesus is the Christ is born of God: and every one that loveth Him that begat loveth him also that is begotten of Him.
> By this we know that we love the children of God, when we love God, and keep His commandments. For this is the love of God, that we keep His commandments: and His commandments are not grievous.
> For whatsoever is born of God overcometh the world: and this is the victory that overcometh the world, even our faith. Who is he that overcometh

---

273 J. Allen, *What the Bible Teaches, Revelation*, John Ritchie Ltd. 1997, p.112.
274 S. W. Jennings, *Alpha and Omega*, Ambassador, 1996, p.131.

the world, but he that believeth that Jesus is the
Son of God? (1 Jn. 5:1-5)

John is clear that every believer is an overcomer. Christians
believe that Jesus is the Son of God and thus recognise that living
for this world is an utter waste. If Jesus were not the Son of God
we would be fools to sacrifice anything for Him, but if He is the
Son of God then we would be fools not to sacrifice everything for
Him. In John's first epistle he presents the world with an alluring
face (2:15-17), and he presents it with an aggressive face (3:13).
The Christian hasn't been taken in by its propaganda or put off
by its intimidation. It is this faith that He is the Son of God that
overcomes the world.

Furthermore, when we look at what is promised to the overcomer
in Revelation it is clear that these promises apply to every saved
soul, so the overcomer cannot be a separate class of Christian.

> He that hath an ear, let him hear what the Spirit
> saith unto the churches; To him that overcometh
> will I give to eat of the tree of life, which is in the
> midst of the paradise of God. (2:7)

> He that hath an ear, let him hear what the Spirit
> saith unto the churches; He that overcometh shall
> not be hurt of the second death. (2:11)

> He that hath an ear, let him hear what the Spirit
> saith unto the churches; To him that overcometh
> will I give to eat of the hidden manna, and will
> give him a white stone, and in the stone a new
> name written, which no man knoweth saving he
> that receiveth it. (2:17)

> And he that overcometh, and keepeth My works
> unto the end, to him will I give power over the
> nations... (2:26)

> He that overcometh, the same shall be clothed in
> white raiment; and I will not blot out his name
> out of the book of life, but I will confess his name
> before My Father, and before His angels. (3:5)

> Him that overcometh will I make a pillar in the temple of My God, and he shall go no more out: and I will write upon him the name of My God, and the name of the city of My God, which is new Jerusalem, which cometh down out of heaven from My God: and I will write upon him My new name. (3:12)

> To him that overcometh will I grant to sit with Me in My throne, even as I also overcame, and am set down with My Father in His throne. (3:21)

> He that overcometh shall inherit all things; and I will be his God, and he shall be My son. (21:7)

We won't go into all of these references, but it is clear that there is no such thing as a Christian who will not have access to the tree of life or who will be hurt of the second death. In Rev.21:8 we find that the alternative to being an overcomer is to be in the lake of fire. This shows that the title *overcomer* is one which embraces every Christian, because every Christian has overcome the world to some degree or another.[275]

To conclude then, this passage is a glorious promise to the genuine Christian that his name will never be erased from heaven's register and he can never be lost. Once again, a passage that has been used to say a believer can be lost actually shows the very opposite.

Final public warning! Revelation 22:18, 19

> For I testify unto every man that heareth the words of the prophecy of this book, If any man shall add unto these things, God shall add unto him the plagues that are written in this book: and if any man shall take away from the words of the book of this prophecy, God shall take away his part out of the book of life, and out of the holy city, and from the things which are written in this book.

The final stroke of the pen is about to be made, the volume of holy

---

[275] We can see that the degree to which a believer practically overcomes will determine the degree to which they enjoy and enter into the blessings promised to the overcomer.

writ is about to close, and we have this parting shot. We can be quite secure in the knowledge that we are not going to encounter anything in the last page of the Bible that is going to overthrow everything its previous pages have taught about the eternal security of the believer.

We need to take notice of a change that ought to be made in v.19. There is no manuscript support for the reading of the Textus Receptus, *the book of life*. The evidence is overwhelmingly clear that *tree of life* is what John wrote.[276] Why is this important? For this reason, having one's name in the book of life is a matter of history, if one is saved then his name is in that book, and so if it said that your part was taken from the book of life it would certainly lend more support to the idea that your name had been in it and had been removed. But access to the tree of life and the holy city is something future.

So, does the warning of someone having his part taken away from the tree of life and from the holy city not imply that this person had a part, i.e. that the person was saved? No, it is stating that what might have been theirs now will never be. It is a bit like the parable the Lord told about the great supper in Lk.14:16-24. The people had been invited and were called. We could say that they had part in that supper; they were wanted and welcome there, but they refused, and their part was taken away and others enjoyed what could have been theirs. The very same thing is in view here. The message of the book of Revelation goes out, people are warned of the terrible judgments ahead, and told of the eternal glory that could be theirs, but if they will not bow to God's Word and accept the message then they will miss the glory and get the judgment.[277]

---

[276] "The Textus Receptus, on which the KJV rests, reads "the book" of life instead of "the tree" of life. When the Dutch humanist Desiderius Erasmus translated the NT he had access to no Greek mss for the last six verses of Revelation. So he translated the Latin Vulgate back into Greek at this point. As a result he created seventeen textual variants which were not in any Greek mss. The most notorious of these is this reading. It is thus decidedly inauthentic, while "the tree" of life, found in the best and virtually all Greek mss, is clearly authentic. The confusion was most likely due to an intra-Latin switch: The form of the word for "tree" in Latin in this passage is *ligno*; the word for "book" is *libro*. The two-letter difference accounts for an accidental alteration in some Latin mss; that "book of life" as well as "tree of life" is a common expression in the Apocalypse probably accounts for why this was not noticed by Erasmus or the KJV translators." Footnote from NET Bible, https://bible.org/netbible/.

[277] It is interesting to notice that Eve both added to and took from the Word of God when she was confronted with the serpent (Gen.3:2, 3), and it resulted in her exclusion from the garden and the way barred to the tree of life.

What about...?

We have gone through the passages that have been used to teach that our security is conditional, but there are one or two loose ends to tie up. Very often when the subject of eternal security is discussed people will bring up incidents of friends or relatives who had professed salvation and seemed to give evidence of reality, but are now unbelievers. How do we respond to that? I have a couple of responses, and the first may sound a bit curt, but it is this: it is my responsibility to interpret Scripture not circumstances. As another said, you can't exegete experiences. All that goes on in the human psyche is far too complicated for me to try to pick apart, but what I do know is what the Bible says, so if someone is not a believer then, on the authority of the Word of God, I can say they never were truly regenerate. I can't read the heart, but one who can read the heart has told us that a true believer continues to believe. If someone objects and says that so and so really was a believer I will have to say, "Let God be true, but every man a liar" (Rom.3:4).

My second response is to say that while we should be sad that this happens, we should not be surprised. The Bible gives us many examples of those who had an inadequate understanding of the issues and consequently a false faith. We need to make sure we don't dilute the gospel, cloud the issues, and coerce professions of faith. Remember, there is no Scriptural example of anyone leading another in a prayer of commitment (or whatever other label you stick on it).

Old Testament examples such as Saul and Solomon seem to lend support to the view that true believers can become unbelievers. These two examples are a bit tenuous because I wouldn't be convinced that the evidence shows Saul ever was truly the Lord's, but it certainly seems Solomon was, though Saul didn't seem to descend to the depths Solomon did. However, what we can say is this, we have made our case for eternal security based on passages that teach on the subject, not on narratives. We draw our doctrine from these didactic passages and use those to understand passages of narrative, we do not do it the other way around. So what we can say is that if Saul and Solomon were ever justified, then the nature of justification necessitates their eternal security.

They didn't have the Holy Spirit permanently indwelling them as believers do today, and thus it could be the case that there was the potential for doctrinal sin that would not be possible for a believer in this age.

We are in the realm of speculation when we go into the fate of these people, and there is no need for us to go there, because in the New Testament we have clear teaching on the matter.

Conclusion

A man-made religion would never have included eternal security amongst its doctrines. It would be utter foolishness. "You have to keep people a bit uneasy or they'll stop attending, working, contributing!" God has a much better way of marshalling a band of willing workers and recruiting an army of devoted soldiers. This is illustrated by the following incident. A friend of mine was doing some door to door evangelism with another believer, and they met a man who was caught up in the Watchtower cult. The man said to them, "Oh, are you two born again?"

"Yes!" came the glad reply.

"Saved, no matter what, eh?" he asked.

"Yes, thank God."

"Well, then, why do you bother doing this? I have to do it, but you're saying you don't, you're saved anyway!"

The brother who was with my friend grabbed the collar of his shirt and said to the Russellite, "Who washed my shirt?"

The man was a bit puzzled and hesitantly said, "Your wife?"

"Aye, why do you think she did that? I'll tell you, she did it because she loves me."

It's a homely illustration but it makes a great point. She wasn't doing those jobs out of fear, to ensure her place in the home or to earn his acceptance. She was doing them out of love, (at least that's what her husband believed!) The believer who knows he is eternally secure has the best of motives for serving the Lord: not fear of rejection, not the earning of credit, but the glory of God and the good of others.

The doctrine of eternal security thus gets things in their proper perspective, and it also puts everyone in their proper place. It shows us that we get none of the credit for our salvation. We will not land in heaven and congratulate ourselves for making it. All the glory goes to the blessed Trinity: we have been rescued by the rich grace of God, redeemed by the precious blood of Christ, and regenerated by the mighty power of the Spirit. This allows us to rest securely in God and compels us to work sacrificially for God. May our lives show our gratitude to such a wonderful Saviour for such a wonderful salvation.

Blessed assurance – Jesus is mine!
Oh, what a foretaste of glory divine!
Heir of salvation, purchase of God;
Born of His Spirit, washed in His blood.

Perfect submission, all is at rest,
I in my Saviour am happy and blest;
Watching and waiting, looking above,
Filled with His goodness, lost in His love.

This is my story, this is my song,
Praising my Saviour all the day long.

(Fanny J Crosby)

How do I deal with someone who says he was a Christian?

In our efforts to reach people with the gospel it is inevitable that we will come across some who will tell us that they used to be a Christian, or that they were saved. We have to ask what the best strategy is for dealing with such people.

I think there are two responses that we would be best avoiding. The first is to say, *If you were truly saved then you still are.* The reason this is not wise or helpful is because all it is likely to do is to give the person vain comfort and false assurance. The fact is, if this person made a profession years ago and it has made no lasting difference in his life then he probably isn't saved. Let us not assume that he had a proper understanding of sin, repentance, faith, Christ and the cross, and has just "backslidden" and is in need of assurance.

The second approach we should avoid is to say, *You were never really a Christian.* This just comes across as arrogant and has the potential to make the person defensive and shut down the conversation. The person we are speaking to will take offence at you making a judgement about something that happened in his own experience. Now we know that we are not making a judgement based on our own opinion or insight; we believe God has told us in His Word, but nevertheless, that's not how it will be taken, and if we want to help the person we will not want to give the impression that we are somehow the arbitrators of people's salvation and the determiners of their eternal destiny.

So how should we proceed? What we can be certain of is this, if someone says he used to be saved it is evident that he has a poor understanding of what the gospel is actually all about. What I think we should do therefore is this: we should put the question to them, *If you were to die tonight, where would you go, heaven or hell?* And then ask them why. This will give us an insight into their understanding of who goes to heaven and hell and upon what basis they go there, and then you can proceed from there with the gospel. Don't bother going back in time and quizzing them on their experience, because then you will be forced to act as the judge as to whether or not that was a bona fide conversion; don't go there. What matters is where they are now, not whether an experience in the past was genuine or not.

APPENDIX 2:
Does the believer have two natures?

It is a common feature of those who subscribe to Reformed Theology to deny that the believer has two natures, and that the flesh after conversion is as incorrigibly and unchangeably corrupt as it was before conversion. John MacArthur, whom we have quoted and who has given helpful teaching on the subject of eternal security, stated:

> I believe it is a serious misunderstanding to think of the believer as having both an old and new nature. Believers do not have dual personalities... there is no such thing as an old nature in the believer.[278]

We need to point out the straw man MacArthur has erected here.[279] He equates the teaching of the believer having two natures with the idea that the believer has two personalities. This is an unjustified equivocation, and this is made evident when we see that MacArthur, in his commentary on John 1-11, quotes with approval the statement of the Council of Chalcedon (AD 451). It speaks about Christ in this way:

> ...recognised in two natures, without confusion, without change, without division, without separation; the distinction of natures being in no way annulled by the union, but rather the characteristics of each nature being preserved and coming together to form one person and subsistence, not as parted or separated into two

---

[278] John MacArthur Jr., *Freedom from Sin – Romans 6,7*, Moody Press, pp.31,32.
[279] He does it elsewhere in even more pejorative language, saying the Christian is "not a spiritual schizophrenic." (See, for example, his commentary on Ephesians, Thomas Nelson, 2006, p.50.)

> persons, but one and the same Son and only begotten God, the Word, Lord Jesus Christ...

MacArthur takes no issue with the reference to Christ having two natures, yet he certainly does not believe our Lord had dual personalities. One wonders then how he can fairly portray the view that the believer has two natures as schizophrenia. These disagreements often are largely matters of semantics, and it is evident MacArthur has defined the term *nature* with reference to the believer in a different way than he does with respect to Christ. If we see the term *nature* as meaning a set of attributes then all the confusion seems to vanish. The Son of God eternally had a divine nature which He never did or could relinquish. Because of His divine nature He has all the attributes of God. At incarnation the Lord took all the attributes essential to proper manhood.[280] That is all that is intended when it is said He took a human nature. So Christ had two sets of attributes – those that belong to God and those that belong to true manhood. Needless to say, this did not make Him two persons. For that reason his objection quoted above vanishes. It seems, with the greatest respect to John MacArthur, he just hadn't taken time to listen carefully to the view he castigated. Look at the following transcript of a discussion on the subject at a meeting of the Independent Fundamental Churches of America (IFCA):

> Harold Freeman: John, are you familiar with Buswell's definition of a nature?
>
> John MacArthur: I'm not sure. James Buswell?
>
> Harold Freeman: Yes. He calls a nature a complex of attributes.
>
> John MacArthur: Yeah. That's good.
>
> Harold Freeman: And if you use nature in that way, you would be right at home with the word nature.
>
> John MacArthur: Sure. Sure. I...

---

[280] Falleness is not an essential attribute of man. Sin is an invader into humanity, so to say the Lord took a human nature does not at all imply He took a *fallen* human nature.

Harold Freeman: Because, now, just a word that is Biblical, you're not uncomfortable with Trinity.

John MacArthur: Right.

Harold Freeman: You use that. But that's not a Biblical term.

John MacArthur: Right.

Harold Freeman: But it's Biblical truth.

John MacArthur: It's Biblical truth. Sure.

Harold Freeman: So, with regard to the nature, if a nature is truly a complex of attributes, we have the attributes of humanness.

John MacArthur: I have no problem with that. I would agree with that.

Harold Freeman: In that struggle in Romans 7. Right?

John MacArthur: Thank you for helping me. That's good. As a complex of attributes, or as, like I mentioned earlier, a disposition which is composed of all those...sure. I have no problem with that at all. I would believe that. Good.[281]

Saying that the believer has two natures is to say he has a set of attributes that belong to fallen humanity, as well as having a set of attributes that belong to the new creation begotten by the Spirit of God. It is evident that the flesh, the sinful nature that we inherited from Adam will always be the same, for the Lord said, that which is born of the flesh is flesh. If the new birth did not give us a new nature, but instead made a change in the nature we had then surely that would be communicated to the next generation, but obviously that doesn't happen.

Where the mistake is made can be seen in the following quotation:

Paul declares 'I have been crucified with Christ,'

---

[281] http://www.gty.org.uk/resources/sermons/90-37/ifca-meeting-62689-part-2.

– that is, my old 'I' is dead and no longer exists.[282]

The problem is that MacArthur, and many others, have totally missed the significance of crucifixion in these contexts. It is not to be taken as synonymous with death. The point is that crucifixion was a judicial act of condemnation; it was a passing of a sentence. The teaching is that God has passed sentence upon Adamic man and has declared it to be condemned. Likewise, the believer at conversion passed sentence upon himself and acknowledged the hopelessness of the flesh to produce anything for God or for his own salvation; in that sense "they that are Christ's have crucified the flesh..." (Galatians 5:24). It does not at all mean the flesh no longer exists. Consider Gal.6:14:

> But God forbid that I should glory, save in the cross of our Lord Jesus Christ, by whom the world is crucified unto me, and I unto the world.

Paul is not saying the world doesn't exist to him or he to the world, but he is saying that he has passed judgment on the world and the world has passed judgment upon him. The cross makes each see the other differently.

So, the flesh is not dead, it is condemned, but it is still present. To say we no longer possess a sinful nature leads to very strange conclusions and serious questions. From where does sin arise then? Since we are born again of incorruptible seed (1 Pet.1:23); sin can never arise from the new life we have received. MacArthur teaches it comes from our unredeemed bodies, but this would imply that the believer's soul is sinless and only the actual physical body is sinful. This leads to one of two troubling conclusions, either we must deny the true humanity of Christ or deny His impeccable sinlessness. Now John MacArthur would rather die than deny either of these two fundamental truths of Scripture, but this only shows an inconsistency in his thinking.

R. C. Sproul spoke of regeneration as being "a vital change in a person's nature...He is still a sinner but is in the process of spiritual reversal that has, by the efficacious work of the Holy

---

[282] John MacArthur Jr. *Romans 1-8*, Moody Press, p.323, cited in John MacArthur's One Nature Teaching, http://www.middletownbiblechurch.org/doctrine/1natjm01.htm.

Spirit, already begun."[283]

C. H. Mackintosh had this to say:

> The Word of God never once teaches us that the Holy Spirit has for His object the improvement, either gradual or otherwise, of our old nature – that nature which we inherit, by natural birth, from fallen Adam. The inspired apostle expressly declares that, "The natural man receiveth not the things of the Spirit; for they are foolishness unto him. Neither can he know them, because they are spiritually discerned" (1 Cor.2:14). This one passage is clear and conclusive on the point. If "the natural man" can neither "receive" nor "know" "the things of the Spirit of God," then how can that "natural man" be sanctified by the Holy Ghost? Is it not plain that, to speak of "the sanctification of our nature" is opposed to the direct teaching of 1 Cor.2:14?[284]

The belief that we have just one nature and it is to be refined, or that practical sanctification is a progressive thing, leads to big problems and major doubts when a man who has lived a godly life and shown the fruit of the Spirit falls into sin. What happened to cause this "spiritual reversal"? The fact is that the sinful nature (the flesh) cannot be refined, and the new nature given by the indwelling Spirit need not be refined. The flesh represents "a fallen nature which knows no eradication, but continues with the believer as long as he is in the world and which is overcome only by a ceaseless appropriation of the power of the indwelling Spirit."[285] The little catchphrase captures the truth of the matter well: *the flesh is not removed, improved or subdued at conversion.* Rather the believer, indwelt by the Holy Spirit of God, needs to focus on and feed the new life he has been given. The believer is therefore still capable of great wickedness and gross sin. That is why Paul frequently warned believers against these sins, because

---

[283] R. C. Sproul, *Faith Alone*, cited in *John MacArthur's One Nature Teaching*, http://www.middletownbiblechurch.org/doctrine/1natjm01.htm.

[284] C. H. Mackintosh, *Sanctification: What Is It? The Mackintosh Treasury*, p.625.

[285] Chafer, *Systematic Theology*, vol.3, p.359.

they were capable of committing them. Some writers in defending the phrase *perseverance of the saints* have cast doubt on whether there can even be carnal Christians.[286] But we need to recognise that the Bible explicitly and implicitly teaches the existence of such Christians (see, for example, 1 Cor.3:1).

The Bible is clear on the fact that the flesh remains present and there is a battle every Christian is engaged in, which continues until death or the Lord's coming.

> This I say then, Walk in the Spirit, and ye shall not
> fulfil the lust of the flesh.
> For the flesh lusteth against the Spirit, and the
> Spirit against the flesh: and these are contrary the
> one to the other: so that ye cannot do the things
> that ye would. (Gal.5:16,17)

This struggle is illustrated with Cain and Abel, Ishmael and Isaac, Esau and Jacob. The first birth produces nothing for God but fights against that which is born second. It is further illustrated in Exodus 17; the Israelites have been redeemed and are freed from Egypt, but it's not too long until they are engaged in battle with Amalek. Amalek is a vivid picture of the flesh, and the battle is one that rages "from generation to generation" (Ex.17:16).

---

[286] John G. Reisinger, *The Perseverance of the Saints – Part 1*, Sound of Grace, available at www. monergism.com.

Scripture Index

He that believeth

He that believeth

He that believeth

He that believeth